The SMART Gardener's Guide to Growing Fruits

Dr. Bob Gough

STACKPOLE
BOOKS

Published by
STACKPOLE BOOKS
5067 Ritter Road
Mechanicsburg, PA 17055

Printed in the United States of America

FIRST EDITION

10 9 8 7 6 5 4 3 2 1

Cover and interior illustrations by Mary Anne Lard
Cover design by Caroline Miller

Library of Congress Cataloging-in-Publication Data

Gough, Bob.
    Smart gardener's guide to growing fruits / Bob Gough.—1st ed.
        p. cm.
    Includes index.
    ISBN 0–8117–2925–7
    1. Fruit-culture. 2. Fruit. I. Title.
SB355.G635 1997
634—dc20   96–33618
                                                                            CIP

Contents

1 Speaking of Fruit   1
2 Cultural Requirements   7
3 Growth and Development   12
4 Flowers to Fruit   15
5 Plant Propagation   28
6 Choosing the Best Site   46
7 Building Your Soil   60
8 Feeding Plants   72
9 Whipping the Weeds   84
10 Watering   89
11 Planting the Plants   92
12 Winter Protection   100
13 Pruning and Training   106
14 Pest Control   116
15 Harvest   133
16 Tree Fruits and Nuts   139
17 Small Fruits and Grapes   194
    Index   250

Speaking of Fruit

Just what is a fruit?

Botanically, a fruit is a ripened, seed-bearing ovary and its accessory parts. Apples, peaches, and gooseberries fit nicely into this definition. Bananas and seedless grapes don't, because they lack fully formed seeds, but botanically they're still fruits. So are tomatoes, peppers, and cucumbers, although gardeners classify them as vegetables.

The popular definition of a fruit—as opposed to the botanical definition—is a perennial or biennial plant with an edible part, which is usually eaten raw as a snack or dessert, rather than as a main-course food. *The SMART Gardener's Guide to Growing Fruits* deals only with those plants that are commonly considered fruits by the popular definition, rather than the botanical.

CLASSIFICATION OF FRUITS

All fruits are given botanical names according to a worldwide taxonomic system. This system of botanical classification, developed in the eighteenth century by Carolus Linnaeus, groups plants into ever more specific categories based upon their common characteristics.

All fruit-bearing plants belong to the plant division Spermatophyta or seed-bearing plants. They also belong to the plant class Angiospermae, or plants that bear their seeds in an ovary, or fruit. Fruit-bearing palms belong to the subclass Monocotyledoneae, plants that have one seed leaf (monocots). All other fruits belong to the subclass Dicotyledoneae, or plants that have two seed leaves (dicots).

The botanical classification of fruits shows their scientific relationships. All temperate-zone fruits belong to several families of the class Dicotyledoneae (dicots). Some common names refer to more than one botanical name.

Actinidiaceae (Kiwifruit family)
Actinidia arguta	Siberian gooseberry
Actinidia chinensis	Kiwifruit
Actinidia deliciosa	Kiwifruit

Betulaceae (Birch family)
Corylus americana	American hazelnut
Corylus avellana	European hazelnut (filbert)
Corylus maxima	European hazelnut

Caprifoliaceae (Honeysuckle family)
Sambucus canadensis	Elderberry
Viburnum trilobum	Highbush cranberry

Ebenaceae (Ebony family)
Diospyros virginiana	American persimmon
Diospyros kaki	Chinese persimmon, kaki

Ericaceae (Heath family)
Vaccinium angustifolium	Lowbush blueberry
Vaccinium corymbosum	Highbush blueberry
Vaccinium macrocarpon	American cranberry

Fagaceae (Beech family)
Castanea mollissima	Chinese chestnut
Castanea sativa	European chestnut
Castanea dentata	American chestnut

Juglandaceae (Walnut family)
Carya glabra	Pignut
Carya illinoensis	Pecan
Carya ovalis	Pignut
Carya ovata	Shagbark hickory
Juglans cinera	Butternut
Juglans hindsii	California black walnut
Juglans nigra	Black walnut
Juglans regia	English (Persian) walnut

Moraceae (Fig family)	
Ficus carica	Fig
Morus alba	White mulberry
Morus rubra	Red mulberry
Morus nigra	Black mulberry
Rosaceae (Rose family)	
Amelanchier canadensis	Juneberry, shadbush
Chaenomeles japonica	Flowering quince
Cydonia oblonga	Quince
Fragaria vesca	Alpine strawberry
Fragaria x *ananassa*	Garden strawberry
Malus pumila	Apple
Prunus amygdalus	Almond
Prunus armeniaca	Apricot
Prunus avium	Sweet cherry
Prunus cerasus	Sour cherry
Prunus domestica	European plum
Prunus institia	Damson plum
Prunus maritima	Beach plum
Prunus persica	Peach, nectarine
Pyrus communis	Pear
Rubus allegheniensis	Blackberry
Rubus idaeus	Red raspberry
Rubus neglectus	Purple raspberry
Rubus occidentalis	Black raspberry
Rubus ursinus	Blackberry
Saxifragaceae (Saxifrage family)	
Ribes grossularia	Gooseberry
Ribes nigrum	Black currant
Ribes rubrum	Northern red currant
Ribes sativum	Red and white currants
Vitaceae (Vine family)	
Vitis labrusca	American bunch grape
Vitis rotundifolia	Muscadine grape
Vitis rupestris	Sand grape
Vitis vinifera	European grape

Gardeners are most familiar with the family classification. Fruits belonging to the same family often have similar cultural requirements and succumb to the same pests. Once you know the common pests of apples, for example, you'll have a pretty good idea of what pests attack many other members of the Rosaceae family, which also includes pears and hawthorns.

A genus is more specific classification within a family. Plants belonging to the same genus have more in common than those merely in the same family. For example, peaches and plums belong to the same genus (*Prunus*) but share a family with apples and quince.

The species is the fundamental unit of botanical classification. Plants belonging to the same species have many characteristics in common. Peaches and nectarines, for example, belong to the same genus and species (*Prunus persica*) and are very similar in appearance and culture.

A variety is a subgroup within a species and is assigned to individuals that differ in small but important ways from others within the species. A variety name is usually preceded by the abbreviation *var.*

When a particular variety becomes stabilized through selective propagation, it is known as a cultivar. Cultivar names are usually enclosed in single quotation marks.

A strain is a subdivision of a cultivar and differs from the parent cultivar by one or more relatively minor attributes. For example, you might have an orchard of 'Cortland' apples. The fruits of one 'Cortland' apple tree might be slightly redder than those of another, or may ripen a few days earlier. If all trees reproduced from that tree produce 'Cortland' apples with the same redder color or earlier ripening date, independent of environmental factors, then the difference is genetic. You have found a better strain of 'Cortland'. Strains are named slightly differently from the parent cultivar, as in 'Gough's Cortland'.

Sometimes a bud mutation causes a single branch of a tree to bear fruit different from the rest of the tree. When plants propagated from that branch pass on those traits, they are known as sports. Sports are often classified as separate cultivars.

When the botanical name of a fruit contains a multiplication sign, such as *Fragaria* x *ananassa* (the garden strawberry), it indicates that the plant is a hybrid of two or more species.

To give you an overview of the entire system, here's the botanical classification of one cultivar of apricot:

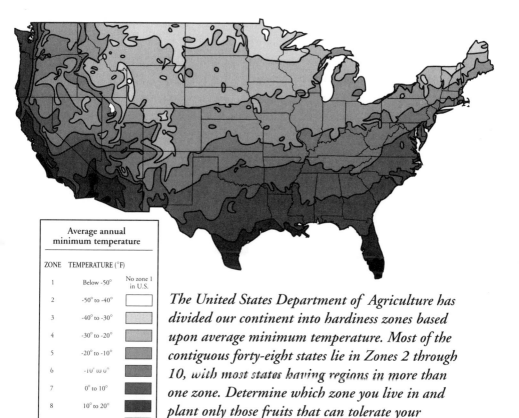

Average annual minimum temperature		
ZONE	TEMPERATURE (°F)	
1	Below -50°	No zone 1 in U.S.
2	-50° to -40°	
3	-40° to -30°	
4	-30° to -20°	
5	-20° to -10°	
6	-10° to 0°	
7	0° to 10°	
8	10° to 20°	
9	20° to 30°	
10	30° to 40°	

The United States Department of Agriculture has divided our continent into hardiness zones based upon average minimum temperature. Most of the contiguous forty-eight states lie in Zones 2 through 10, with most states having regions in more than one zone. Determine which zone you live in and plant only those fruits that can tolerate your winters.

Division	Spermatophyta
Class	Angiospermae
Subclass	Dicotyledoneae
Family	Rosaceae
Genus	*Prunus*
Species	*armeniaca*
Cultivar	'Moorpark'

Most of the fruits grown in the home garden are temperate-zone plants. (I've not dealt with tropical and subtropical fruits because their culture is limited to very small portions of the United States.) Within the temperate-zone group, some plants are classified as very cold hardy, while others can tolerate only slight amounts of cold. Temperature hardiness is indicated by the numbered USDA hardiness zones to which various plants are adapted. The home gardener often can create a microclimate that is a zone or two warmer or cooler than the surrounding area, so that he can grow plants that might otherwise be only marginally adapted to the area.

Fruit plants are long-term investments. Learn all you can about a particular variety before you plant—its soil and water requirements, its need for fertilizer and pruning, its preference for chilling, and its cold tolerance. If you make a mistake in choosing an annual vegetable to plant, you've wasted only one year. A mistake in a fruit planting may waste several years of effort.

Cultural Requirements

It's important to understand the cultural requirements of fruit plants so that you can provide the optimum conditions for production. Your selection of a planting site and the climatic features of that site can significantly affect the amount and quality of fruit you harvest.

LIGHT

All green plants need light to conduct photosynthesis. Photosynthesis is the process by which plants manufacture simple sugars from a combination of carbon dioxide and water, using sunlight to fuel the process. The simple sugars are used for the growth and development of shoots, flower buds, roots, and fruit. Lack of adequate sunlight causes reduced photosynthesis, which in turn causes weak new growth, slow root development, and reduced flower bud formation. The general health of the plant is also affected. The stress of inadequate light may also decrease insect and disease resistance and reduce cold hardiness.

Photoperiodism

Besides the intensity of light a plant receives, some fruits—notably strawberries—are sensitive to the relative length of daylight during the course of the year. *Photoperiodism*, or day-length sensitivity, influences the amount of sugar produced during photosynthesis, which in turn affects the plant hormones that regulate growth and flower bud formation. June-bearing strawberries set flower buds during the shortening days of late summer; runner growth, however, is most active during the long days of early summer. Everbearing strawberries form flower buds during long summer days, and day-neutral strawberries form flower buds without regard to day length. Day-length sensitivity is affected strongly by temperature, latitude, elevation, cloud cover, and humidity. Cooler temperatures or a lack of rainfall, for example, can partially substitute for shorter days. Because of the influence of photoperiod on flower bud formation in strawberries, it's important to plant only "northern" cultivars in northern gardens and "southern" cultivars in southern gardens. You should choose your onion cultivars with similar thoughts.

TEMPERATURE

Temperature affects the rate of respiration in plants, thus influencing the speed at which simple sugars are chemically converted into carbohydrates, fats, and proteins for growth and storage. In general, the higher the temperature, the faster these chemical reactions proceed, and the faster the plant grows. Most plant respiration is carried on at night. During warm nights, respiration is high and the sugars made by photosynthesis during the day are quickly broken down and used to build leaves, new growth, and immature fruits. Cool night temperatures slow this process so that some sugars accumulate in the ripening fruit and make it sweet. Accumulated sugar is also turned into red pigment, so fruits ripening during cool nights often are more colorful and look more desirable.

Although most temperate-zone fruits will tolerate a wide range of temperatures, most won't grow well at temperatures above 85 or below 60 degrees Fahrenheit. Temperatures between 30 and 40 degrees F can chill some shoot tips and stop growth, even without a frost. The temperature requirements of fruits vary among species. Figs, for example, require a long growing season and warm temperatures. Gooseberries, on the other hand, do better where summer temperatures are cool and will drop their leaves if they become too warm.

Most temperate-zone fruits benefit from a period of freezing or near-freezing temperatures during the winter. Cold hardiness varies among species, but as long as the cold is not too severe, most fruits will do fine. Fluctuating winter temperatures, however, can cause much damage to your plants, especially if they occur after the first of the year. An unseasonable warm spell can cause buds to open prematurely, making them susceptible to frost and freeze damage.

NUTRIENTS

In addition to sunlight and proper temperatures, plants need to absorb certain essential nutrients from the soil in order to thrive. These nutrients are dissolved in water and taken up into the plant through the small white root hairs and actively growing white root tips. Older, brown root tissues have corked over and can-

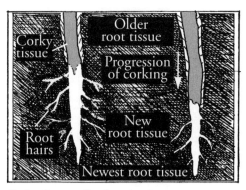

Only the small white region containing root hairs near the root tip can absorb water and nutrients from the soil.

not absorb this nutrient-rich solution. If a root stops growing, the corky tissue develops nearly to the tip, further reducing the root's ability to absorb and in turn further reducing root growth. A healthy, actively growing plant will have many new roots to absorb the water and nutrients it needs to support its growth. Damage to the roots reduces the amount of nutrients a plant can take up and has a stunting effect on growth. The roots of some fruit trees are very slow to regenerate and grow, so use extreme care in transplanting them.

You may need to add supplemental nutrients to your soil before you set out

Soil pH causes chemical reactions that can increase or reduce the availability of certain nutrients to the plant. For example, iron becomes less available to the plant as the soil pH increases.

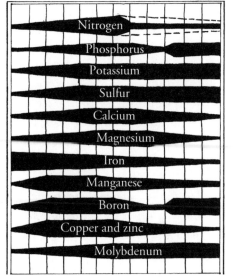

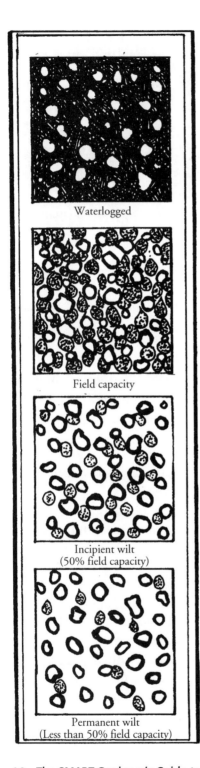

Waterlogged

Field capacity

Incipient wilt
(50% field capacity)

Permanent wilt
(Less than 50% field capacity)

your plants. These nutrients must be available to the plants in the proper proportions. Too much or too little of any nutrient can have a significant negative impact on the plants' health. You can supplement your plants' nutritional needs through the application of balanced fertilizers and by maintaining a proper soil pH level.

SOIL pH

Soil pH is the measure of relative acidity or alkalinity in the soil. Many nutrients become chemically tied up in the soil and unavailable for plant growth when the pH level is too high or too low. A soil pH near neutral is about right for most plants, except the acid-loving blueberries, lingonberries, and cranberries. Most fruiting plants grow best in slightly acid soil at pH 6.5. In soil above 5.5, blueberry roots cannot extract iron from the soil, and the plants suffer iron-induced chlorosis. In excessively acid soil, with a pH of 3.5 or below, aluminum and manganese can become highly available and toxic to plants, causing

The less soil water there is, the more tightly it is held by soil particles and the less able plants are to absorb it. Roots grow poorly in waterlogged soil because all air spaces are filled with water.

stunted roots with a decreased ability to absorb nutrients and water. Low soil pH can also cause manganese toxicity, resulting in "measles" on apple trees.

WATER

Water is necessary for all plant functions. Without water, nutrient uptake ceases, growth stops, and the plant dies. Water is constantly being absorbed by actively growing root tips. Some of it is broken down during photosynthesis and its oxygen content emitted into the atmosphere; some is stored in plant tissues; and the rest is eliminated as water vapor through small pores, called *stomata,* in the leaves. This process is known as *transpiration,* and it plays an important part in the water, or hydrological, cycle of the planet. Most plants retain only about 10 percent of all the water they absorb. Unless the roots can replace water lost during transpiration, growth is checked, leaves wilt, flowers drop, and root and shoot growth cease. During prolonged drought, nutrient deficiency symptoms may begin to show, caused not by an actual deficiency but because there is not enough water for the plant to absorb the nutrients from the soil. Because most fruits are nearly all water (blueberries are about 87 percent water), it is important for plants to have all the water they can use. Fruits won't grow to a good size if water is lacking, and they'll shrivel and drop if the shortage becomes severe.

When the soil carries all the water it can hold without any draining away, it's said to be at *field capacity.* Plants absorb this water easily. As the soil dries, plants have greater difficulty in extracting moisture. When the soil is at about half field capacity, plants may wilt at midday and recover at night, known as *incipient wilt.* Even if you water immediately when you first observe incipient wilt, yields and plant growth will already have been affected. If the drought continues, plants will not recover during the evening and may be lost or severely damaged. This is called *permanent wilt,* and it is usually fatal to newly transplanted trees, which don't have deep root systems yet.

3

Growth and Development

I watched my children being born and grow through their childhood into adults, and now they're ready to have children of their own. Plants, too, pass through life cycles that are analogous to those of humans. Let's consider an apple tree.

A seedling apple tree begins as an embryo in the seed held in the fruit of an adult apple tree. In autumn, the ripened fruit falls to the ground and rots, releasing the seed onto the soil. This seed is dormant and cannot germinate until that dormancy is broken by freezing winter temperatures. In the spring, when temperatures are best for growth, the seed will germinate. The emerging seedling has a complement of juvenile hormones that allow it to make vigorous vegetative growth for several years. It also has other juvenile characteristics that are easy to see. For example, it won't form flower buds, its leaves may have serrated (sawtoothed) edges, and it will have long thorns that look like those of the hawthorn. Gradually, over a period of twenty to fifty years, the plant begins to produce adult hormones and passes into its adult phase.

During its first few years in the adult stage, the apple tree begins to produce leaves with smooth edges, drops its thorns, and slows its vegetative growth. Because it still produces no flower buds, we call this the *vegetative adult phase*. Depending upon the apple cultivar, this stage can last from two to fifteen years before passing into the reproductive adult phase. Only during this reproductive adult phase will the apple tree blossom and bear fruit.

Grafting or vegetative propagation sets a fruiting plant back a bit, so

Different species of fruits come into bearing at different ages, counted in years from planting. The precise time is variable and depends upon cultivar, rootstock, pruning technique, and cultural practices.

Species	Time After Planting (Years)
Apple	2–5
Apricot	2–5
Cherry, sour	3–5
Cherry, sweet	4–7
Chestnut, seedlings	6–8
Chestnut, grafted	2–3
Fig	2–3
Filbert	6–8
Pawpaw, northern	5–7
Mulberry	Highly variable
Peach	2–4
Pear	4–6
Pecan	4–7
Persimmon	6–8
Plum	3–6
Quince	5–6
Strawberry	Immediately
Walnut	Highly variable
Most small fruits	1–2

those you purchase at the nursery drop back to the vegetative adult phase. The time it takes for a grafted or cutting-rooted plant to pass again from vegetative to reproductive adult is known as the time needed to come into bearing and is influenced by type and amount of pruning, fertilization, and rootstock. For example, severe pruning, too much nitrogen, and standard rootstocks prolong the vegetative adult phase and delay the onset of bearing. In addition, some cultivars mature more rapidly than others. A 'McIntosh' apple on a given rootstock will come into bearing earlier than a 'Northern Spy' planted next to it on the same rootstock. Once a plant flowers and enters the reproductive adult phase, it will ordinarily produce annually from then on.

The transition from vegetative to reproductive adult may be an uncertain time for many plants. Because fruit-forming hormones may fluctuate, some young, highly vigorous plum trees may produce flowers with defective pistils that inhibit fruiting. Other species may drop all their immature fruits for the first few years as a reproductive adult. During this stressful time, some plant species even change sex. Oriental persimmon (*Diospyros kaki*) seedlings at first produce only male flowers, then both male and female, and eventually mostly female flowers.

Any condition that delays the onset of flowering will also lead to irregular flowering later on. Balance is important in all things. As the plants mature and hormones stabilize, all fruiting plants produce better crops.

The bottom line is to give your plants time to develop as they will. In general, grafted trees should begin to bear fruit by their sixth year. Small fruits, like currants and blackberries, usually bear by their third year. Don't be impatient; don't try to push them into premature bearing. Give them time to develop a strong framework and root system before you require them to bear fruit. The stress of early bearing has ruined many orchards.

Flowers to Fruit

Once a plant has entered the reproductive adult phase, it will normally form flower buds every year. Most temperate-zone fruits form their flower buds during the growing season prior to spring bloom, often during the summer or early autumn. (Everbearing cultivars of raspberries and strawberries are exceptions.)

FLOWER BUD FORMATION

In general, the exterior, vegetative parts of the bud form first, then the interior, reproductive parts. We don't know all the factors that influence the formation of flower buds, but we do know a few:

- The physiological age of the plant is important in the development of flower buds. A plant must be in the reproductive adult phase to produce the proper hormones for flower bud formation.
- The ratio or balance of carbohydrates to nitrogen in plant tissues has long been thought to be an important factor in the formation of flower buds. Carbohydrates are the sugars formed during photosynthesis, along with their related products. Nitrogen is supplied by soil nutrients. If a plant's tissues contain a low amount of carbohydrates and a high amount of nitrogen, vegetative growth is poor and only a few fruits of poor quality will be produced. This situation is found in defoliated plants and plants that have been excessively pruned or fertilized. If carbohydrates are moderate and nitrogen high, the plant produces rank vegetative growth but few fruit. This is often caused by excessive pruning or fertilization. A high carbohydrate and moderate nitrogen content pro-

duces moderate vegetative growth and good fruiting. This is the result of proper pruning and fertilization. A very high carbohydrate and very low nitrogen balance results in poor vegetative growth and reduced fruit set. This is usually caused by insufficient nutrients.

- Light intensity has an important effect on flower bud formation. The interior limbs of many fruit trees receive only about 500 foot-candles of light, not enough for good

The upper outside areas of a tree or bush receive the most sunlight and produce the best fruit. Fruits toward the interior of the plant often are smaller, have less color, and ripen later than those near the outside. The area of the plant near the bottom receives less than $1/3$ of full sunlight; it often is barren.

flower bud formation, while the exterior limbs receive 5,000 to 10,000 foot-candles. Therefore, it's the exterior of the plant that usually produces most of the fruit. You can't change this entirely, but you can help to even out the areas of flower bud formation by opening up the center of the plant with judicious pruning.

Light duration also influences flower bud formation through the photoperiodic response in plants like strawberries.

- Proper pruning has a major influence on the formation of flower buds. Excessive pruning during the vegetative adult phase delays the onset of the reproductive adult phase. Excessive pruning during the reproductive adult phase reduces the amount of foliage so much that carbohydrates are reduced and fruit production is impaired. In response, the root system supplies too much water and too many nutrients for the reduced top, which forces the

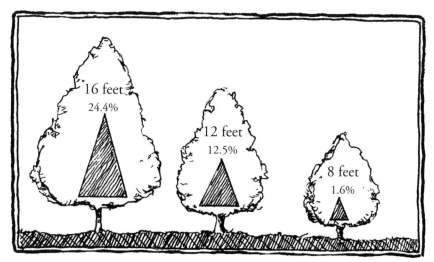

Dwarf trees are often more productive than larger trees because a larger portion of their total area is exposed to light. By reducing a tree's height from 16 to 8 feet, the heavily shaded, unproductive portion is reduced from about ¹/₄ of the tree volume to about a ¹/₅₀, so use dwarf trees whenever you can.

growth of excessively vigorous shoots and water sprouts. These shade the leaves of the bearing branches, reducing their production of carbohydrates. The low carbohydrate and high nitrogen content in the tissues of the bearing branches reduces flower bud formation and fruit set.

- Root injury from cold damage or root pruning can sometimes *increase* the formation of flower buds by limiting vigorous shoot growth.
- Summer pruning stops shoot growth and increases the formation of flower buds. (This is a little tricky, and you need to be careful not to knock off the young fruits.)
- Defoliation, especially in early summer, decreases the formation of flower buds. If defoliation occurs during late summer and autumn, it can decrease the size of the flower buds that have formed. This is especially troublesome in areas plagued by Japanese beetles, gypsy moths, or other foliage-eating insects.
- Water influences all functions in a plant. A slight deficiency in soil

moisture during the summer can actually increase the number of flower buds formed, probably by slowing vegetative growth. A severe deficiency will decrease the number of flower buds because it will stop growth altogether and may cause partial defoliation.

- Either an overabundance of nutrients or a deficiency of nutrients, particularly zinc, copper, or boron, can interfere with flower bud formation. Keep soil nutrient levels in balance through careful soil testing, fertilization, and pH modification where necessary.

FORCING FLOWER BUD FORMATION

Suppose you do everything right and in moderation, and after you've waited the requisite amount of time, your plant still doesn't bloom. Is there anything you can do to force it into bearing? Yes. Here are a few things you can try, but only do so as a last resort.

Limb Bending

Limb bending should be part of the normal pruning process for pear and apple trees. Spread young branches so that their limbs leave the trunk at a 35- to 45-degree angle (the *crotch angle*). Bending branches toward the horizontal increases their ability to flower, while reducing their vegetative growth. You can even bend the tips of young branches to the ground, but this may lead to excessively vigorous shoot growth behind the bend and flower bud formation only on the tips of the limbs.

Phloem Interruption

Ringing the trunk or major limbs by completely removing a small strip of bark from around them will sometimes force flower buds to form. This occurs because carbohydrates cannot bridge the gap in their movement down the plant's phloem tissue into the roots. Instead, the carbohydrates back up into the top and cause the formation of flower buds. This is also called *controlled girdling*. Be warned, however, that if you remove too much tissue the girdled limb or tree will die.

    Scoring is safer than ringing and produces similar results. Instead of removing a strip of bark, use a knife to score two rings about an inch apart in the trunk or branch. Push your knife blade into the branch as far as it will go, then move it completely around the trunk. Do this twice to be sure the phloem is completely severed. Remove no bark. The cuts will heal

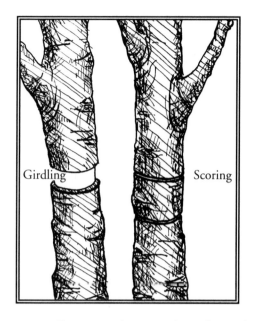

Girdling   Scoring

Girdling (ringing) or scoring a tree trunk or a major branch causes carbohydrates to pool in the upper areas of the plant, forcing it to form flower buds.

in a couple of weeks but will cause backup of carbohydrates for a sufficient time to produce enhanced flower bud formation.

If you do get desperate enough to try phloem interruption, here are a few things to remember:

- Carry out the procedure about three to four weeks after petal fall on trees of the same species growing in your area.
- Don't score or girdle very young or very old trees, stressed trees, defoliated trees, or any trees of the stone fruit species, like cherries, plums, and peaches.
- Remove any shoots or water sprouts that develop near the score line to reduce the chances of aphid buildup or fire blight infection.

FRUITING HABITS

Each species has its own fruiting habit. Some, like peaches and blueberries, bear their flower buds on the current year's wood and fruit on one-year-old wood. Others, like apples and pears, bear on spur wood two years old or older. (Spurs are short, thick little branches that form along major limbs and carry fruiting buds.) Still others, like gooseberries, bear on wood up to three years old. You must know which limbs will produce flower buds in order to care for your fruiting plants properly.

Most plants bear annually and some bear more than one crop each season. The cultivars of some fruits, however, particularly those of apples and pears, bear good crops only biennially. This habit is known as biennial bearing, or alternate bearing. The year in which the crop is heavy is called the "on" year, and the light year is called the "off" year. Many older cultivars have this habit of alternate bearing, and it is one of the reasons they have been omitted from commercial production orchards.

Trees that have been neglected or grown in a poor environment also may resort to this habit of biennial bearing, because during the "on" year, the heavy fruit load drains carbohydrates from the tree, leaving little for flower bud formation. Because bud formation is light, the crop is sparse the following year. This leaves plenty of carbohydrates for the tree to set a heavy crop of buds for the next year, and so on. If your tree gets into this habit, thin the fruit heavily during "on" years to even out the demand for carbohydrates and keep the tree healthy and growing vigorously throughout the season. If thinning doesn't work, you may have a cultivar that is genetically inclined toward biennial bearing.

POLLINATION

Getting a plant to set flower buds is half the battle; getting it to set fruit is the other half. Once the plant has bloomed, there must be a transfer of pollen from the male to the female parts of the flowers to complete fertilization and start the actual formation of fruits. If no pollination occurs, the flowers drop and no fruit will set.

Types of Pollination

Self-pollination is the transfer of pollen from the male structure or *anther* of a flower on one cultivar to the female structure or *pistil* of a flower on the same cultivar to complete fertilization. This transfer might occur within the same flower, to another flower on the same tree, or to a flower on another tree, so long as it's the same cultivar. Transfer of pollen from one 'McIntosh' apple blossom to another 'McIntosh' blossom is an example of self-pollination. A plant that can set fruit through self-pollination is said to be either partially or completely self-fruitful, depending on whether a full or partial crop of fruit is set.

Cross-pollination is the transfer of pollen from the anther of a flower on one cultivar to the pistil of a flower on another cultivar of the same kind of fruit. For example, transfer of pollen from a 'McIntosh' apple blossom to a 'Red Delicious' apple blossom is a form of cross-pollination. Cross-pollination between a 'Red Delicious' and a 'Golden Delicious' will not result in a bunch of pink apples, because the results of the cross are in the seeds only. The variety of the fruit produced is determined by the variety of the tree on which it is borne: 'Golden Delicious' trees bear only 'Golden Deli-

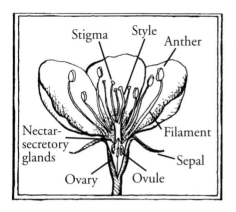

Stigma Style Anther

Nectar-secretory glands

Filament

Ovary Ovule Sepal

This apple blossom is typical of many fruit flowers, although not all flowers have all parts. The anthers and filament together form the stamen—the male part of the flower. The stigma, styles, and ovary form the female part of the flower. Sepals and petals are asexual.

cious' apples, regardless of what cultivar pollinates them. Plants that can set fruit only through cross-pollination are said to be self-unfruitful or self-incompatible.

Types of Pollen

The type of pollen produced by a fruiting plant also varies by species and cultivar. Some cultivars, like 'Mutsu' apples, produce sterile pollen. To achieve fertilization and fruit formation, a *pollen-sterile* cultivar must be pollinated by another, similar cultivar. In the case of 'Mutsu' apples, pollination by another apple cultivar, such as 'York Imperial', is necessary to produce fruit.

Self-incompatible pollen will not result in fruit set after self-pollination but could set fruit in cross-pollination. Some cultivars of apples and sweet cherries are self-incompatible.

Cross-incompatible pollen will not result in fruit set if it lands on the pistil of some cultivars within a species but will result in fruit set if it pollinates the blossoms of certain other cultivars. Sweet cherries, plums, and pears are notorious for having groups of cross-incompatible cultivars. When planting these species, research their pollen compatibility carefully.

Methods of Pollination

The pollen of most fruit species is commonly transferred from blossom to blossom by honeybees. A single bee can carry one hundred thousand pollen grains at a time and visit up to five thousand flowers in a single day during good weather. Other insects, including bumblebees and wasps, also pollinate plants.

Some fruit plants need insects to pollinate them; others need wind; and some need both.

Wind Pollinated	Wind and Insect Pollinated	Insect Pollinated
Mulberry	Strawberry	Apple
Chestnut	Italian prune	Pear
Pecan	Grape	Quince
Filbert	Raspberry	Plum
Walnut	Persimmon	Cherry
		Peach
		Cranberry
		Blueberry
		Kiwi
		Nectarine
		Ribes
		Blackberry
		Apricot

Any condition that interferes with the flight of these insects will interfere with fruit set. Honeybees often don't fly during rainy and windy periods or when temperatures fall below 65 degrees F. Bumblebees fly in more inclement weather, but both types of bees work closer to the ground on cold days. You may notice your crop borne low on the plant if weather conditions were poor during bloom. Pollination is best when the weather during bloom is sunny and calm and the air temperature is above 70 degrees F.

Competing flowers also can interfere with pollination. For example, dandelions often bloom at the same time as apples and pears. With all the dandelion flowers present, bees may not visit the fruit blossoms. The problem is especially difficult with pears, which produce flowers unattractive to bees. Try to limit the presence of any plants that flower at the same time your fruiting plants bloom.

Some fruiting plants, particularly those of the nut species, are wind pollinated, so you don't have to worry about bee activity or competing flowers.

Improving Pollination

Although many plants will set fruit by their own pollen when self-pollinated, cross-pollination usually results in larger, better-tasting fruits with better shape and color. These fruits also usually ripen slightly earlier than those produced by self-pollination. It is best, therefore, to always provide for cross-pollination. Cross-pollination is easily achieved by planting at least two cultivars (the more the better) of the same kind of fruit within 50 feet of each other. The bloom times of all cultivars must overlap; in general, early-ripening cultivars bloom early and late-ripening cultivars bloom late. To be sure you have overlap in bloom time, plant at least one early-, one midseason-, and one late-fruiting cultivar. If one cultivar is pollen-sterile, plant at least two others to compensate.

If you have only a single tree and no room for another, graft a scion from a different cultivar onto a branch near the top of the tree to provide pollen for cross-pollination. A simpler, though less permanent, method is to place a bouquet of blossoming branches from a different cultivar in a vase at the base of the tree, or in one of the major limb crotches. One bouquet per tree is usually enough.

FRUIT SET

Once pollination is completed and all conditions are favorable, the pollen that has been deposited atop the stigma germinates, forming a pollen tube that grows down through the pistil to the ovary and its ovules. Sperm cells travel down the tube to fertilize the egg cells, which are contained within the ovules. If most of the ovules are not fertilized, the fruit will drop before ripening. If most, but not all, of the egg cells are fertilized, the fruit will set but will be lopsided, with only the tissue on the fertilized side developing normally. Well-formed, undamaged blossoms on vigorous, healthy plants have the best chance of setting fruit, provided that pollination occurs within the first few days of bloom, when egg cells are most receptive.

Assuming satisfactory pollination, there are several factors that can influence fertilization and subsequent fruit set.

- Proper pruning, which removes some flower buds and reduces competition, increases fruit set.
- Insufficient nitrogen reduces fruit set, so fertilize before bloom.
- Temperatures below 60 degrees F may reduce pollen germination and subsequent fruit set.

- Wind, in addition to influencing bee activity, may dry the stigma, reducing the chances of the pollen tube penetrating to the ovule. Wind can also damage blossoms.
- High humidity or rain may cause pollen to clump together, making it difficult for bees to transfer it to the stigma. If humidity is too low, dried-out stigmas may not allow pollen grains to germinate.

FRUIT DROP

If conditions are terrific for pollination and fertilization, your fruit plants may set too heavy a crop. If the plant tries to mature all the fruit it sets, each individual fruit will be small and unlikely to produce viable seeds. Nature has devised a way to rid a plant of excess fruits by causing hormonal fluctuations that allow excess or poorly fertilized fruits to drop off.

Apple and pear trees go through four small drop periods. These are usually lumped into two larger periods: the *first drop* and the *June drop*. The first drop occurs soon after petal fall and consists of fruits that are incompletely fertilized. Because the fruits are so small, most gardeners don't notice this drop. During the June drop, which occurs a week or two after the first drop, excess fruits are shed to reduce competition. These larger, nickel-sized fruits are more noticeable, and I always know when June drop occurs because I'm deluged with phone calls from nervous gardeners wanting to know why their trees are losing so much fruit. Believe it or not, an apple tree needs to set only 5 percent of its fruit in order to produce a good crop.

Peach trees experience two drops. The first begins shortly after bloom, lasts for two to three weeks, and consists of aborted flowers and small fruits. The second drop begins about five weeks after bloom and is made up of partially developed fruits that can't compete for water and nutrients.

Plum and cherry trees undergo three drops. The first consists of unfertilized fruits, and the second and third of insufficiently fertilized, partially developed fruits.

THINNING

In some years of heavy fruit set, normal drops may not remove enough fruits. Those that survive to maturity will be undersized and of poor

Some fruit plants may need to be thinned even though they have undergone natural drops. If fruits are crowded, thin them to the following spacings. Thinning reduces competition among fruits and increases fruit size and quality.

FRUIT	PROPER SPACING
Apple	Thin to one fruit per cluster, or space fruit about 7 inches apart on a branch
Pear	Thin to two fruits per cluster, or space fruit about 5 inches apart on a branch
Peach, plum, apricot	Thin the fruit annually so that they hang about 7 inches apart on a branch
Nuts	Not usually thinned
Small fruits	Thinned by removal of some flower buds during pruning; not usually hand-thinned, with the exception of some grapes

quality. Because fruiting is exhausting for a plant even under normal conditions, a very heavy fruit load can be detrimental. You need to thin out excess fruits.

Removing excess fruits improves the size and appearance of those that remain, helps maintain annual bearing habits and a favorable balance between fruit and leaves, reduces limb breakage from excessive fruit load, maintains plant vigor, and removes poor or misshapen fruits. Although the process decreases total yield, it increases the yield of high-quality fruits.

The best time to thin is right after the last natural drop, and never later than one month following petal fall. The longer you delay, the less influence the process will have on plants or fruits.

The simplest way to thin is to pick the fruits off by hand. Some gardeners beat on the limbs with a rubber hose or shake the plant to dislodge excess fruits, but that can cause damage.

DORMANCY AFTER BEARING
Once harvest is over and flower buds have been set for next year, the top portion of a plant slowly enters dormancy for the winter. Roots do not enter a true dormancy but merely stop growing when soil temperatures

get too cold. Dormancy begins in early autumn as the weather cools and the days shorten. Vegetative growth slows and finally stops, and plant tissues become more resistant to extreme cold. This process is called *hardening*, and it's important to let a plant go through this natural cycle. Beginning in late summer, don't do anything that stimulates vegetative growth: don't water or fertilize your fruiting plants, and don't cultivate the soil around them—cultivation may release nitrogen into the plant's root zone and stimulate late growth. New growth that develops late in the summer is very susceptible to frost and freeze damage.

As autumn progresses, plants become increasingly less responsive to their environment, until finally nothing will stimulate growth. At about the time of leaf drop, the plants enter a period of *true rest*.

During true rest the top of a plant is unresponsive to environmental stimuli, although the roots may still be able to absorb water and nutrients. Even if you were to move a completely dormant plant into a warm greenhouse and water and fertilize it, it would not grow at this time, because the internal mechanisms that allow for growth have been turned off and must undergo a certain cold treatment before they can turn on again. Because roots remain active even during true rest periods, it is important to continue watering your plants until the soil freezes to reduce winter desiccation. Watering at this time will not encourage them to grow.

COLD HARDINESS AND CHILLING

By the time a plant has entered true rest, it can withstand extreme cold. The degree of cold it can withstand is determined by the plant's genetics and modified by the prevailing conditions immediately preceding rest.

Not all parts of a plant are equally hardy. Roots, because they don't enter true rest, are most tender and are killed when soil temperatures drop to about 15 degrees F. Other tender spots include branch crotches, shoot tips, flower buds, and the entire cambium (the green growing tissue just beneath the outer bark). During very cold winters, flower buds may be killed while the rest of the tree is unaffected.

Once a plant has entered its rest period, it must undergo a certain number of hours of temperatures below 45 degrees F to satisfy its rest requirement. When the requirement has been satisfied, the plant once more becomes responsive to the environment and can begin to grow if the temperatures warm.

This *chilling requirement* varies for different cultivars and explains why some fruits, like most apples and peaches, cannot be grown in the Deep South, where temperatures aren't cold enough to satisfy their chilling requirement.

Most orchard-tree species will break their rest reliably if the average temperature of the coldest nine weeks of the year is 42 degrees F or below. In general, most fruit plants in the northern United States have accumulated enough chilling hours by January to break their rest. The plants may still remain dormant because of cold temperatures, but they are no longer in true rest. As the days lengthen and warm, the plant *dehardens,* emerges from rest, and blooms.

If a plant enters rest but does not receive enough cold to satisfy its chilling requirement, you may see some problems in the spring. If temperatures have remained warm all winter, there will be no bloom. If chilling time was only slightly inadequate, the bloom will be delayed a few days—not entirely bad, because you'll have a better chance of escaping damage from a late frost. Also, because shoot buds require slightly more chilling than flower buds, the plant may bloom but have sparse foliage. If chilling was moderately inadequate, both bloom and shoot growth will be spotty and weak.

Some species, like apricots, will shed their flower buds in the spring if chilling was inadequate. In species with mixed buds, like pears and apples, the flower parts may die from inadequate chilling so that the spur produce only leaves. In borderline years, shaded shoots will have met their chilling requirement, but those that were in the full sun will not have.

Midwinter Thaws

Entering rest is how a plant survives the cold, dry conditions of winter. Midwinter thaws can be tough on plants if they occur after rest has ended. Fruit plants begin to deharden when temperatures rise into the mid-twenties. Apples respond slowly to warm temperatures and aren't likely to be injured by a thaw unless the temperatures remain near 60 degrees F for a couple of weeks. Peaches, nectarines, and apricots deharden rapidly and can be injured after only a few days of warm temperatures. The injury comes not from the heat but from the rapid drop in temperature that often follows a warm spell. The more rapid and severe this temperature drop, the greater the degree of injury to the plant.

Plant Propagation

Some gardeners enjoy amateur plant breeding, making their own crosses, then planting the seeds to see what comes up. Other gardeners simply want to save money by propagating their own plants. It's an easy process, but the results can be disappointing if the work is not done carefully.

STARTING PLANTS FROM SEEDS

When started from seeds, most fruit plants won't reproduce true to type. If you plant a seed of a 'McIntosh' apple, you may not get an apple tree that produces 'McIntosh' fruit. Cherries and peaches come close to reproducing true to type, so we have Morello- and Montmorency-type cherries and Elberta-type peaches. Some minor species, such as buffaloberry, are normally propagated by seed because no superior selections have been made. Other plants, such as nuts, are usually propagated from seed because they usually come true to type.

Besides the problem of not reproducing true to type, seed-started plants can take many years to grow through the juvenile period, and they may have variable habits. Some apple seedlings may grow to be 15 feet tall, some 40 feet tall. An orchard of trees of such varying sizes is difficult to maintain and harvest.

Despite their problems, seed-started plants have valuable uses. They are often used as rootstocks, on which cuttings or scions of named cultivars are grafted. Because seed-started plants often revert back to the sturdy characteristics of their ancestral stock, they usually produce tough, cold-hardy, pest-resistant root systems.

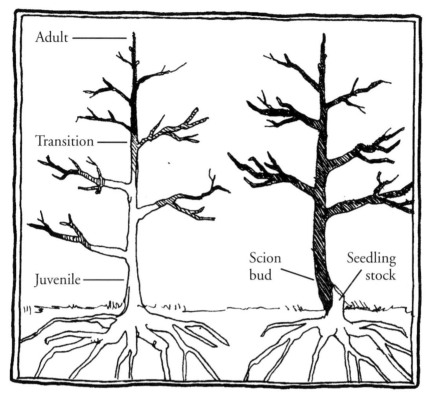

Adult

Transition

Juvenile

Scion
bud

Seedling
stock

Seedling fruit trees pass through the juvenile stage into the adult stage gradually. For example, the seedling tree (left) has juvenile zones at the crown and the lower regions, a transition zone near the middle of the tree, and adult zones at the top and near the ends of the branches. The grafted nursery tree (right) is completely adult above the graft union. That means that the entire tree has the capability of producing fruit. It's much easier, then, to propagate the adult stage of any fruit plant and get it into production in only a short time. If you start your fruit plants from seeds, you'll have to wait for the plant to pass through its juvenile stage before it will bear fruit. This may take decades.

The stems of seed-started plants may also have certain dwarfing characteristics, and because the main stem or trunk of the seedling does not grow to great size, scions grafted to it will produce a shorter mature tree.

The very variability that makes seedlings so unpredictable can also be an asset. New and superior cultivars sometimes are discovered among a large group of seedlings that have been allowed to grow to full maturity.

If you want seedlings to use for rootstocks or if you just want to try selecting superior seedlings, start with ripe fruits from healthy trees.

Stratification

Seeds right out of a ripe fruit are dormant and will not germinate until they have completed an after-ripening period of cold and thaw to break their dormancy. This occurs naturally over the winter. *Stratification* is a method to artificially duplicate these conditions. Each species has its own temperature requirement and length of stratification treatment needed to break dormancy. Begin by moistening, or *imbibing,* the seeds. Soak dry seeds in water for twelve hours. (If you're using fresh seeds, you can skip this step.) Place the imbibed seeds in a container or plastic bag of moist sawdust or peat moss. Plastic bags are ideal because they allow a certain amount of air to pass through to the seeds, even when tightly sealed. If you use a can or jar, don't seal it tightly; it's essential for a small amount of air to reach the seeds. The seeds must be held for several months at a temperature below 45 degrees F but above freezing. A root cellar or refrigerator works well, or you can bury the packages containing the seeds about 12 inches deep outdoors in a sheltered area and leave them over the winter. Whichever procedure you follow, never let the seeds dry out. If for some reason fully imbibed and chilled seeds dry, they will enter a secondary dormancy and you'll have to stratify them all over again. Check the seeds every few weeks, and plant them in the garden as soon as they

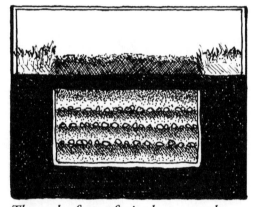

The seeds of most fruit plants must be dampened and exposed to cold before they can germinate. This process is called stratification. You can do it by placing seeds in a shallow box in layers separated by sand. Moisten the entire mass and keep it in the refrigerator or buried outside in a well-drained place until spring. Then remove the seeds and plant them in a nursery bed.

show signs of sprouting. If the weather is still too cold to plant outdoors, hold the sprouted seeds for a week or two in the refrigerator.

Seeds of plums, peaches, and other stone fruits may not always crack open for germination, so it's a good idea to crack them carefully in a vise or with a hammer before stratification, discarding any that appear shriveled.

If you wish to follow a more natural path, in September or October, take seeds from ripe fruits and plant them immediately. Space them 1 to 3 inches apart and 3 to 4 inches deep in shallow trenches. Smaller seeds like those of currants and blueberries should be planted closer and more shallowly. Cover the seeds with fine soil or, if your soil tends to crust, start with 2 inches of moist peat moss or sawdust, then finish covering with soil. Squirrels and rodents are always a problem, so protect your seeds by covering them with fine screening, placed directly atop the seeds before you cover them with soil. Be sure the screen covers both the tops and sides of the seeds. Just before the soil freezes, mound it 6 inches high over the rows to protect the seeds during the winter. Remove this extra soil in the spring before growth begins.

ASEXUAL PROPAGATION

Because so many fruit plants don't come true to type from seeds, named cultivars can be reliably propagated only *asexually*, or *vegetatively*. Some plants naturally reproduce by asexual means. Suckering in red raspberries and tip layering in blackberries are examples of natural asexual propagation. Plants can reproduce asexually thanks to *totipotency*. Each cell in the plant body is genetically the same as every other cell. A single cell in the root carries all the genetic information to reproduce an entire plant exactly like the parental type. To get a plant that naturally reproduces through seeds (sexual propagation) to reproduce asexually, all we have to do is provide the right environment to encourage these totipotent cells to reproduce the whole plant.

Cuttings

Cuttings are lengths of young shoots or roots that are detached from the parent plant and rooted to produce new plants identical to the parent. There are several types of cuttings.

Hardwood cuttings are usually taken from healthy, dormant, one-year-old wood. They should be about 6 inches long, pencil thick, and contain

Many fruit plants can be propagated from hardwood cuttings. Take 6-inch-long cuttings of dormant, pencil-thick, one-year-old wood that contain at least three nodes.

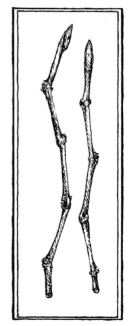

at least three nodes. Cuttings from the basal end of a shoot (the point where the shoot begins to grow out of a main limb) will root much more easily than those taken from the middle portion. Tip portions root poorly. Because roots will form only at the base of each cutting, it is standard practice to cut the base end off straight and the top end at a sharp angle, so there's no chance of planting a cutting upside down.

Take hardwood cuttings in late winter after severe cold has passed but before the buds break their dormancy, and store them upside down in damp peat moss in a cool cellar until planting time. Putting them in a plastic bag in the refrigerator also works well. During this storage period, the basal ends form a *callus*, or enlarged nodule, and may begin to form roots. Plant the callused cuttings in good soil outside in early spring, as soon as the soil can be worked. Delaying planting for a month or more will decrease the percentage of successful rootings. Set the cuttings right side up in rows 3 inches apart and deep enough that only the top bud remains above the soil. Successful rooting is indicated by the appearance of vigorous new growth.

Quince and currants are easy to root by hardwood cuttings; the latter even has partially formed young roots in the stem *nodes,* or points where new stems emerge from old growth. You only have to supply the proper environment for them to grow. Apples, pears, peaches, plums, and cherries are difficult to root by hardwood cuttings. These species may root more readily if the cuttings are treated with rooting hormone, although this is more often useful on softwood cuttings. Scratching or nicking the basal end of a hard-to-root cutting sometimes helps, because the wounding causes the plant to release ethylene gas, which stimulates root formation.

Softwood cuttings are used to propagate a very few deciduous fruit plants, among them blueberries, mahaleb cherries, and some myrobalan

A homemade frame for propagating softwood cuttings is inexpensive and effective. Use a wooden flat or box and attach bent coat hangers to form hoops over the flat. These support a piece of clear polyethylene to form a miniature greenhouse. The plastic helps keep the humidity high in the propagating frame.

and European plums. If you want to try softwood cuttings, take soft shoots of new growth from June to late July. Cut them 4 to 6 inches long, with the basal cut just below a bud and the upper cut just above a bud or leaf. Remove the lowest leaf. Moisten the basal end and dip it into rooting hormone, usually a preparation of indolebutyric acid (IBA). After dipping, push the cuttings into a sterile medium of sand, peat, vermiculite, perlite, or a combination of two or more of these. The lowest remaining leaf should be just above the surface. Press the medium very firmly around the cutting.

You must keep the cuttings moist until they have rooted. In well-equipped professional greenhouses, an intermittent mist system similar to those you see sprinkling fresh vegetables in the grocery store is used to maintain a constant level of humidity. Home gardeners can construct a propagation box from decay-resistant wood, with a fairly tight-fitting glass lid to keep the humidity high and let sunlight in. (The more sunlight that hits the softwood cuttings, the better they'll root.)

A simpler method is to plant the cuttings in a standard flat or box and cover it with a tent of clear plastic supported with wire hoops made from coat hangers. Attach a room humidifier or cool-mist vaporizer to the tent so that the atmosphere inside is saturated with moisture.

Moderate 75 degree F bottom heat, supplied by approved thermostatically controlled mats or cables, will hasten rooting. Don't let cuttings get too hot, however, or they will die.

After several weeks, check softwood cuttings by giving them a slight tug. If they don't move readily, roots have started to form. Give them a few more weeks to root completely before moving them to an outdoor nursery bed.

Root cuttings work well on blackberries, raspberries, and huckleberries. Collect pencil-thick roots in the autumn, pack them in damp peat or sand, and keep them cool in a root cellar or refrigerator until spring. As soon as you can work the soil, plant the root cuttings horizontally in a shallow furrow and cover them with a few inches of fine soil. The appearance of new growth indicates successful rooting.

Layering

Layering is a simple way to propagate new fruit plants. Strawberries and other species do this naturally through the formation of runners. Instead of removing a cutting, a stem is encouraged to root while still attached to the mother plant. It's then cut off and transplanted as a new plant.

Mound layering, or stooling, is an easy way to propagate fruit plants. Plant the mother plant in spring. By fall it will have established a good root system and put out vigorous growth. In the second spring, cut back the top to force vigorous production of side shoots. Mound soil or sawdust over the shoot bases until the mound is several inches high. Never cover the shoot tips. By late fall of the second year, the side shoots will have rooted and can be separated from the mother plant. Where winters are severe, wait until the next spring to separate them.

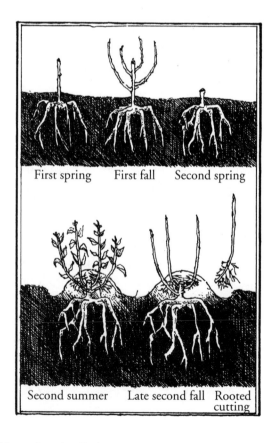

First spring   First fall   Second spring

Second summer   Late second fall   Rooted cutting

Mound layering, or *stooling,* is commonly used to propagate root-stocks for apples, plums, quince, and sometimes cherries. You can also use it to propagate many other kinds of fruit plants. To begin, cut the top off the mother plant. As side shoots form, begin mounding them gradually with moist sawdust until about 12 inches of the shoots are covered. (Use sawdust instead of soil because it's easier to remove without damaging the newly formed roots.) Never cover the shoot tips, and always keep the sawdust moist. Mounding should be complete by midsummer, and the shoots should be well rooted by autumn. In warmer climates you can brush away the sawdust and cut the rooted shoots from the mother plant in autumn; in cooler climates wait until spring. Leave the mother plant exposed until new shoots form, then begin the mounding process again.

Tip layering and *simple layering* are similar and work well on most plants, particularly grapes, gooseberries, blackberries, and black raspberries. In the spring, bend a new shoot to the ground and either stick the tip into the soil (tip layering) or leave the tip bare and cover the middle section of the shoot, about 6 inches back from the tip, with soil (simple layering). Use a rock or a U-shaped wire to hold it down. The shoot will root where it touches the soil. By the following spring you can detach the daughter plant and transplant it. Girdling, notching, or scraping the shoot where it enters the soil may speed rooting.

Many fruit plants can be propagated by tip layering, but it's usually reserved for bush fruits. In spring, scrape a bit of bark from a new shoot about 6 inches back from the tip. Place the injured area on the soil, mound soil over it, and hold it in place with a rock. Roots will form from the injured tissue. The daughter plant can be separated from the mother plant the following spring.

You can propagate plants that sucker freely by digging the suckers in the early spring. Be sure to get as much of the root system directly under the sucker as you can without overly damaging that of the mother plant.

Division

Division is perhaps the simplest method of propagation and is commonly used on strawberries, currants, gooseberries, and blueberries. Lift mature plants in the spring and divide their crowns into a few pieces. Treat each piece as a new plant. The separation of suckers in blueberries and raspberries is also a form of division.

GRAFTING

Grafting forms new plants by merging the top of a desired cultivar to the rootstock or branches of another. There are several types of grafting, all of which depend upon the proper selection of scion wood.

Choose dormant, pencil-thick wood of the previous season's growth from shoots that were at least 12 inches long. Be sure the buds are plump, that there are no flower buds present, and that the shoots are dormant. Collect the wood when the temperature is above freezing and wrap it in moist paper towels. Place this into a plastic bread bag and put it in a cool basement or refrigerator until the following spring. Never let the wood freeze after it is cut.

In the spring, begin grafting preferably just as the leaf buds begin to break on your fruit tree stocks. The stock may or may not be active, but the scions must be dormant during the grafting process. In all grafting, the actual point of union occurs where the cambia of both scion and stock meet. The cambium is near the thin, green layer found just under the outer bark. To form a successful graft, the cambia of the two pieces must be kept moist and in close contact until they grow together. To hold the graft together, special stretchy tapes and ties are used that provide the necessary support while at the same time allow the unrestricted flow of

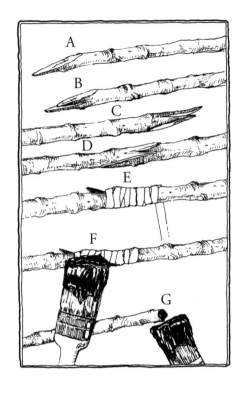

Whip grafting is an easy way to propagate apple and pear trees. Be sure the scion and stock are about the same diameter ($1/2$ inch or less). Cut the scion from the midportion of a dormant, pencil-thick, one-year-old shoot; it must have at least two good buds. (A) Make a slanting cut about $1^1/2$ inches long at the scion's base. (B) On the slanting surface, make another cut about $3/4$ inch long and parallel to the shoot's long axis. (C) Prepare the stock's end as you did the scion. (D) Fit the scion and stock together tightly, matching the cambia. (E) Tie the graft with raffia or grafting tape. (F) Wax the unions completely and (G) also the cut surface at the scion's tip. About a month after growth begins, run a knife along the wrapping, severing it. Don't remove it or you might damage the graft. Rewax the graft through the summer. If more than one bud grows, remove all but the most vigorous shoot. Remove all competing shoots from the stock below the graft union.

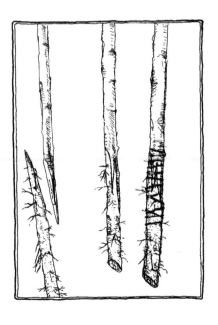

(Left) The completed whip graft looks like this. Here, a scion has been grafted to a root piece.

water and nutrients between the stock and scion. Once tied, the graft is usually coated with special grafting wax to further retain moisture.

Whip grafting, also called *bench grafting* because it's often done on a bench in the workshop, is the most common type of grafting. To make a good bench graft, both stock and scion should be about the same diameter, usually ¹/₂ inch or less. On both stock and scion, make a slanting cut with a single stroke of the knife; if you make more than one stroke, you're likely to change the angle of the blade slightly, resulting in a cut with ridges and hollows, and the stock and scion will not fit together well.

Cleft grafting is used for *topworking* trees when you wish to change a fruit's cultivar without planting a new tree. In this case the stock may be larger in diameter than the scion, though stocks less than 2 inches in diameter work best. The scion cut consists of two angled cuts instead of the single one used in the whip graft. Be sure to make each angled cut with just one stroke. Slightly cant the angle cut so that one side of the scion is thicker than the other, to help in matching the cambia.

Budding is a type of grafting in which a leaf bud replaces a scion. It's commonly used on stone fruits, nuts, and some grapes, and also in cases where there is not enough good scion wood to graft by other methods.

The best time to bud graft depends upon the maturity of the buds and the ease with which the bark

Cleft grafting is often employed in changing the scion cultivar of a fruit tree in a process called topworking. Here, an old apple tree has had most of its branches removed and the stubs topworked. This is an easy graft to make, and you can use this method to add many different cultivars to your tree.

All cleft grafts use a scion(s) inserted into a split in the stock stub of a branch or a small tree too large to whip graft. The scions should be dormant, one-year-old, pencil-thick wood. A stock 2 inches or less in diameter works best. The best time to cleft graft is just before spring growth begins. Saw off the stock squarely with a fine-toothed saw. (A) Split the stock across the center of its diameter and about 2 inches deep with a grafting chisel and mallet or a hatchet. (B) Hold the split (cleft) open with the chisel or a screwdriver. (C) Cut the scion's bottom end into a wedge shape, with one side of the wedge thicker than the other. Make the slanting cuts about 1¹/₂ inches long using single strokes. (D) Insert the scions with the narrow edge toward the center of the branch, being sure to match the cambia of the scion and stock. You can insert two scions into larger stocks. (E) Remove the chisel, and the spring of the stock will hold the scions in place. (F) Coat all cut surfaces, including the scion tips and the cleft sides, with wax. Rewax them if necessary throughout the first season, but don't wax over the buds. Let all growth develop the first year. Select the more vigorous shoots the next year and remove all others. If you allow two scions to remain and grow, they'll develop a bad crotch angle.

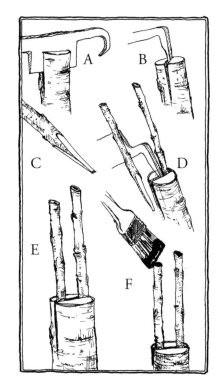

slips, or separates from the rest of the wood. Species that complete their vegetative growth late in the summer are usually budded in September. Those that complete their vegetative growth earlier can be budded in May or June. June budding is more common in the southern states, where the growing season is longer.

In selecting good budwood, choose only growth from the current season with vigorous leaf buds but no flower buds. Shoots with terminal

If you want to try grafting fruit to various rootstocks, use the following combinations. Most cultivars are compatible with the suggested stock.

SCION	STOCK
Apple	Apple
Pear	Pear, quince, hawthorn, medlar, serviceberry
Quince	Quince, mountain ash
Hawthorn	Hawthorn
Medlar	Pear, quince, hawthorn, medlar
Serviceberry	Mountain ash, serviceberry

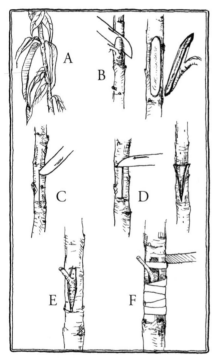

T-budding is used to propagate many fruit trees but is most popularly used on the stone fruits. (A) Select a healthy, vigorous shoot of current year's growth for use as a budstick. Remove it from the tree and snip off the leaves, leaving only the petioles attached. (B) Cut a shield from the budstick. Cut through the bark about ¹/₂ inch below a bud, then upward beneath the bud and out ¹/₂ inch above the bud, leaving the bud and petiole attached to the shield. (C) Make a vertical cut through the bark of the stock about 1¹/₂ inches long. (D) Make a horizontal cut at its top to form a T, then spread the bark from the T-cut. (E) Insert the bud into the slit and beneath the bark. If the shield extends above the upper horizontal cut, snip it off. (F) Wrap the bud firmly with budding rubbers to hold it in place. Start below the bud and wrap up. Don't cover the bud. Budding rubbers are thin and will crack and fall off in a couple of weeks.

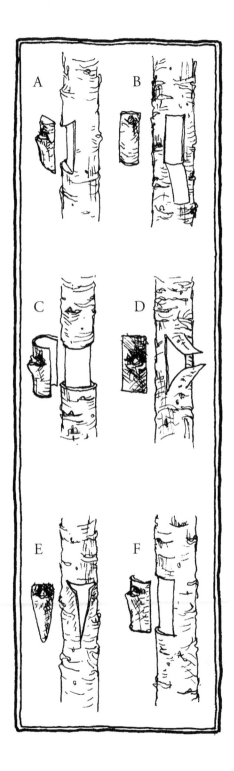

Other budding methods are similar but involve different cuts. (A) Chip budding is used on thick-barked trees, such as the nuts, and on grapes. (B) Plate budding for nut trees. (C) Ring or annular budding. (D) H-budding. (E) Prong (T-budding). (F) Flute budding. Nearly any type of budding will work on any type of fruit tree.

buds generally work best. Cut the budstick, clip off the leaves to reduce transpiration, and wrap the sticks in moist toweling. You can use them immediately or store them in the refrigerator for later use. Cut plump buds from the midsection of the budstick for best results.

The most common type of budding is the *T-bud,* also called the *shield bud.* Other types of budding, including *chip budding, patch budding,* and *flute budding,* vary only in the type of cut made and the method of insertion. All budding and grafting techniques are variations on the same theme and all have the same basic requirements.

Interstocks are used when a tree is *double-worked,* or grafted twice. A stem piece is added between the rootstock and the scion to impart some special character to the tree. Interstocks are used to overcome some incompatibility between stock and scion. For example, a graft between 'Stayman' apples and M9 dwarfing rootstocks don't unite well; an interstock overcomes this. The interstock may also impart hardiness to the trunk or provide dwarfing on a vigorous rootstock. One major problem with the use of interstocks is that instead of one graft union, you have two, and hence two areas of weakness.

Once you learn how to graft, you'll want to graft everything to everything. But the scion and the stock must be compatible. Compatible plants will form a good, strong union. Usually, closely related varieties, species, and sometimes genera are compatible, but more distant relatives are almost always incompatible. A 'Bartlett' pear scion on a quince rootstock makes a weak union that breaks. A 'Bartlett' scion on an ornamental sand pear (*Pyrus pyrifolia*) rootstock forms a strong union, but is vulnerable to a disease known as black end, ultimately making it incompatible.

Some incompatibilities are caused by viruses or fungi. For example, English walnut scions on black walnut rootstocks succumb to black line

Double-working involves the use of an interstock to lend special characteristics to the tree. The name comes from the fact that the tree has to be grafted twice. The strength of the characteristic imparted to the tree by the interstock depends upon the length of that piece. For example, an M9 interstem piece that is 12 inches long will have a stronger dwarfing effect on the tree than one only 6 inches long. Double-worked trees are useful in some specialized situations.

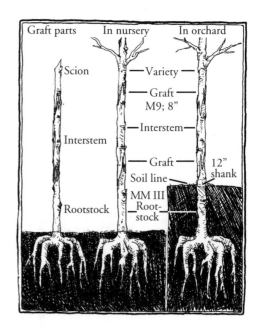

disease, which is caused by the cherry leaf-roll virus. Sweet cherry scions on *Prunus mahaleb* (another cherry) rootstocks develop buckskin disease, a fungal infection.

BUYING READY-TO-PLANT

Unless you're really interested in experimenting with propagation and grafting, it's much easier to buy plants that have already been started. There are a few things to consider.

- Start shopping early. At least one year before you plant, decide what you want. While you're making up your mind, get soil tests, work the soil, and add any amendments it might need.
- Select fruits that are right for your area. Check the USDA zone numbers for cold and heat tolerance. If you garden in southern Florida, for example, don't plant apples. Also, the cultivation of certain plants may be restricted in your area, so check with your state department of agriculture or your county cooperative extension service office before you order.
- Study catalogs for all the information they offer. Read the descriptions given under each fruit. Which rootstock is right for you? Will you need an interstock? Consider soil, climate, irrigation, and the level of care you'll give your plants.
- Check out local nurseries to see what they offer. Compare prices and quality—the cheapest plants are not always the best buy.
- Decide whether you want grafted plants or plants on their own roots. Sometimes you won't have a choice. Shrub-type fruiting plants will be available only on their own roots, and most tree fruits will be available only as grafted plants. Nut trees may be offered as either grafts or self-rooted.
- Always purchase disease-free plants. This is especially important with strawberries and brambles because so much of the stock is virus infected. Apples and pears also have a high incidence of disease, especially fire blight. Whenever you can, plant pest-resistant cultivars.
- Buy only certified plants that have been inspected and found to be healthy and true to type.
- Avoid buying "pedigreed" trees, a sales scam that simply means that the tree has been propagated from a mother plant that has

shown exceptional characteristics such as good vigor or freedom from pests. Since there is no evidence that those traits are necessarily inheritable, there's no guarantee that your tree will also be vigorous or pest-free, even if you do pay the extra money.

- How old a plant will you buy? Most fruit plants are sold as one- or two-year-olds. Sometimes you'll find a "ready-to-bear" plant or tree offered for sale. I've seen full-grown eight-year-old blueberry bushes sold for exorbitant prices just so people can take them home, plant them, and pick fruit the first year. Most of the time this doesn't work. Any flowers or fruit on the plant usually abort due to transplant shock, and the shock may be enough to set the plant back several years or kill it outright. Older plants do not guarantee a faster harvest. Even four- or five-year-old plants will be set back considerably by transplanting. I once experimented by planting some one-, two-, three-, and four-year-old blueberries; after five years in the field, you couldn't tell the difference.

- Order your mail-order plants in the fall prior to spring planting. If you garden in the South where fall planting is okay, order them in the spring. Placing your order several months in advance gives you the best chance of getting the cultivar and/or stock you need.

- Purchase only dormant plants. Planting stock that is not dormant is always risky.

- Should you buy bare-root or container-grown plants? Bare-root plants are packed in damp peat or sawdust and shipped in a cardboard box with a plastic liner. There's little or no soil on the roots, so these are light and easy to ship. This is typical of most mail-order stock.

   Local nurseries may offer container-grown plants or balled-and-burlapped (B&B) plants. Container-grown plants usually are sold in metal cans or plastic pots and have a compact root ball with plenty of soil clinging to it. B&B plants are dug from the field and have their root balls held intact by a wrapping of burlap or woven plastic material. These plants suffer less root disturbance than bare-rooted stock, but slightly more than container-grown stock. Choose only B&B plants with moist, healthy root balls.

   Potted or canned stock is a good choice if the plant is not root bound. If you see roots at the surface encircling the tree, choose another plant. Both potted plants and B&B plants have a better chance of surviving transplanting than bare-root stock.

- Whenever possible, buy locally. You'll have a chance to look over the stock, there will be only a short time between purchase and transplanting, and you'll establish a relationship with the local nursery or garden center. If you need to order special cultivars from a mail-order firm, be sure the company is in the same geographical region as your garden. Stock from a nursery in a different climatic zone may not be well adapted to your area, even though they may be plants of an adapted cultivar. And if you live in the North and order from a southern nursery, your plants may arrive too early. Holding them may encourage them to break dormancy.

- Watch out for new cultivars that aren't adapted to your area. When 'Granny Smith' apples hit the market, everyone in Rhode Island was planting them while I was telling them they shouldn't. 'Granny Smith' is a 200-day apple and Rhode Island has, on average, a 160-day season. The tree will survive, but the fruit won't ripen. Check with your county extension agent and plant only those cultivars whose growing-season requirements match your region.

- Choose only cross-fruitful cultivars. Some cultivars of apples, pears, plums, and sweet cherries are cross-incompatible and require a different cultivar planted nearby to ensure pollination. Plant the right combination for the best crops.

- Beware of novelty fruits. Those five-in-one grafted apple trees are fun to have but expensive. Why not do the grafting yourself? You'll have more pride in a tree you "built" yourself. (A friend of mine whip grafted over a hundred cultivars onto his 'McIntosh' apple tree. He didn't pay a dime extra for his novelty.)

People love bargains. Everyone wants to get a deal, but the best deal is to purchase your plants from a reputable nursery. You may find cheaper plants at local discount stores, but they may be rootbound, overly mature, mislabeled, or underwatered. Don't take chances. You're not planting radishes. Fruit plants are long-term investments.

Choosing the Best Site

Careful site selection is an important step in making a successful fruit planting. Because fruit plants must occupy the same site for years, you don't have the luxury of changing the planting location every year until you happen on the right spot.

PLANNING AND LAYOUT

Begin by laying out your planting to scale on paper. Consider not only plant spacing, but also mature height and spread, so that you avoid having plants shade each other when they mature. Also, make sure your plants are far enough from nearby buildings so that they won't be shaded when young, and so that their roots won't crack foundations as they mature. If you have a vegetable garden, consider the shade and root competition your fruit trees and shrubs may give your vegetables. Fruit trees should be set back from the garden a distance equal to their mature height plus 20 feet. For example, if you plant a standard-size apple tree, expect it to reach a height of about 30 feet. Add 20 feet to that, and you should plant your vegetable garden no closer to the tree than 50 feet. To further decrease shading, plant fruit trees on the north side of the garden where possible.

How big a planting do you want? It's nice to dream of a beautiful apple orchard in bloom, but who's going to care for it? How much time can you spend in the strawberry patch? With what equipment will you care for your chestnut trees? How many apples can your family use? Do you have room to store excess produce? Does your family like and eat the varieties you want to plant? Will you plant full-size or dwarf cultivars?

Fruit plants can be influenced by the shade and root competition of a nearby tree. Always locate your fruit plants well away from competing vegetation. If you must plant fairly close to a shade tree, sever the tree's roots to eliminate competition with your fruit plants. Fruit trees can also create problems for the vegetable garden if they're planted too close.

Approximate yields from your home fruit garden. Harvest fruits at peak quality and store only sound fruit.

FRUIT	AVERAGE ANNUAL YIELD
Apple	
Standard	8 bushels per tree
Semidwarf	4 bushels per tree
Dwarf	1 bushel per tree
Blackberry	
Erect	30 quarts per 100 feet of row
Evergreen	10 quarts per plant
Blueberry	5 pints per bush
Cherry	
Sour	60 quarts per tree
Sweet	75 quarts per tree
Nanking	15 pounds per bush
Currant	5 quarts per bush
Dewberry	60 pints per 100 feet of row
Elderberry	15 pounds per plant
Grape	
V. vinifera	25 pounds per vine
V. labrusca	15 pounds per vine
Muscadine	15 pounds per vine
Gooseberry	8 quarts per bush
Jostaberry	12 pounds per bush
Jujube	100 pounds per tree
Juneberry	12 pounds per plant
Mulberry	10 bushels per tree
Pawpaw, northern	1 bushel per tree
Peach	4 bushels per tree
Pear	
Standard	3 bushels per tree
Dwarf	$^1/_2$ bushel per tree
Persimmon, American	75 pounds per tree
Persimmon, kaki	400 pounds per tree
Plum	2 bushels per tree

Quince	1 bushel per tree		
Raspberry			
Black	50 pints per 100 feet of row		
Purple	50 pints per 100 feet of row		
Red	65 pints per 100 feet of row		
Yellow	65 pints per 100 feet of row		
Strawberry	70 quarts per 100 feet of row		

You can't grow all fruits in all gardens. How much of what you should plant depends upon how much you like the fruit and upon what grows well in your area. Here are some ballpark figures on how many plants of each fruit are right for a medium-size fruit planting.

FRUIT	NUMBER OF PLANTS	FRUIT	NUMBER OF PLANTS
Apple	3–6	Strawberry	100
Pear	2–4	Blackberry	25
Quince	2	Dewberry	30
Peach	6	Fig	4
Plum	6	Raspberry	40
Sour cherry	2–3	Grape	4–6
Sweet cherry	3	Jujube	3–6
Apricot	2	Gooseberry	2
Pecan	4–8	Currant	2

A 5-foot pear tree is a cinch to care for, but when that tree matures, it's another story. Consider questions like these very carefully before you plant. It is usually best to start small and add plants as you become more experienced. If you have a small yard, plant dwarf fruit trees or stick to small fruits and berries. If you're just beginning to grow fruit, a dozen fruiting shrubs or four to six trees are enough to care for.

Fruit plantings are usually rectangular in shape, but they don't have to be. Straight, regular rows allow for the most efficient use of large equipment, but home orchards can be any shape or pattern you like. You may even choose to incorporate some of your fruiting plants into the landscape.

Most fruit trees and bushes are arranged in squares for convenience in cultivating, but you don't have to plant in this scheme if you're short on space. Planting in a square with a fifth tree in the middle (quincunx scheme) allows you to fit 20 percent more plants into a given area. Planting in a hexagonal arrangement allows 15 percent more trees in a given space.

Strawberries and lingonberries make great borders for flower beds and walks. Use grapes and kiwifruit for arbors and dividers, currants and gooseberries for hedges, and blueberries for landscape specimen plants.

A space-saving *quincunx system* spaces plants on the points of a square with a fifth plant in the middle. This allows you 20 percent more plants in a given space. A *hexagonal system* allows plants to be set equidistantly, and you can get 15 percent more plants into a given area.

Generally, allow enough space between young plants so that the mature plants don't touch each other. Of course, you can't do this with raspberries or other brambles that will naturally spread and crowd each other, but in other plants, flower bud formation and fruit production will suffer where plants shade each other. In hedgerow plantings—a common practice with berry bushes and grapes—leave out one plant every 50 feet to allow for air drainage and for bees to cross between rows during bloom.

Precise spacings depend upon soil type, cultural conditions, species, and rootstock. Plants on poor soils, dwarfing rootstocks, and those grown where the season is short can be spaced slightly closer.

Whatever pattern you choose, plant taller trees and vining fruits on the north side of your property to reduce shading. Arrange taller plants in rows running north to south where possible to reduce in-row shading and increase yields.

Throughout all your planting, remember that proper exposure to sunlight is a key element of success. With few exceptions, always plant fruits in full sun.

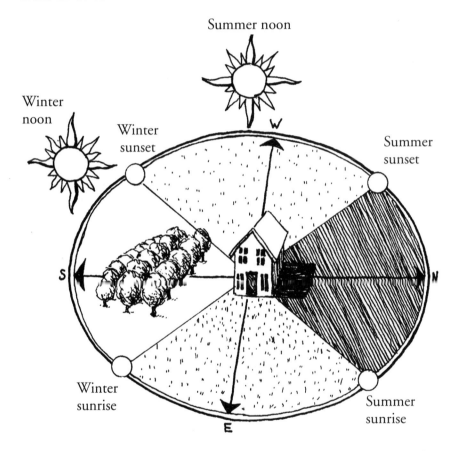

All fruit-bearing plants usually do best in full sun. Planting on a southern exposure will ensure that they receive all the sun they can use. Eastern exposures receive morning sun and are cooler than western exposures, which receive the hot afternoon sun and often are exposed to prevailing winds. Northern exposures are not good for most fruit plants, except perhaps Ribes *planted near their southern limit. Never plant within 10 feet of a single-story building or within 20 feet of a two-story building.*

MICROCLIMATES

Microclimates are small areas whose environmental conditions can differ substantially from the overall climate (macroclimate) of your location. The microclimate of a paved patio or driveway can be brutal, even though your macroclimate may be moderate. If you live near the northern limit of a fruit species, plant it near your house, a chimney, or a heated building to take advantage of the heat lost through the walls, but don't plant it on the shady north side of any building. If you garden near the southern limit of a species, plant it in a cooler area of light shade.

Slopes

Sloping land creates microclimates warmer or cooler, windier or calmer than surrounding areas. Depending on where you live, taking advantage of the microclimates created by sloping land can help you produce better fruit.

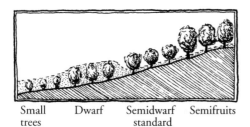

Small trees   Dwarf   Semidwarf standard   Semifruits

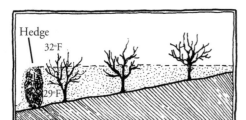

Hedge
32°F
29°F

Cold air is heavier than warm air and always flows downhill. Planting small fruit at the bottom of a hill and tree fruit at the top means that the smaller plants are more likely to be engulfed by colder air and have a greater probability of suffering frost damage. A physical block, such as a row of thick brush or a hedge at the bottom of the hill, will cause the colder air to back up and become deeper, and will increase the chances of frost damage to flowering trees. Plant smaller bushes near the top of the hill and the tallest ones farther down. The greater height of the flowering branches is some insurance against frost damage.

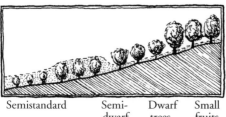

Semistandard   Semi-dwarf   Dwarf trees   Small fruits

Cold air, being heavier than warm air, flows downhill. If you plant on a gentle slope, cold air will drain away from your plants, lessening the chances of frost damage. Frost pockets usually accumulate at the bottom of a hill, so avoid planting early-blossoming cultivars there.

Generally, southern and western slopes are warmer and drier than northern and eastern slopes and fruits planted there will usually bloom, set fruit, and be ready to harvest earlier. If you live in an area where late-spring frosts are common, you may find that this earlier bloom exposes your plants to a risk from late frost. In areas with hot spring and summer temperatures, planting on cooler eastern slopes may allow your fruits a longer blossoming time and a better chance at pollination.

Study the lay of the land carefully before you plant. Avoid exposed, windy sites and heavily shaded slopes. Hot, sunny sites usually dry out quickly, and if you plant on southern and western slopes, you may need to pay close attention to watering.

Elevation

To gardeners in mountainous regions, the microclimates created by elevation are equally important as those created by the slope of the land. A difference in elevation of 100 feet can mean a difference of 5 to 10 degrees F in temperature. As you move up in elevation, it gets colder, and as you move down, it gets warmer, unless you move down into a frost pocket or shaded canyon.

Bodies of Water

Water can also create microclimates. Even a small pond has an influence on the surrounding area, and a large lake or ocean creates significant climatic changes. Depth of water is more important than area covered, because deep water holds heat and releases it slowly to the air, warming and moderating the microclimate near the shore.

Springtime is usually cooler and later in coastal areas than a few miles inland, so fruits planted there often escape late frosts. Autumns are warmer along coastlines, and the chances of an early frost are less. Many fruits grown along the shores of the Finger Lakes and the Great Lakes can't be grown a few miles inland. You can grow figs along the Atlantic shore of southern Rhode Island, but they won't survive in wooded western Rhode Island only 25 miles away.

WINDS AND WINDBREAKS

Light winds promote air circulation and lessen the incidence of disease. Strong winds, however, can cause problems for a fruit grower. It's difficult and dangerous to spray in windy conditions, bees won't fly in strong wind and so pollination may be light and incomplete, and a dry wind reduces fruit set by drying the pistils, making fertilization impossible. Also, trees grow lopsided in continual strong wind and may topple.

Those who garden in urban and suburban areas usually get enough protection from surrounding homes and trees to eliminate the need for a windbreak. Orchards in wide open spaces, however, may need extra protection.

In the United States, prevailing winds come from the southwest during the summer and the northwest during the winter. Planting a windbreak on the south, north, and west sides of your orchard gives it protection from hot south winds, cold north winds, and strong west winds. A traditional windbreak consists of five rows of plants: The outermost and innermost rows are shrubs, the center row is tall evergreens, and the two rows in between are small trees. In cross section the windbreak looks like a pyramid. Shrubs like Siberian pea tree (*Caragana arborescens*), common lilac (*Syringa vulgaris*), Tatarian honeysuckle (*Lonicera tatarica*), and buffaloberry (*Shepherdia argentea*) work well. Small trees like Russian olive (*Elaeagnus angustifolia*), green ash (*Fraxinus pennsylvanica*), and chokecherry (*Prunus* spp.) are fine. For large evergreens, try Colorado blue spruce (*Picea pungens*) and Norway spruce (*Picea abies*). Set the plants about 6 to 10 feet apart, in staggered rows about 10 to 15 feet apart. Windbreaks take up a lot of space, and you should plant no closer to the windbreak than a distance equal to the height of the tallest tree species. If you don't have the room (or the need) for a traditional five-row break, a single row of Russian olives or other dense shrubs spaced 4 feet apart makes an excellent single-row windbreak. Snow fences, picket fences, hedges, and even a double row of tall sunflowers can all be used to protect small plants. Don't use solid fencing, however; it creates a dead air space that may increase pest damage by encouraging bugs to nest there.

Wind protection on the leeward side of a windbreak extends to five

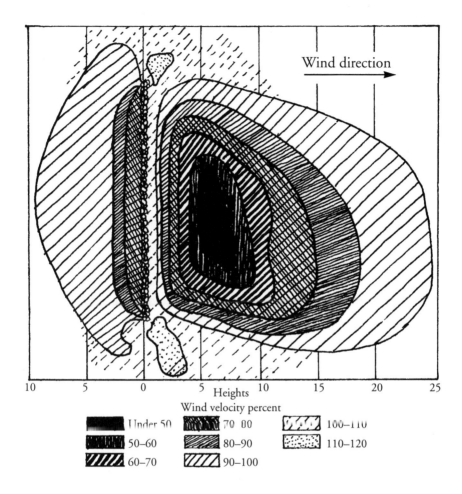

Wind direction

10   5   0   5 Heights 10   15   20   25

Wind velocity percent

▅ Under 50	▓ 70–80	▒ 100–110
▓ 50–60	▨ 80–90	░ 110–120
▥ 60–70	▨ 90–100	

The actual field of protection afforded by a windbreak depends upon the height of the break and the speed of the wind. In general, a windbreak with about 50 percent of the wind blocked will afford some wind protection to plants to a leeward distance equal to about 19 times the height of the break. The degree of protection varies with distance from the break, with the slowest wind speed and therefore the greatest protection about 6 heights from the break. For example, a windbreak that is 20 feet high will slow wind out to 380 feet (20 x 19) to leeward of the break. The area of greatest protection will be about 120 feet (20 x 6) to leeward.

to ten times the height of the break. If the tallest trees in the break are 60 feet, you'll have wind protection for 300 to 600 feet to the leeward. Windbreaks also cause snow to drift over plants located leeward of the break. This snow cover protects plants and roots from extreme cold and drying winter winds. A windbreak can also reduce the summer temperature by several degrees through the evaporative cooling effect of all that massed greenery and may result in a better fruit crop.

On the down side, windbreaks take a lot of space, need a long time to become established, and provide great nesting sites for fruit-eating birds.

DRAINAGE

Drainage is an important consideration, because tree fruits and grapes have roots that can go down 20 feet into the soil. A very high water table can cause these deep-rooted plants to rot. If your water table is high, stick to shallow-rooted small fruits like cranberries and blueberries and plant on elevated ridges to improve draining.

To test the depth of your water table, dig a hole several feet deep. Soil color can tell you a lot about the drainage. Dig a second hole 2 to 3 feet deep and fill it with water. If the water remains in the hole longer than twelve hours, you have poorly drained soil.

You can improve the drainage in most soils by adding about 3 inches of coarse sand at a depth of about 10 inches. If the soil is heavy and wet, you may have to install drain pipes to remove the excess water.

Bush fruits, such as strawberries and blueberries, can be grown in raised beds constructed over extremely wet soils.

What color is your soil? You can tell a lot about soil drainage by looking at its color. Dig a hole several feet deep and examine the soil at its sides. If you're in a poorly drained area that experiences flooding, plant elsewhere.

Soil Color	Characteristics
Uniform bright red, yellow, or brown	Good, well-drained soil
Mottled or deep gray	Short-term, periodic flooding
Uniform light gray	Prolonged flooding

The water infiltration rate and a soil's water-holding capacity are very important. If you apply water at a faster rate than the intake rate of the soil, it will run off and can cause erosion. The heavier the soil, the more water it can hold.

Texture	Intake Rate (in./hr.)	Holding Capacity (in./ft.)
Sand	1.0–5.0	0.5–0.7
Sandy loam	0.7–1.0	0.8–1.4
Loam	0.6–1.0	1.0–1.8
Silt loam	0.5–1.0	1.2–1.8
Clay loam	0.3–0.8	1.3–2.1
Clay	0.1–0.5	1.4–2.4

Some fruits are more tolerant to flooding and poor soil drainage than others, but none do well under very wet soil conditions.

Most Tolerant	Least Tolerant
Apple	Peach
Apricot	Almond
Pear	Cherry
Blueberry	Blackberry
Gooseberry	Currant
Grape	Raspberry
	Plum
	Strawberry
	Quince
	Juneberry

POTTED PLANTS

If you have a very small property, or if no part of your property is suitable for fruit plants, you can still have a miniature orchard—in pots.

Container-grown fruits fit very well in small gardens and let you grow fruits that might otherwise be marginal in your area. Most small fruiting shrubs and dwarf trees can be grown in pots, but they require a great amount of care.

The root systems of container-grown plants are greatly restricted, and they require more attention to watering and fertilizing than plants in the garden. Also, because the roots have less insulating soil around them, summer temperatures can get too hot and winter temperatures too cold. Apple tree roots will tolerate soil temperatures only as low as about 10 degrees F; peaches, cherries, and most other fruit plants will tolerate soil temperatures only as low as 15 degrees F. When winter air temperatures drop into the twenties, move potted plants indoors.

Fruiting plants must have a period of chilling, so place them in a cool basement area where the temperature remains between 35 and 45 degrees F until spring. If you can't do this, plant them outside, pot and all, and mulch them heavily for the winter months.

Summer protection is essential, too. Root ball temperatures in potted plants can reach 130 degrees F if the pots are set in bright sun on a paved surface. Because most plants stop growing at temperatures above 85 to 90 degrees F, and because plant tissues begin to break down at about 110

A wet-soil tolerance scale. The best soil types fall about in the middle of this scheme. Rubus *and strawberry species are not fussy about their soils, although wet soils can promote diseases in these crops.*

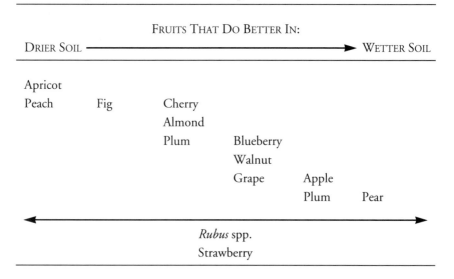

		FRUITS THAT DO BETTER IN:			
DRIER SOIL ──────────────────────────────▶ WETTER SOIL					
Apricot					
Peach	Fig	Cherry			
		Almond			
		Plum	Blueberry		
			Walnut		
			Grape	Apple	
				Plum	Pear
◀──────────────────────────────────▶					
		Rubus spp.			
		Strawberry			

degrees F, your potted plants are not long for this world in those conditions. In hot summer weather, move your plants to a cooler spot off the pavement and water them deeply and often.

Potted fruit plants can be grown even indoors. Plant dwarf fruit trees in 9- to 14-inch-diameter pots and hold them in a cool cellar for two weeks after potting. Then move them into a cool, sunny area of the house and treat them as you would a houseplant during the spring and summer. Move them into a cool area for three or four months each autumn to satisfy their chilling requirement. In about three years, they will bloom, usually about a month after being brought back into the house from their cool rest period.

Unless you want to keep a beehive in the house, you'll have to pollinate the flowers by hand. Use a camel hair brush to collect pollen from the anthers of one cultivar and brush it onto the pistils of another.

Keep your potted trees in shape with careful pruning. Repot all container-grown fruit plants every few years in fresh soil.

Building Your Soil

The condition and fertility of your soil are probably the most important considerations when selecting a site for your fruiting plants. All fruit plants do best in deep, well-drained, fertile silty loam. Fruit trees need a soil depth of at least 5 to 6 feet; small fruits, 3 to 4 feet; and strawberries, 1 to 2 feet. Building your soil with the addition of proper amendments, organic matter, and carefully applied fertilizers will help you grow better fruit.

TYPES OF SOIL
Soils are classified as loam, sandy, clay, or silt, depending upon their composition.

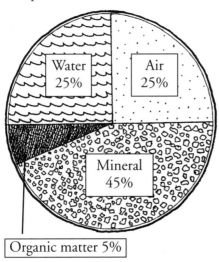

Water 25%

Air 25%

Mineral 45%

Organic matter 5%

Loam soils, dark, rich, and high in organic matter, are ideal. Fertile, friable, and well aerated, loam is well drained yet holds sufficient moisture for plant growth. If you have

The perfect soil for fruit plants is made up of half solids and half pore space. The pore space is filled half with water and half with air. The solid material consists of minerals and about 5 percent organic matter.

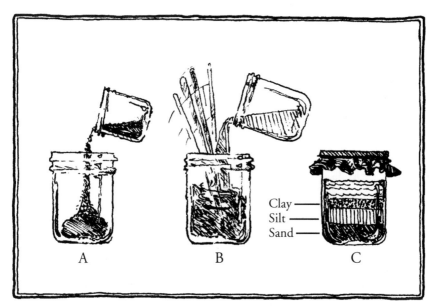

Clay
Silt
Sand

A   B   C

To estimate the percentage of sand, silt, and clay in your soil, (A) put ¹/₂ cup of soil in a jar. (B) Fill the jar with water and swirl the contents for one minute. Let them settle, swirl several times more, fasten the top and let sit for one week. (C) Then examine the contents without moving the jar. Sand will have formed a layer at the bottom, silt in the middle, and clay at the top. Estimate the percentages of each in your soil. If the thickest layer is sand, you have a sandy soil; if clay, a clayey soil.

loam soil, preserve its tilth with annual applications of compost, organic matter, and balanced fertilizers.

Sandy soils warm quickly in the spring, are well aerated, and don't compact readily. They don't hold water well and are more prone to summer drought, and they tend to be infertile because nutrients leach away quickly. Plants in sandy soils start growth earlier in the spring and ripen their fruit earlier in the fall, but they are also more susceptible to late-spring frost damage. If you have very light, sandy soil, amend it with peat moss, compost, or other organic matter, and pay great attention to the water and fertilizer needs of your plants.

Clay soils are heavy and feel slick when wet. They warm slowly in the spring, retain nutrients well, are poorly aerated, and compact easily. Because they drain slowly, they're less droughty in summer but can quickly become waterlogged during rainy periods. Plants in clay soil start

How wet is your soil? Here's an easy way to gauge your soil type and its moisture-holding capacity.

Moisture Available	Sand (Gritty When Wet)	Sandy Loam (Gritty When Wet, Dirties Fingers)	Clay Loam (Sticky When Wet)	Clay (Like Modeling Clay When Wet)
0%	Dry, loose, flows through fingers	Dry, loose, flows through fingers	Dry clods break into powder	Hard, cracked, clods hard to break
Less than 50% (irrigate at once)	Dry, will not form ball	Dry, will not form ball	Crumbly, forms loose ball	Pliable, forms loose ball
50%–75% (irrigate)	Same as 50%	Forms loose ball	Forms ball; feels slick under pressure	Forms ball; ribbons between thumb and forefinger
75% to field capacity (okay)	Sticks together, forms very weak ball	Forms loose ball; does not feel slick	Forms pliable ball; may feel slick	Easily ribbons between fingers
Field capacity (saturated)	No free water upon squeezing; hand moist	Same as sand	Same as sand	Same as sand
Above field capacity (Water-logged)	Free water appears when soil is bounced in hand	Free water appears when soil is kneaded	Squeeze out free water	Puddles and free water on surface

growth later in the spring and have fewer problems from late-spring frosts. Fruit also ripens later. Amend these soils with crushed stone, sand, peat, or compost. Be careful not to overwater or overfertilize.

Silty soils are fine grained, usually fertile, easily compacted when wet, and very prone to wind erosion when dry. Amend silty soils with peat moss, compost, and organic matter to loosen and aerate the soil structure and to help hold moisture and nutrients.

pH LEVELS

The pH level of your soil—its degree of acidity or alkalinity—will influence how well your plants absorb nutrients. The pH scale runs from 0 to 14; 7 is neutral. A pH of less than 7 is acid; the smaller the number the more acid the soil. A pH greater than 7 is alkaline; the greater the number the more alkaline the soil. The scale is logarithmic, so there is a factor of ten between numbers. A soil with a pH of 5 is ten times more acidic than one with 6, and one hundred times more acidic than one with 7.

Most fruit plants do best in slightly acid soil, with a pH between 6 and 7—the range in which most nutrients are readily available. If soil pH is too high, iron can become unavailable to plants, resulting in iron chlorosis. If soil pH is too low, aluminum and manganese can become too available to plants, resulting in toxicity and poor growth.

Some fruiting plants, such as apples and pears, are not fussy about soil pH and will grow in soil with a pH range between 4 and 8. Other plants, notably the acid-loving blueberries and lingonberries, need a moderately acid soil with a pH of about 4.5 to 5.2. They have difficulty absorbing iron at a soil pH above this range, making it difficult to interplant these fruits with others.

Test your soil pH and adjust it prior to spring planting. Most areas east of the Mississippi have acid soils. If yours is too acidic, wood ashes, ground limestone, or hydrated lime can be added to raise the pH level. It takes about 50 pounds of wood ash or limestone per 1,000 square feet per year to raise the pH by one number.

Ground limestone (calcium carbonate), also called agricultural limestone or garden lime, is the safest to use but takes several months to work. Hydrated lime (calcium hydroxide) works much faster but can burn plants if it is applied too close to them. Wood ashes supply potassium as

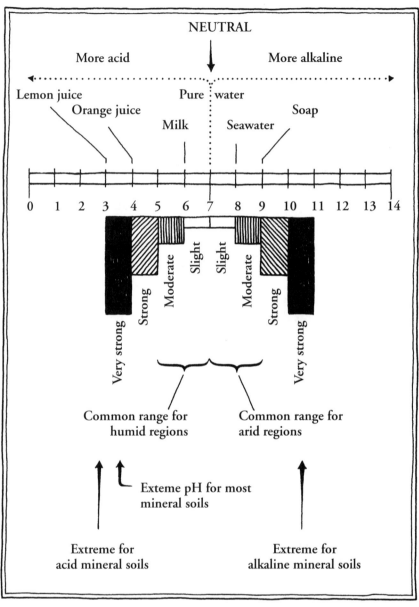

The pH scale expresses the degree of acidity or alkalinity of a substance. Seven is neutral; less than 7 is acid; greater than 7 is alkaline. Soap, at a pH of 9, is alkaline; lemon juice, at a pH of 3, is acid. Most fruit plants do best in a slightly acid soil with a pH of 6 to 6.5, although many will grow at higher soil pHs. Blueberries and lingonberries need acid soils with a pH range of 4.5 to 5.2.

The correct soil pH is necessary for the best growth of fruit plants. If a fruit is not listed here, its best range for growth is not known or it grows over a wide pH range. When in doubt, adjust your soil pH to 5.5 to 6.5. If it is an ericaceous plant, adjust it to 4.5 to 5.5.

CROP	BEST RANGE
Apple	5.5–6.5
Apricot	5.5–6.5
Blackberry	4.5–7.5
Blueberry	
Highbush	4.2–5.2
Rabbiteye	4.2–5.5
Cherry	5.5–6.5
Cranberry (highbush)	6.0–7.5
Currant	6.0–7.0
Fig	7.0–7.5
Gooseberry	6.0–7.0
Grape	
V. labrusca	4.0–7.0
Hybrid	5.0–7.0
Muscadine	5.5–7.0
V. vinifera	5.5–7.0
Juneberry	6.0–7.5
Lingonberry	4.2–5.5
Medlar	5.5–6.5
Nuts	5.0–6.0
Peach	5.5–6.5
Pear	5.5–6.5
Plum	5.5–6.5
Quince	5.5–6.5
Raspberry	5.5–7.0
Strawberry	5.0–6.5

they dissolve, but before that happens they form a lye solution in the soil that can harm plants for several days after application. Apply pH-adjusting materials in the autumn to avoid burning growing plant tissues.

If you live west of the Mississippi, your soil is probably alkaline. Sul-

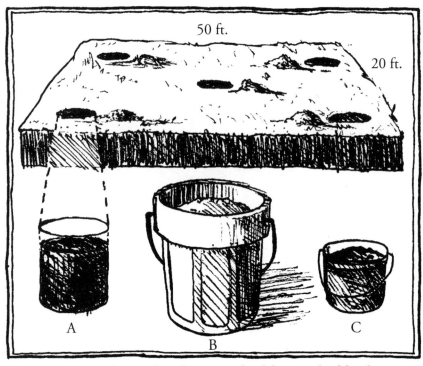

To sample your soil properly, take a cup of soil from each of five locations around your planting. In each case, discard the top 2 inches of the soil and (A) use that from a depth of 2 to 5 inches only. This is the feeder root zone of many fruit plants. (B) Mix the five samples in a clean plastic bucket and (C) take 1 cup of the composite sample for testing. Areas of the planting that have markedly different soils should be sampled separately.

furic materials are used to lower pH levels. Wettable garden sulfur and ferrous sulfate are commonly used soil acidifiers. Ammonium sulfate adds nitrogen and works faster than sulfur, but you'll need twice as much. Stay away from sulfuric acid, and never use aluminum sulfate. All the gardening books recommend it, but they shouldn't; it acidifies the soil, but it also adds aluminum, which is not a nutrient and can become toxic to plants. Oak leaves and peat moss also are soil acidifiers, but they are only slightly acidic and won't have much effect on very alkaline soils.

Regardless of which materials you use to raise or lower soil pH, the speed of the reaction depends not only upon the compound, but also

If your soil pH is too low, raise it to about 6.5 using ground agricultural limestone if possible. Avoid the harsher hydrated lime.

CHANGE pH	POUNDS OF LIME PER 1,000 SQUARE FEET		
FROM	SANDY SOIL	LOAM	CLAY
4.0	65	175	250
4.5	55	145	210
5.0	45	115	165
5.5	30	85	115
6.0	15	45	60

Lowering soil pH to about 4.5 is easy. If you substitute ferrous sulfate for sulfur, multiply the amount of material applied by six. Adapted from R. E. Gough, The Highbush Blueberry and Its Management, *Binghamton, NY: The Haworth Press, 1994.*

CHANGE pH	POUNDS OF SULFUR PER 1,000 SQUARE FEET	
FROM	SANDY SOIL	LOAM
7.5	24	70
7.0	19	60
6.5	15	48
6.0	13	38
5.5	9	25
5.0	4	13

upon the fineness of the grind (finer material works faster) and upon the levels of organic matter and clay in the soil. The higher the organic matter and clay content, the slower these compounds work.

Some areas of the western United States have soils with a high calcium content. High-calcium, or *calcareous*, soils have a pH of about 7.5. Apply dilute acid to them and they'll fizz. If you can lower the pH to within an acceptable range, they can be used to grow some fruits.

ALKALI SOILS

Soils with high salt levels are known as *alkali soils*. There are two types: *saline soils*, which contain enough salt to impair plant growth, and *sodic soils*, which contain enough sodium to restrict soil drainage through compaction. Sodic soils often have pHs above 8.4, far too high for fruit plants. Alkali soils also contain other salts, notably carbonates, chlorides, and sodium and potassium sulfates, which form different-colored crusts on the soil's surface. A white crust indicates the presence of calcium and magnesium salts, and black, the presence of sodium salts.

Most woody plants are very sensitive to sodium and chloride, which will cause marginal and tip leaf burn, leaf mottling and shedding, and deformed new leaves. The partial defoliation caused by leaf damage exposes the fruits to the direct rays of the sun and may cause sunburn. Affected plants will be intolerant of adverse weather conditions.

You can ameliorate alkali soils, but sometimes it's not worth the aggravation. Adding gypsum (plaster of paris), sand, and organic matter will condition the soil, and the application of sulfur or ammonium sulfate will acidify it. Use iron chelate or an iron-containing fertilizer, like ferrous ammonium sulfate, to help prevent iron chlorosis. You can make ferrous ammonium sulfate by adding 4 ounces of ferrous sulfate and 4 ounces of ammonium sulfate to 3 gallons of water. Periodically water your plants with this. If you get too much on your lawn it may turn your grass blackish green for a few weeks. The grass will eventually regain its color.

These amelioration techniques are only temporary, because water in these areas is usually salty as well, and each time you water your plants, you add more salt to the soil. Also, soil pH will rise naturally over time and you'll have to constantly reacidify the soil. If your soil is severely salty, grow salt-tolerant plants like buffaloberries, or use salt-tolerant rootstocks. Check with your county cooperative extension service for salt-tolerant varieties that will do well in your area.

INCREASING HUMUS CONTENT

Organic matter, made of complex carbon compounds from plant and animal residues, is an important part of soil. Humus increases the soil's water-holding capacity, porosity, and aeration. It also increases the availability of nutrients (particularly nitrogen) and decreases nutrient leaching and the solubility of toxic aluminum.

In the soil, given enough time, all organic material decays. When the soil is cultivated or turned, it becomes oxygenated, making organic matter decay faster. Every season of cultivation depletes the soil's organic matter. Because perennial fruiting plants occupy the soil for a long time, it's difficult to incorporate enough organic matter after planting. That's why its important to add plenty before you plant—you may never have another chance to get it into the root zone, where it does the most good.

When adding anything to the soil to increase the organic matter, consider its C:N ratio, the proportion of carbon to nitrogen. High-carbon materials decay slowly, and the microorganisms that decompose them must use some of the soil's nitrogen for food. This may cause a nitrogen deficiency that adversely affects plant growth. To prevent nitrogen deficiencies caused by the slow breakdown of carbon, it's always best to use partially composted material or material with a low carbon-to-nitrogen ratio. If you use dry leaves or other high-carbon materials, chop them so they won't mat and will break down faster. If the C:N ratio of the material you're adding is less than about 25:1, you won't have to add more nitrogen. If above that, add nitrogen when you incorporate the material into the soil, at the rate of about 2 pounds of 10–10–10 (or its equivalent) per 100 square feet.

Manure is more valuable as a soil amendment for increasing organic matter than as a fertilizer. If you have only a couple of fruit plants, you can buy bags of composted manure. Never apply fresh manure near growing plants or it will burn them. For large plantings, either locate a local source of bulk manure or use another humus-building material.

Cover crops are a good way to add organic material to the soil. A cover crop of buckwheat or millet will crowd out weeds and add plenty of organic matter when plowed under. Cover crops should be planted on tilled, amended soil the summer before you plant fruit. Plow the summer cover crop under in late summer or early autumn and plant a winter cover crop, such as winter rye or spring oats, to hold the soil. If you plant winter rye, turn it under in the spring before it gets taller than about 8 inches or it will dry the soil and be tough to incorporate. If you want to add compost or rotted manure, do it in the fall after you've put down your summer cover but before you plant your winter one. Remember, this is the last time you'll be able to strongly influence the soil's organic matter content in your fruit planting.

In small areas, where cover cropping is impractical, improve poor soil by digging a hole at least 3 feet wide and 3 feet deep and refilling it with

Approximate carbon-to-nitrogen (C:N) ratios of some common materials. If you use material with a C:N ratio of 25:1 or greater, you'll have to add supplemental nitrogen fertilizer to aid decomposition.

MATERIAL	C:N RATIO
Wood chips	600:1
Sawdust	300:1
Paper	125:1
Timothy	80:1
Cornstalks	80:1
Oat straw	75:1
Autumn leaves	65:1
Peat moss	58:1
Horse manure	35:1
Rotted manure	20:1
Cow manure	18:1
Table scraps	15:1
Grass clippings	15:1
Mature compost	15:1
Normal soil	10:1
Hen manure	7:1
Dried blood	4:1

a fifty-fifty mix of pH-amended topsoil and peat moss or compost in the autumn prior to spring planting.

GETTING SOIL READY TO PLANT

You should prepare your planting site by plowing or tilling well ahead of planting. If the area is in sod, till it at least a year ahead of time to incorporate all the organic material and to kill the grass. Better still, kill the grass before you turn it under by using a commercial product like glyphosate or by covering the entire area with black plastic early in the summer before spring planting. Anchor the plastic securely. By autumn, all vegetation beneath the plastic should be dead. You can then turn it under with other organic matter and plant a fall cover crop.

Final spring plowing or tilling should be done as soon as the ground

Some cover crops do well on acid soils. Check with your county cooperative extension service for those that will do well in your area. Adapted from R. E. Gough, The Highbush Blueberry and Its Management. *Binghamton, NY: The Haworth Press, 1994.*

CROP	SEEDING RATE	SEEDING TIME	NOTES
Alsike clover	4 lbs./acre	Late spring	Nitrogen-fixing
Annual ryegrass	30	Spring	Heavy root growth; rapid establishment
Buckwheat	60	Late spring	Reseeds when mature
Hairy vetch	40	Late summer	Nitrogen-fixing
Japanese millet	20	Early summer	Cut and till when growth exceeds 20 inches
Perennial ryegrass	25	Spring	Produces much organic matter
Spring oats	100	Early spring	Frost-kills; easy to incorporate
Sudan grass	80	Late spring	Cut and till when growth exceeds 24 inches
Winter rye	80	Late summer	Till in early spring

can be worked but at least two weeks before planting. This means as soon as the ground has dried out enough that turned soil doesn't form large clumps or compact when worked, not as soon as the ground has thawed. After it thaws, the ground will be too wet to work for some time.

Finishing your tilling at least two weeks ahead of planting gives the soil a chance to settle. Planting in soil that is still fluffed up from tilling may cause plant roots to be exposed when the soil settles around them.

When you turn the soil, break up all clods and clumps to create a fine texture for planting. If you've plowed a large area, use a disk harrow; in larger beds, a rototiller turns and pulverizes the soil in one operation.

If you're setting a small number of plants, individual holes can be prepared by turning the soil deeply with a spade, breaking up the clods, and incorporating peat moss or other organic material into the holes.

8

Feeding Plants

A plant and its fruits are composed of carbohydrates, minerals, and water that has been absorbed from the soil through the plant's roots. When the plant dies, its minerals return to the soil. But if any part of the plant, including the fruit, is removed, so are the minerals it contains. For example, a 100-foot row of blackberries yielding 350 pounds of fruit has accumulated nearly a pound each of nitrogen and potassium and $1/4$ pound of phosphorus in its fruit. When we harvest the fruit, we are effectively removing these nutrients from the soil. The same applies every time we prune and remove the clippings. Over time the soil is drained of nutrients unless we apply fertilizers to replace them.

There are sixteen elements essential for the growth of fruit plants. Carbon (C), hydrogen (H), and oxygen (O) are supplied by the air and water and are available in unlimited supply. Plants also need nitrogen (N), phosphorus (P), potassium (K), calcium (Ca), magnesium (Mg), and sulfur (S) in large quantities. These are called *macronutrients.* Plants use the first three—known as the primary macronutrients—in the greatest amounts. Calcium, magnesium, and sulfur, the secondary macronutrients, are needed in smaller amounts. Boron (B), zinc (Zn), copper (Cu), chlorine (Cl), molybdenum (Mo), manganese (Mn), and iron (Fe) are *micronutrients;* they're needed in trace quantities. Micronutrients are usually found in plentiful supply in most soils. All nutrients are equally important; a lack of a micronutrient can stop plant growth just as fast as a lack of a macronutrient. The margin between deficiency and toxicity of micronutrients is very small, however; don't add any micronutrients to your soil unless you're sure that a real deficiency exists.

FERTILIZERS

Nitrogen, phosphorus, and potassium make up the bulk of nutrients in commercial fertilizers. The three numbers appearing on a bag of fertilizer represent the percentage of nitrogen, phosphorus, and potassium contained in that bag. For example, a bag of 5–10–10 fertilizer contains 5 percent nitrogen, 10 percent phosphorus, and 10 percent potassium, always in that order. If the bag weighs 80 pounds, that's 4 pounds of nitrogen and 8 pounds each of phosphorus and potassium. The remaining 60 pounds is filler. Adding these elements in their pure form would be difficult (nitrogen is a gas) and dangerous (pure phosphorus and potassium could explode or cause severe burns).

Concentrated fertilizers are often less expensive. For example, an 80-pound bag of 10–20–20 contains twice the amount of nutrients as an 80-pound bag of 5–10–10 but probably won't cost twice the amount. Purchasing fertilizers with higher analyses is usually a better deal, but don't apply them at the same rate you would a fertilizer with a lower analysis.

In the example above, the two fertilizers have different analyses but the same ratio, or proportion of one nutrient to another. Various plants may respond differently to fertilizers of different ratios, and so recommendations often include the ratio. Both 5–10–10 and 10–20–20 fertilizers have a 1–2–2 ratio.

COMMERCIAL VERSUS ORGANIC FERTILIZERS

Commercial, or chemical, fertilizers are nutrients in mineral form as they are mined from the earth or manufactured as a by-product of the petroleum industry. They contain no organic material. Sometimes the nutrients undergo further treatment to make them more concentrated. This type of fertilizer became popular after World War II because it's concentrated and dry, less expensive to ship, easier to handle, has no odor, and can be used in smaller amounts than organic fertilizers.

Organic fertilizers are by-products of living plants or animals. Manure is one example, fish emulsion another. Organic fertilizers can be bulky and tough to handle or have an offensive odor. They have lower analyses than commercial fertilizers. For example, a bag of dehydrated cow manure has a typical analysis of 1–1–1, so it would take 5 pounds of it to supply as much nitrogen as 1 pound of 5–10–10 fertilizer.

A great debate rages over the use of commercial versus organic fertilizers. Each has its advantages and disadvantages. Studies done years ago

Classes and analyses of some fertilizers. In general, commercial fertilizers are more concentrated and can more easily burn the plant.

Type	N	P	K
Inorganic			
Ammonium nitrate	33	0	0
Ammonium sulfate	21	0	0
Calcium nitrate	16	0	0
Sodium nitrate	16	0	0
Superphosphate	0	20	0
Treble superphosphate	0	45	0
Diammonium phosphate	18	47	0
Muriate of potash	0	0	60
Potassium sulfate	0	0	50
Potassium magnesium sulfate	0	0	21
Potassium nitrate	13	0	44
Synthetic organic			
Urea	45	0	0
Ureaform (aldehyde)	38	0	0
Organic			
Manure	See table on page 76		
Bat guano	10	1.8	1.7
Blood	13	0.9	0.8
Bone meal (raw)	3	6	0
Bone meal (steamed)	2	12	0
Compost	2	1	1
Cottonseed meal	6	1.3	0.8
Fish meal	10	3.8	0
Seaweed	0.2	0.1	0.6
Wood ashes	0	1	5
Granite meal	0	0	3
Greensand	0	1	7
Feather meal	12	0	0

How do organic fertilizers compare with commercial fertilizers? A lot depends upon your source of material, what you want it to do for the plant, and your philosophy.

ORGANIC FERTILIZERS

PROS	CONS
Organic matter	Bulky
Relatively nonburning	Odor
Long-lasting	Long-lasting
Cheap (if you know	Expensive (if you buy them
a friendly farmer)	at a garden-supply store)

COMMERCIAL FERTILIZERS

PROS	CONS
Concentrated	Can burn
No odor	No organic matter
Inexpensive	Can deplete organic matter
Fast acting	Fast acting

with vegetables showed that the best yields resulted from the use of a combination of both. The latter supplied the bulk of the major nutrients and the former the micronutrients and organic matter needed to improve soil structure and keep soil microorganisms healthy.

Commercial fertilizers are salts—small molecules that dissolve readily in water and are quickly taken up by plant roots. This makes them fast-acting. If you apply too much at one time, too high a salt concentration will develop in the soil and root systems may be injured.

Organic fertilizers are slow-acting because the nutrients are locked up in large organic molecules that must be broken down by soil microbes before the plant can utilize them. Because this happens over time, there is less chance of burning the roots through misapplication. Some fresh manures, however, contain large quantities of urine. Decomposing urine releases ammonia, which can burn plants just as easily as a heavy application of commercial fertilizer. Other organic fertilizers become available to

The moisture and nutrient content of manure depend upon the animal and its feed, bedding, and the way the manure was stored. The nutrients are given in pounds per ton of manure.

ANIMAL	MOISTURE (%)	APPROXIMATE COMPOSITION		
		N	P	K
Fresh manure				
Cow	86	11	4	10
Duck	61	22	29	10
Goose	67	22	11	10
Hen	73	22	22	10
Hog	87	11	6	9
Horse	80	13	5	13
Sheep	70	20	15	21
Turkey	74	26	14	10
Dried commercial				
Cow	15	30	40	25
Hen	13	31	35	40
Hog	10	45	42	20
Rabbit	16	26	31	32
Sheep	10	32	25	41

the plant so slowly that they are practically useless. Rock phosphate is not much use to the plant for the first year or so after application.

APPLYING THE RIGHT AMOUNT

You must apply fertilizers at the right time and in the right amounts for best results. If you fertilize too early or too late, you may stimulate the wrong type of growth or not stimulate growth at all. If you apply too much, you may stimulate excessive, soft vegetative growth that is more prone to attack by pests, won't harden in time for winter, and may produce poorly colored, soft, perishable, bland-tasting fruit. Too little fertilizer may result in stunted growth, small or yellow leaves, poor root growth, and small, off-colored fruit.

How do you know when and how much to apply? Observe your plants carefully for signs of deficiency, and never apply fertilizer if you see no need for it. Do your plants look good? Are they vigorous, with a good number of large, dark green leaves? Are new shoots thick and relatively long? Is fruiting regular? Do the fruits look good? Are trunks and scaffolds stocky, thick, and green-brown? Are nonbearing spurs putting out about $1/2$ to $3/4$ inch of new growth each year?

If you answer yes to most of these questions, your plants probably don't need fertilizer. If some of the answers are no, look further before applying fertilizer. Check your watering schedule and the soil's moisture

How can you tell whether your fruit trees need fertilizer or are getting too much? Although the plants need many kinds of nutrients, the one most often lacking is nitrogen. Look at different parts of the plant to assess its nitrogen status. Nitrogen deficiency symptoms are similar in all fruit plants, though normal shoot lengths and fruit colors and set vary according to species.

PLANT PART	LOW N	NORMAL N	EXCESS N
Terminal shoot length			
Bearing plants	Thin; length less than 4 inches	4 to 12 inches	12 to 20 inches
Nonbearing	Less than 10 inches	10 to 24 inches	24 to 40 inches
Leaf size	Small, thin	Medium to average	Large, thick
Leaf color	Pale, yellow-green	Normal green	Dark green
Autumn leaf drop	Early; some red color in veins	Normal time; green to light green	Late; dark green to severe frost
Bark color	Light reddish brown	Gray to dark gray-brown	Green-gray to gray
Fruit set	Poor; heavy drop	Normal	No effect or slightly reduced
Fruit size	Small	Normal	Large
Fruit overcolor	Highly colored; early color	Average color	Poor color
Fruit undercolor	Yellow earlier than normal	Yellow develops normally	Green or green-yellow
Fruit maturity	Slightly early	Normal	Week later than normal

Nutrient deficiencies cause general symptoms that are similar in all fruit plants, though not all plants show exactly the same set of symptoms.

NUTRIENT	DEFICIENCY SYMPTOMS
Potassium	Leaf margins of older leaves on current season's growth turn olive-brown, then reddish brown, and eventually die. This is called marginal leaf scorch. Next to the dead area the leaf will show an olive-brown discoloration, while the rest of the leaf becomes dark green. On grapes, early symptoms include marginal and interveinal chlorosis of basal leaves, while the terminal leaves remain green. Leaves turn black in 'Concord'. Scorch, leaf rolling, and marginal chlorosis common in stone fruit. High levels of magnesium can interfere with uptake of potassium.
Magnesium	Appear in middle to late season, first in older leaves at the base of current season's growth, then progressing toward the terminal. Yellowing of the leaf margins progresses through the interveinal tissues. Necrosis may follow in severe cases. The veins remain green, giving the leaves a Christmas tree pattern. High levels of potassium fertilizers can interfere with uptake of magnesium.
Phosphorus	Deficiency of this nutrient is rare and usually shows only on strawberry. In this plant, the leaves become dark green and dull. Later, they turn bronze or red, especially at the margins, and mature and fall early in the autumn.
Calcium	Deficiency of this element is rare and doesn't show up in the leaves. Instead, root growth is greatly restricted and the tips turn brown. Deficiency in apples results in bitter pit, the development of small, brown, dried corky pits beneath the skin, especially in the blossom half of the fruit. Bitter pit normally develops within a month or two after harvest.
Boron	Apples develop small, tan, corky spots anywhere in the flesh of the fruit. These develop while the fruit is still on

the tree. In pears, the fruit may become dry and black and crack near the blossom end. Foliage symptoms are rare, as are deficiencies in other fruits.

Manganese and iron	Deficiencies can occur in many plants when soil pH is above 7, or above 5.5 for ericaceous plants. High soil pH causes these elements to become unavailable for absorption. Young terminal leaves show interveinal chlorosis and later turn a bright lemon yellow with iron deficiency. Manganese deficiency causes a pattern similar to but more intense than that of magnesium deficiency, but it shows first on the terminal leaves. Manganese toxicity can happen when soil is very acid (below pH 5.0). This can show up as measles in apples, causing a bumpy, pimply appearance on the bark of two- or three-year-old wood. It usually begins to show up in midsummer. As the pimples enlarge, they crack and the bark scales at the base of the cracks.
Zinc	Zinc deficiency is rare in most garden soils. It is most evident on sandy soils. Internodes are short, and the leaves small and narrow with interveinal chlorosis. Shoots die back. In severe cases, the small terminal leaves are arranged in whorls typical of a rosette. Only a few shoots may show the symptoms, which may disappear as the season advances.

content. Unless plants get enough water, they can't absorb nutrients. If the soil is dry, water immediately and regularly. If soil moisture is sufficient but your plants are still suffering, then you need to fertilize. Unfortunately, if you can see visual symptoms of a nutrient deficiency, the plant's yields and growth will be off even if you fertilize immediately.

A special word of caution here. Don't apply fertilizer just because you think it's the right thing to do. And never apply special fertilizers containing micronutrients unless you are absolutely sure your plants need them, as there's a very small margin between deficiency and toxicity with these, and some, like boron, can sterilize your soil if you goof up.

Fertilizer requirements vary according to the fruit species, age of the plant, rootstock, crop load, soil, and climate. I'll give you some broad recommendations here, but you'll have to fine-tune your applications to fit your conditions. Take a soil sample and have it analyzed to see what nutrients are lacking or out of balance. And watch your plants: Visual inspection can pinpoint deficiencies quickly and accurately. The ancient adage still holds true: "The footsteps of the master are the best manure."

Pounds of Actual Nitrogen

There are so many types of fertilizers around that application recommendations are often given in *pounds of actual nitrogen* (lbs./N_a)—you are told how many pounds of actual nitrogen to apply per acre, or per 100 square foot, or per tree. You decide which type of fertilizer to use.

For example, you may be told to apply 1 pound of actual nitrogen per inch of tree trunk diameter measured chest high. Your tree is 5 inches in diameter chest high, so you need 5 pounds of actual nitrogen for that tree. If you are using 5–10–5, the nitrogen content is 5 percent. You will need 100 pounds of 5–10–5 to supply 5 pounds of actual nitrogen (100 x .05 = 5). If you use 10–10–10, you'll need only half that amount, because it contains twice the nitrogen. If you use cow manure—typically rated at 1–1–1—you'll need to apply 500 pounds.

Pounds per Foot of Row

This refers to applications per foot of row of the entire plantation, not to each side of the row. For example, if the recommendation calls for applying 100 pounds of fertilizer per 1,000 feet of row of raspberries, apply 50 pounds to each side of the row, not 100 pounds to each side.

Pounds per Acre

There are 43,560 square feet in an acre. Round that to 40,000 for easy figuring. Recommendations that call for applying 500 pounds of fertilizer per acre include the space between the rows, so you don't have to subtract the amount of ground used for walkways.

WHEN AND HOW TO APPLY FERTILIZERS

Fertilizer is usually applied in the early spring after the ground thaws and buds begin to swell. That's just about the time the roots begin to grow and can absorb nutrients. Some plants may require additional fertilizing at other times in some situations.

Once plants are in the ground, the only way to apply dry fertilizers is by *side dressing*. To side dress a tree or single bush, encircle the plant with a broad band of fertilizer at least a foot wide, at the dripline of the plant. Fertilizers applied too close to the trunk or canes may burn the shallow roots there; fertilizers spread farther away than the dripline may not contact the roots at all. Side dress rows of small fruit plants at the dripline, on both sides of the rows. On cultivated ground, rake the side dressing into the surface of the soil. In mulched areas, rain or irrigation water will wash the fertilizer into the soil.

If your trees or bushes are in a lawn area, use a crowbar to punch a number of 12- to 18-inch-deep holes around the tree directly beneath the dripline. Fill the holes with fertilizer only to within 2 inches of their tops, to reduce the chances of the grass taking up the fertilizer. If you prefer, fertilizer spikes can also be used. They are easy to use and supply the proper balance of nutrients for specific types of plants.

Foliar Fertilizers

Foliar fertilizers have been dissolved in water and thus are taken up quickly through the leaves. They can work to immediately correct a deficiency, but they supply only small amounts of nutrients and their effect is temporary.

Indiscriminate use of complete foliar fertilizers can result in lush vegetative growth that will attract more pests, cause excessive shading, and may not harden in time for winter. Some foliar sprays may russet the finish on certain fruits, especially 'Golden Delicious' apples, and the water may cause other fruits to crack, particularly blueberries and cherries, if applied at the wrong time of year.

Foliar applications of specific micronutrients have their place, however, and are useful if done correctly and in conjunction with soil-applied amendments and fertilizers. Emergency foliar applications of iron to correct chlorosis is especially common, but to permanently correct the problem, you must lower the soil pH. Emergency foliar applications of calcium, boron, zinc, and copper can give you better fruit in the season in which you notice a deficiency of these nutrients, but again, soil correction is the best long-term remedy. Always consider foliar applications as temporary fixes and soil applications as long-term fixes.

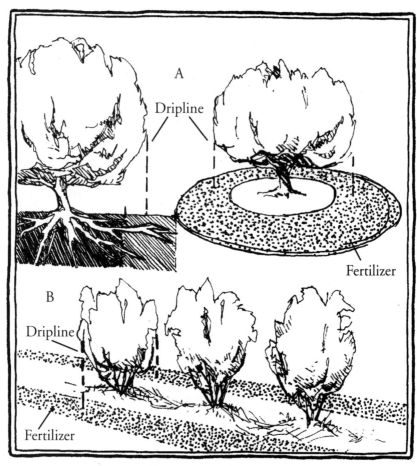

(A) To side dress a fruit tree, apply the necessary amount of fertilizer in a broad band around the tree beneath its dripline. (B) To side dress a row of berry bushes, apply the fertilizer to each side of the row in a broad band beneath the dripline of the plants. If your fruit plants are growing in sod, punch holes about 18 inches deep in the sod and fill them with fertilizer to within a few inches of the top. This will reduce the chances of the grass using all the nutrients and growing in an unsightly lush band.

TIPS FOR FERTILIZER USE
- If you can see a nutrient deficiency, the plant is already suffering and crop yields will be reduced
- If you use an organic mulch, add about one and a half times more

The chelated forms of micronutrients can contain up to the percentages indicated in the table.

Carrier Material	% Average Content
Manganese	
Manganese sulfate	32
Manganese chelate	12
Iron	
Ferrous sulfate	20
Ferric sulfate	27
Iron chelate	10
Boron	
Sodium borate (borax)	11
Solubor; Polybor	21
Copper	
Copper sulfate	25
Copper sulfate monohydrate	35
Copper chelate	13
Zinc	
Zinc sulfate	22–36
Zinc oxide	75
Zinc chelate	14
Molybdenum	
Ammonium molybdate	49
Sodium molybdate	39

nitrogen fertilizer to compensate for that used by soil microorganisms as they break down the mulch. Apply about 2 pounds of 5 percent nitrogen per 100 square feet of mulch surface.

- If you must prune a plant severely, reduce the amount of nitrogen fertilizer by half. Top growth will already be vigorous because of the increased root-to-shoot ratio, and adding nitrogen fertilizer will exacerbate the problem and cause excessive shoot growth.
- Never mix foliar fertilizers with pesticide sprays, because one may neutralize the effectiveness of the other.

9

Whipping the Weeds

Weeds will be with you always, and your battle against them will be constant. Thorough preparation of the soil before planting will go a long way toward suppressing them for the first couple of years, but they'll be back. Plan your long-term weed-control strategy before you plant.

Weeds rob young plants of sunlight, water, and nutrients and can harbor pests that attack fruit. Slugs love thick weed cover from which they can creep at night to feed on strawberries, and grassy weeds are a winter haven for voles and mice that chew the bark off trees, girdling and killing them.

Keep weeds at least 2 feet away from newly planted trees. For small plants such as strawberries, keep both the rows and the spaces between the rows weed-free. Although the presence of weeds is a little less critical with mature fruit trees, it's still a good idea to keep a weed-free 4-foot-diameter circle all the way around the trunk.

Because weeds are plants—just like your currants and kiwifruit— any measure you take to kill them can also kill your fruit plants if you're not careful. Home fruit gardeners should avoid herbicides in most cases. Instead, use a combination of cultivation, hand pulling, and mulching to control weeds.

The temptation to use weed killers (herbicides) is sometimes great, but don't give in to it. The only effective herbicide safe enough for use in a home fruit planting is glyphosate, and that only under desperate conditions where the weeds are out of control and are too close to plantings to grub out. Although this herbicide is relatively mild and easy to use, it's nonselective: It will be absorbed by any green plant tissue that it contacts.

The compound then circulates throughout the plant, breaks down its tissues, and causes it to die in a week or two. There is no margin for error.

CULTIVATION

Tilling the soil in the autumn turns under trash and organic matter and buries weed seeds deeply so they won't germinate. It also exposes long-buried seeds to winter conditions that can kill them. A final tilling in the spring before planting turns under and destroys any weeds that might have sprouted in late fall or early spring. Recently, researchers have found that tilling at night discourages some weed seeds from germinating. Try it.

After planting, cultivation with tillers or hoes loosens the soil, breaks the soil crust, and aerates plant roots. This aeration boosts the activity of soil microbes that break down organic matter to release nutrients to the plants. Cultivation also loosens the soil surface to reduce runoff and slows the migration of moisture to the surface from deeper soil layers. Also, because compact soil is a better heat conductor, cultivating lowers soil temperature slightly. All of these benefits are incidental to the primary value of soil cultivation—the control of weeds.

The key to proper cultivation is to disturb no more than the top inch or so of soil to avoid damaging the plants' root systems and bringing deeply buried weed seeds to the surface where they may germinate.

Cultivate as soon as weeds break through the soil. The old saying is that for every day you let a weed grow, you add another hour to your weeding time. If the weeds around your young plants get so big that you want to pull them, don't. By that time the weed's roots have intertwined with those of the fruit plant, and pulling the weed will injure the fruit plant's roots. Instead, cut the weeds off at the soil surface and leave the roots intact, or spot treat them with a systemic herbicide such as glyphosate, being extremely careful not to let the compound contact the green tissue of the fruit plant.

A hoe is a wonderful but too-little used tool. Keep it sharp and use it to cut small weeds at the soil line. Be sure to buy one that is not too heavy and has a handle long enough for you to stand nearly straight while you work. And remember, a hoe was meant for scraping, not chopping.

Keep string trimmers far away from your fruiting plants. The whirling nylon strings can girdle a young tree faster than mice, and the damage is just as complete and lasting. The same goes for lawn mowers. I've seen many fruit trees killed by "mower disease," which, like mouse damage and winter injury, doesn't show up until well into the next growing season.

MULCHES

Mulches are an excellent alternative to constant cultivation and the use of herbicides. Mulches retain soil moisture, sometimes by half again as much as bare soil, increase the rate of water absorption into the soil, and smother weed seedlings. But for a mulch to be effective as a weed control, you must remove all weeds before you apply it.

Mulches can also influence plant growth. An organic mulch keeps the soil cooler longer in the spring. This delays the initiation of growth and gives the plant a better chance of escaping damage from a late frost. It also means you'll get a somewhat later crop. Because several inches of organic matter create a good insulating blanket, the soil remains warmer longer in the autumn and through the winter, thus reducing the chances of winter damage to the roots from extreme cold.

Inorganic mulches, on the other hand, are poor insulators. Soils warm faster in the spring, reach higher temperatures in the summer, and cool faster in the autumn. Fruit plants begin root growth earlier in the spring and bloom earlier, making them more susceptible to damage by late frosts. If your plants escape frost damage, the crop will ripen a few days earlier than with an organic mulch.

Organic Mulches

Organic mulches add organic matter to the soil as they decompose. When maintained 4 to 6 inches deep, they can provide effective weed control. A thick organic mulch also prevents soil crusting and compaction and encourages feeder roots to grow up into the lower, rotting layers of the mulch to form a denser root system. When you apply an organic mulch, slope it toward the plant to decrease water runoff away from the root zone. You'll need roughly 5 bushels per plant—about 30 cords to mulch a 4-foot-diameter area around an acre of bushes or about 50 cords to mulch an acre of 5-foot-wide rows of fruit plants.

Straw is often recommended as a mulch, but don't use it for fruit trees because it is a great place for mice to overwinter while they feed on tree bark. The same is true for legume hay, salt hay, and grass clippings.

Compost and *well-rotted manure* are weed-free and make excellent mulches. Never use fresh manure or chicken manure in any form as a mulch. The latter can burn tender plants such as strawberries, and the former will host a great crop of weeds.

Peat moss makes a good mulch but may crust when dry. It is also too expensive to use in large quantities; it's better used as a soil amendment.

Wood chips rot slowly, making them a great mulch for fruit plants. Apply them right after planting and maintain them several inches deep. Pine and hemlock bark work well as mulches, but you may want to add a finer-textured material to fill in the large spaces left by these coarsely textured chips.

Wood shavings are relatively inexpensive but lightweight. If you use them, apply a couple inches of the shavings and cover them with a couple inches of chips to hold them in place.

Bagasse, or dried and shredded sugarcane, makes a good mulch for trees and shrubs, but its stickiness makes it hard to handle and may cause problems with ripening strawberries and other fruits that grow low to the ground.

Sawdust is an excellent mulch for all fruit plants. Under sawdust, the readily available ammonium form of nitrogen increases. Years of study on blueberry plants show that plant size and crop yields substantially increased when sawdust mulch was used. And one of the beauties of this material is that often it's free for the taking. To decrease the likelihood of nitrogen deficiency problems, compost fresh sawdust for a year before using it or mix a little nitrogen fertilizer with it and use it fresh.

Be sure to get the right kind of sawdust. Dust from a furniture factory or woodworking shop is too fine and will crust and compact. Sawdust from a sawmill works best. Softwood sawdust is usually coarser, fluffier, and decomposes more slowly than hardwood sawdust. Some gardeners question the use of cherry sawdust because of toxins it might contain, but most sawmills cut a variety of species and you won't get pure cherry sawdust, so don't worry about it. I would not apply large quantities of pure black walnut sawdust, however, for the real fear of the juglone it might contain. Juglone is excreted by black walnut roots and inhibits the growth of many plants. I know of no research on the toxic effects of black walnut sawdust, but as a precaution stay away from it.

Inorganic Mulches

Inorganic mulches are long-lasting, easy to apply, and often less expensive than organic mulches.

Inexpensive black *polyethylene plastic* mulch is best used for small row plants such as strawberries. It's sold by thickness measured in mils (thousandths of an inch). Three-mil poly is common. The black plastic blocks sunlight from hitting the soil and prevents weed seeds from germinating. It also makes the soil surface 10 to 15 degrees warmer than bare soil. This heat, along with the soil moisture conserved by the plastic, promotes strong root growth, especially in the spring when soil temperatures are cold. The soil beneath black plastic can sometimes get too hot for good root growth. I found that the temperature beneath the plastic can rise 25 percent above that of ambient air. Thus, when air temperatures are 90 degrees F, the soil beneath the mulch can approach 113 degrees F, the critical point at which plant enzymes break down. If you provide no supplemental irrigation, plant death is more likely with plastic mulch than with organic mulch.

When plastic is used to mulch strawberries and raspberries, the natural formation of suckers and runners is suppressed along with the weeds. If you mulch your raspberries and strawberries with plastic, you'll have to punch holes in the plastic where you wish to set offshoots, and the holes will reduce the mulching efficiency of the material. Plastic films also break down and must be replaced every couple of years.

Landscape cloth or *fabric* is great for mulching fruit trees and bushes that you don't want to sucker. This thinly woven material resembles fine nylon window screen or woven fabric. It allows air and water to penetrate the soil but blocks weed growth. Put this down before your organic mulch for double protection.

A 2- to 3-inch layer of *crushed stone* or *pea stone*, applied over landscape fabric and held in place by plastic curbing, makes an attractive mulch that keeps the soil cool and moist and prevents weed growth. Don't apply crushed marble chips to acid-loving plants like blueberries or lingonberries. Marble is a form of limestone, and it will slowly raise the soil pH to an unacceptable level for these plants. Don't mulch your strawberry patch with stones either, because they'll be too difficult to remove when you renovate or replant every few years. Also keep in mind that light-colored stones can reflect too much winter sunlight, resulting in an increased potential for sunscald damage to tree trunks.

10

Watering

Most living things are 70 to 90 percent water by weight. Water powers biochemical reactions, including some of the reactions of photosynthesis. Scientists estimate that it takes about 500 pounds of water to make 1 pound of dry plant matter. A peach tree needs about 11 tons, or 3,000 gallons, of water each year to grow and produce a crop. An apple tree needs a whopping 16.5 tons, or 4,500 gallons, of water to set a crop. Water, applied at the right time and place and in the right amount, can mean the difference between a good crop and a dead plant.

The amount of water required depends upon the crop, soil type, climate, management practices, plant spacing, and other considerations. Mature plants need more water than young plants, bearing plants more than nonbearing plants, and those with shallow root systems more than those with deep root systems. Because roots grow only in moist soil, insufficient water leads to stunting, stress, poor fruit size, preharvest drop, premature fall coloration and leaf drop, and the potential for increased winter damage. 'Golden Delicious' apples are only three-quarters full size when grown on dry soils, even though the trees don't evidence any wilting of shoots and leaves.

Too much water, on the other hand, can delay fruit maturity, cause lush growth that attracts pests, and delay autumn hardening, which results in increased winter damage. Excessive water to the point of prolonged soil saturation can cause root death. The symptoms of root rot are similar to those produced by insufficient water. In a sense, the plant is suffering physiological drought because the dead roots cannot absorb water and nutrients.

Fruit plants that mature their crops early, such as cherries, get most of the necessary water from spring rainfall and snowmelt and often don't require supplemental irrigation. But during dry periods, and particularly with plants that mature their crops later in the summer and fall, you must supplement natural rainfall to get the best production. Water is most critical during fruit sizing and ripening. A lack of water at this time may lead to undersize fruit or no fruit at all. On hot days, water is actually drawn out of the fruit through transpiration and is replaced at night only if soil water is sufficient.

For deep-rooted trees and shrubs, soil should be kept moist at least to a depth of 1 to 2 feet. On shallow-rooted small fruits like strawberries and lingonberries, don't let more than an inch or two of the surface soil dry out. To test soil moisture, feel the soil. Properly moistened soil forms a loose ball when squeezed. For a more accurate test of soil moisture, use a soil water meter. Follow the manufacturer's instructions to calibrate it properly, then plunge it into the soil to root depth. If it indicates soil at 70 percent or less of field capacity, water immediately. Most fruiting plants need this amount of soil water to make the best growth, and if soil moisture falls below 50 percent, growth will be substantially reduced. To maintain these levels of soil moisture requires approximately 1 inch of water per week, either from rainfall or supplemental watering. During hot, dry, windy periods, your plantings may lose as much as 3 or 4 inches of water per week, and unless that water is replaced, your crop will suffer.

To keep track of rainfall, invest in a rain gauge. If rainfall exceeds an inch per week, you may not have to water. Gentle, slow, soaking rains are best. Violent, heavy rains can injure crops and often run off before soaking in. Light showers that supply less than a $1/4$ inch of rain are useless, as much of the water evaporates before it reaches the root zones.

IRRIGATION METHODS

Trickle irrigation and *soaker hoses* are the most efficient ways to water plants. Place the emitters and hoses to provide water only to the root area of your plants. A flow rate of as little as 3 to 7 quarts per hour will keep the soil near field capacity. Because you're not applying water between rows, water is not wasted and weed growth is discouraged. The gentle seepage from trickle irrigation and soaker hoses won't disturb the fine roots of young plants.

In mild-winter regions, lay trickle lines and hoses beneath mulch. In areas with cold winters, where you may want to remove and store the irrigation system between growing seasons, lay the lines on top of the mulch so that they are easy to pick up. Trickle irrigation lines can be buried beneath mulch and left in place even during severe winters, but you must clear all water from the lines at the end of each season with a blast of compressed air to prevent freeze damage. Soaker hoses are nearly impossible to drain completely, so you'll have to take them up each autumn and store them.

Overhead and *hose-end sprinklers* are great for watering small fruits. They provide frost protection in late spring and can cool the plants when temperatures exceed 85 to 90 degrees F. Because they wet fruit and foliage, however, plants are more susceptible to disease, and some fruits, particularly cherries, blueberries, and gooseberries, may crack if they're wet while maturing. And because this type of sprinkler throws water into the air, some is lost to evaporation and some is applied to vacant areas and weeds. Use overhead sprinklers only when the temperature is rising, never in late afternoon. Evaporation is usually less in the morning, so you'll waste less water, and turning sprinklers off by noon will give the foliage a chance to dry before nightfall. Wet foliage and fruit going into a cool evening are a welcome mat for disease.

The distribution pattern of most hose-end sprinklers is uneven, dropping more in the center of the stream than at the edges. Check the distribution and amount applied by placing empty tuna fish cans around the planting. Move the sprinklers around until the cans are filled equally.

When debating whether or not to water, remember that mature fruit plants, because of their extensive root systems, can pull water from deep in the ground, but young plants are especially vulnerable to damage from lack of water. Pay particular attention to your young, unestablished plantings and water them well and often. A weekly deep soaking is far better than frequent, light waterings, which may encourage shallow root development.

Planting the Plants

If you've ordered your plants from a mail-order nursery, open the packages as soon as they arrive and pull back the plastic shipping liner. If the packing material around the roots is dry, moisten it. If you must hold the plants for a day or two, leave them in the box with the plastic liner replaced. Move the box to a cool area in the garage or shed. If you must wait a week or more before planting, *heel in* the plants in an area sheltered from direct sunlight and strong wind. To heel in plants, place the roots in a shallow V-shaped trench with the tops of the plants resting at an angle slanting toward the south. Cover the roots with moist soil, peat moss, or sawdust. If the roots are very dry, soak them for a few hours in a bucket of water before heeling in. Heeling in is a temporary holding measure when planting must be delayed for a week or two.

If you purchased B&B or container-grown plants from a local nursery, you won't have to heel them in. If you can't plant them for a few days, water them well and set them in a cool, shaded area. If you have to keep them longer, cover the root balls or containers with damp peat moss or sawdust. In either case, don't remove the plants from their burlap or container until you are ready to plant them.

Once you are ready to plant, protect the roots of your nursery stock from bright sunlight and drying air. Bare-root plants should be set in a bucket of water and carried with you as you plant. They'll replace whatever water they lost during transit and storage, and the roots won't dry during the planting process. Leaving them in the water for up to several hours won't harm them a bit.

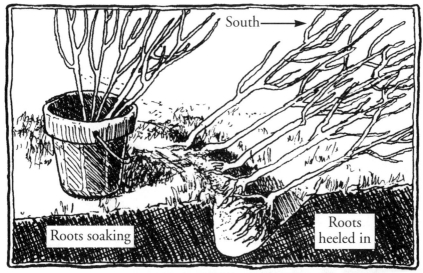

South ——→

Roots soaking

Roots heeled in

If you can't transplant your plants to the garden right away, heel them in. If the roots appear to be dry, soak them in water for several hours or overnight, then lay the plants in a shallow trench and cover their roots with soil. Orient the plants to the south to reduce the amount of sun and heat they'll be exposed to. Heeling them in a shady spot is a good idea.

If you don't have the strength to lug a large bucket, set your plants in a wheelbarrow and cover them with a wet towel or a piece of wet burlap. Rewet the cloth as it dries, and if the telephone rings while you're planting (as it always does), move the plants to a shaded spot until you return.

WHEN TO PLANT

Depending on whether you are planting bare-root, balled-and-burlapped, or container-

Heel in strawberry plants by placing their roots in a shallow trench with the crowns at ground level and packing soil firmly around their roots. Don't bury the crowns.

grown fruiting plants, early spring and late autumn are the only times to plant.

Bare-root plants have had much of their root systems removed, and it will take some time to get them back. Before they can absorb water, new root hairs and branchlets must form. This takes up to several weeks. The plants are not equipped to deal well with moisture stress, so conditions should be as optimal as possible. In areas with tough winters, where the ground freezes deeply, soil water is unavailable, and the temperatures plummet, bare-root plants set in the autumn will not have time enough to reestablish a good root system and survive the winter. If you garden north of a line extending roughly from Norfolk, Virginia, to Fresno, California, plant bare-root stock in the spring.

Balled-and-burlapped plants and container-grown plants arrive with more of their root systems intact, and they'll be able to absorb water right away. They can be planted in either the spring or fall, although if you live in an area with tough winters, spring planting is best.

Most plants should be dormant when they go into the ground. Sometimes you can successfully transplant balled-and-burlapped and container-grown plants in full leaf, but those leaves will substantially increase the plant's need for water. You must water conscientiously until the plant is established.

PLANTING HOLE SIZE

Your soil should be prepared before your plants arrive, and you may already have your planting holes dug. A common mistake is digging a hole too small for the plant. You have invested a lot of money in your plant, and you will invest a lot of time. Your plant is going to be in that hole for a long time. Take time to prepare it right.

Dig the hole at least twice the diameter and twice the depth of the root ball. A hole about 4 feet wide and 2 feet deep is adequate for most fruit plants. Loosen the soil at the bottom and be sure there are no rocks, ledge, or hardpan there. If the soil is heavy, the sides may have compacted during digging, especially if you used a posthole digger. Rough up the sides of the hole with your spade to break that compacted layer.

Temporarily set your plant in the hole and determine how much fill you need to add to the bottom so that the plant will be at the same depth as it was in the nursery. Remove it and put in the required amount of a

Dig your planting hole wide and deep enough that there will be plenty of loosened soil on all sides of the root ball. Place the topsoil and the subsoil in separate piles. Loosen the soil at the bottom and sides of the hole, especially important when digging in heavy soils.

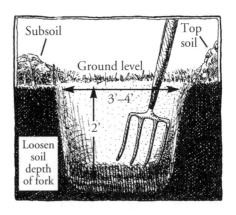

loam and peat moss mixture, forming a mound on which the plant will sit. You can determine planting depth by looking at the soil line on the trunk or canes. A slight change in bark color marks the planting line. Plant strawberries so that the soil surface cuts the middle of the crown. Set standard grafted trees so that their graft unions are 2 inches below ground level. Trees on dwarfing rootstocks should be set so that their bud unions are 2 inches above the soil lines; burying the union of a dwarf stock may allow the scion to root and overcome the effect of the stock. Instead of a 10-foot tree, you'll wind up with a 35-foot tree and blame the company for sending the wrong plant.

If you're planting balled-and-burlapped trees or shrubs, examine the wrapper. If it's a woven plastic fabric, remove it completely before you plant the tree. If it's old-fashioned burlap, loosen it at the top of the ball but leave the material intact. (Be sure that no burlap shows above the soil line after planting, or it will wick water away from the roots.)

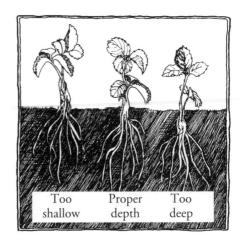

Set strawberry plants so that their crowns are neither too shallow, which can cause them to dry out, nor too deep, which can cause them to rot.

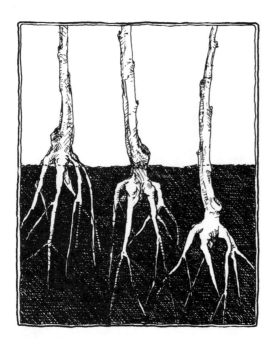

Set standard, grafted trees so that their graft unions are a couple of inches below ground; set dwarf trees or those on other special rootstocks so that their graft unions are a couple of inches above the ground. Burying the graft union of dwarf trees can cause their scions to root and overcome the dwarfing effect of the stock, resulting in a standard-sized tree.

If you can, set your fruit trees so that the lowest limb is on the southwest side to reduce sunscald. If you're planting in a windy location, lean your trees slightly into the prevailing wind.

Fill the planting hole with water. When the water drains, set the plant and spread out its roots, trimming any that are damaged or too long. Don't ever wrap long roots around the inside of the hole. They'll continue to grow in that fashion and in time will girdle the plant. Fill the hole halfway with soil and gently tamp with your hands, working it around the roots. Fill the hole again with water. When it's drained, fill the rest of the hole with soil and water liberally again.

After you have set the plant and firmed the soil, make a shallow ridge of soil at the dripline to form a water-holding basin.

Don't skimp on water. Liberal applications will ensure that root hairs get all the water they can absorb. In addition, the water will move the soil into close contact with the roots, eliminating air pockets in the planting hole. Roots in air pockets can't absorb water and will dry out and die.

Water deeply two or three times each week— more often if the weather is hot and dry—for the first several weeks. Don't overwater! Prolonged saturation will suffocate the roots and kill the plant. Reduce watering in late summer to allow the plants to harden for the winter.

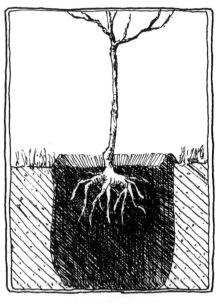

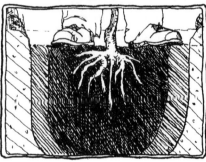

Backfill the hole with a mixture of topsoil and peat moss or compost. Don't add any dry fertilizer or other amendments to the planting hole. When the hole is half filled with soil, fill it to the top with water. When that has soaked in, fill the remainder of the hole with soil mix, tamp it well with your feet, and water it again. In lighter soils, make a basin around the planting hole to catch and hold rain water.

The trick to getting a good take on your transplanted fruit trees and bushes is to be sure that soil and roots come into firm and close contact. Tamping the soil with your feet and watering well after transplanting help ensure this.

Never add dry fertilizer or fresh manure to the planting hole. Without root hairs, bare-root plants can't absorb it, and the few root hairs that B&B and container-grown plants have might be burned. Compost or well-rotted manure won't do any harm, and you can substitute them for peat moss in your soil mixture. Dilute liquid transplant fertilizers won't harm your plants, but their efficacy is questionable.

STAKING AND SUPPORT

Stake your trees at planting. One method is to drive a 2 x 3 stake into the ground about 6 inches from the tree at planting, taking care not to damage the roots. Tie the tree to the stake with wide, soft strips of cloth. An old nylon stocking works well.

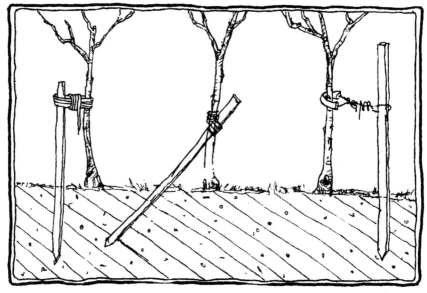

Stake young trees firmly right after planting and tie them with soft strips of cloth. Here are several good ways to stake and tie your tree.

You may also position three small stakes around the tree several feet out from its base and run guy wires from the stakes to the tree. Pad the wires where they touch the trunk with lengths of old rubber or plastic garden hose. Never apply wire or other small-diameter material directly to the tree. As the tree grows, and when it moves in the wind, the wire will cut through the bark and into the conducting tissue, partially or completely girdling the tree.

For the same reason, remove all sales and name tags from the plants right away. I emphasize this because it's so often overlooked. Copper wire tags, and to a lesser extent plastic tags, allowed to remain on the plant's trunk or branch will girdle it in a few years. This small act of carelessness can disfigure or kill an otherwise beautiful plant. If you're afraid of forgetting what the plant is, make a map listing the cultivar, stock, and date of planting.

With the exception of a few dwarf trees, which have brittle root-stocks and remain poorly rooted throughout their lifetime, support is necessary only until the root system has become established. By the beginning of the second or third season in the field, the root system is established enough that support can be removed.

Protect the bark of young trees from winter sunscald damage by wrapping them with flexible plastic especially made for the purpose. This also gives some protection from rodents. Be sure the plastic has plenty of holes in it for the trunks to breathe. Painting the trunks with white latex paint will also work.

CARE AFTER PLANTING

In late summer, wrap tree trunks with plastic or cardboard tree wrap to reduce winter sunscald damage, or paint the trunks with white latex paint. Rodents gnaw the bark on fruit trees in winter. Protect the trunks by positioning cages of ¹/₂-inch mesh hardware cloth around them. Extend the cages into the soil and at least 18 inches up the tree trunks, and at least 2 inches away from the trunks all the way around. As your trees grow, the cylinders can girdle them. Beware of this and replace the cylinders with larger ones as necessary

Winter Protection

If you garden in the South, you'll have little to worry about come winter. But northern gardeners have to take precautions to help their plants get through tough winters.

AUTUMN WATERING

Give your plants enough water during summer to allow them to grow and produce effectively. To let plants harden for winter, stop watering between harvest and leaf fall unless you are in a severe drought. After the leaves drop, water your plants deeply once each week until the ground freezes. Because the plant tops have entered dormancy, they won't respond to the water with new growth. The roots remain active, however, absorbing water from the soil and moving it throughout the plant to prevent small shoots and buds from drying out.

BURYING PLANTS

To get marginally hardy fig trees, grapevines, and other moderate-size plants through severe winters, bury them. After autumn leaf drop, dig a shallow trench beside the plant and gently bend the plant into it. Be careful not to disturb the root system or break the stems. Hold the plant in place with a stone or piece of bent wire and fill the trench with soil. Mound soil about a foot high over the trench, then cover it with another foot of leaves, cornstalks, straw, or other organic insulating material. Moisten everything to hold it in place. Mound and insulate the soil directly above the root system as well. After snowfall, shovel snow over the plant for further insulation.

Cold resistance depends upon plant genetics, how sharp the drop in temperature is, when it occurs, and the prior condition of the plants, among other factors. Roots are the most sensitive to cold damage, followed by the collar tissue. But cold damage is most noticeable when it kills the flower buds.

FRUIT	CRITICAL MINIMUM TEMPERATURE (°F)	
Almond	-15	Zone 5
Apricot	-15	Zone 5
Apple	-30	Zone 3
Blackberry	-25	Zone 4
Blueberry		
Highbush	-25	Zone 4
Rabbiteye	-10	Zone 6
Buffaloberry	-35	Zone 3
Cherry		
Sour	-30	Zone 3
Sweet	-20	Zone 5
Chestnut	-15	Zone 5
Cranberry, Highbush	-30	Zone 3
Currant	-35	Zone 3
Elderberry	-25	Zone 4
Fig	+15	Zone 8
Filbert	-10	Zone 6
Gooseberry	-35	Zone 3
Grape		
V. vinifera	0	Zone 7
V. labrusca	-25	Zone 4
Muscadine	+5	Zone 7
Lingonberry	-25	Zone 4
Mulberry	Variable	Zones 4–8
Peach	-20	Zone 5
Pear	-20	Zone 5
Plum		
American	-30	Zone 3
European	-20	Zone 5
Japanese	-20	Zone 5

Raspberry		
Red	-25	Zone 4
Black	-10	Zone 5
Purple	-15	Zone 5
Strawberry	-25	Zone 4
Walnut (Persian)	0	Zone 7
Carpathian strains	-10	Zone 5

When the ground thaws in the spring, uncover the plants and gently raise them to an upright position again. Remove the mound of soil above the root ball, and you're back in business for another year.

WINDSCREENS

In areas with very windy, cold, dry winters, give your fruit plants individual protection. Gently wrap the sides of bushes with burlap or plastic-weave fabric. This side wrapping breaks the wind and decreases the drying of small branches. Leave the top open. If you cover the top, heat may build up inside and cook your plants. Don't use plastic garbage bags, either. On a bright sunny, windless day in late February, the temperatures inside the bag can reach 100 degrees F or more. And because plastic gives no insulation, temperatures will plummet after sunset, resulting in all sorts of winter damage. Remember, the idea of wrapping the plant is simply to block the wind, not to try to keep it warm. Be sure the plant is well ventilated, whatever wrap you use.

Young, thin-barked trees and trees with dark reddish or brown bark are sus-

Winter winds can dry the small shoots of a fruit plant. Pound four stakes into the ground around the plant, then wrap burlap, tar paper, or other material around them to block the wind. Don't cover the top of the plant.

ceptible to winter sunscald damage, sometimes called "southwest disease." In late winter, when the sun is higher in the sky and the days are getting longer, the sunny side of a tree trunk warms. The warming is greatest on the southwest side, which is exposed to afternoon sun. By this time of year, the tree has satisfied its rest requirement; its cells warm substantially and may begin to metabolize and deharden. As the sun sets, the temperature drops dramatically. The dehardened cells die, and bark cracks, scales, and may peel off the affected area. If the wound becomes infected or bugs invade it, the tree is lost.

Protect your trees by preventing the bark from heating. Situating a tree with its lowest limb on the southwest side helps shade the trunk. Tree wraps do the same. Painting the trunks with white latex paint causes the sun's rays to be reflected and keeps the bark cool. Do not use oil-based paint. It can damage the tree's cambium and cause a fate worse than sunscald.

Shrubs and vines are not usually affected by sunscald because they have canes and branches that shade their lower portions.

EARLY-SPRING PROTECTION

Late-spring frosts and freezes can destroy blossoms and negate your fruit harvest entirely. Early-blooming varieties, and small fruits that grow close to the ground, are most susceptible to frost and freeze damage.

Flower buds are hardiest during deep rest. They lose hardiness as they approach bloom. A fully dormant flower bud on a highbush blueberry can survive -20 to -25 degrees F. As the bud breaks dormancy and begins to swell, it may be damaged by a temperature of 20 degrees F. Partially open blossoms may survive 23 degrees F. Flowers in full bloom can survive 28 degrees F for four hours and 26 degrees F for two hours. After petal fall, critical temperature for injury rises to 29 to 30 degrees F because berries lose heat faster than the flowers. Critical temperatures vary for different fruit species and depend upon the length of time the flowers are exposed to cold and upon the temperature immediately preceding the frost. If it was warm before the frost, damage will be greater.

To protect your blossoming plants during a frost, cover or sprinkle them. Products such as agricultural fleece or garden fabric are lightweight and insulative. Covering your small fruit with garden fabric, old sheets, buckets, or even newspaper will trap ground heat and may keep the flowers a couple of degrees above freezing.

Sprinkling is another quick and easy way to protect plants. Position

As flower buds come out of rest and develop toward bloom, they become less resistant to cold. Here are the critical temperatures at which you can expect substantial damage to flower buds in various stages of development. The precise amount of damage depends upon the length of time temperatures were at the levels indicated, whether the buds were moist or dry, and preceding temperatures. Not all stages occur in all fruits. The stages are descriptive of the development of the flower bud, often relying upon the color of the petals to illustrate the stage of development.

STAGE	APPLE	PEAR	CHERRY	PEACH	APRICOT	PRUNE	GRAPE	STRAWBERRY
Buds emerge	—	—	—	—	—	—	—	10°F
First crack	—	—	—	—	—	—	19°F	—
First swell	—	—	7°F	9°F	—	6°F	21°F	—
Scales separate	—	—	8°F	—	—	—	—	—
Tips separate	—	—	—	—	15°F	—	—	—
Silver tip	6°F	—	—	—	—	—	—	—
Calyx green	—	—	—	12°F	—	—	—	—
Buds closed	—	—	—	—	—	—	25°F	—
Side green	—	—	15°F	—	—	—	—	—
Side white	—	—	—	—	—	8°F	—	—
Cluster showing	—	12°F	—	—	—	—	—	—
Green tip	12°F	—	19°F	—	—	11°F	—	—
Calyx red	—	—	—	15°F	15°F	—	—	—
Half-inch green	17°F	—	—	—	—	—	—	—
Full swell	—	—	—	—	—	—	23°F	—
Tight cluster	21°F	17°F	22°F	—	—	17°F	—	—
Open cluster	—	—	25°F	—	—	—	—	—
First pink	24°F	—	—	20°F	—	—	—	—
First white	—	20°F	25°F	—	20°F	21°F	—	—
Full pink	26°F	—	—	—	—	—	—	—
Full white	—	24°F	—	—	—	—	—	—
First bloom	27°F	25°F	26°F	23°F	20°F	21°F	—	—
Full bloom	27°F	25°F	26°F	25°F	24°F	24°F	23°F	30°F
In shuck	—	—	—	—	26°F	—	—	28°F
Postbloom	28°F	26°F	27°F	26°F	27°F	26°F	—	—

your sprinklers to cover the entire plant or planting, then turn the water on when the temperature drops to 35 degrees F. Ice forms on the plants as the temperature falls below freezing. Water liberates heat as it freezes, and as long as continual freezing occurs, the temperature around the plant tissue remains about 32 degrees F—high enough to reduce freeze damage to the blossoms. Keep the sprinklers running until the temperature rises and the ice melts. Ice itself is a poor insulator. If you turn off the water while the freeze is still on, the temperature beneath the ice coating will drop until it equals that of the air. If that's below about 30 degrees F, you'll lose your flowers just as fast as if you hadn't sprinkled at all. But if you continue to run the sprinklers, the continuous freezing process actually generates enough heat to keep your blossoms from freezing. The weight of the ice cover may cause a little mechanical damage, but it is minor compared with losing your crop. Prune out any damaged branches after the ice melts.

ASSESSING COLD DAMAGE

In late winter, check for suspected damage to unopened buds from severe cold or late frosts. Snip off a few random branches bearing flower buds and bring them into the house. Set them in a bucket of water to warm for a couple of days, then remove the flower buds and cut them open. If a bud's inner tissue is brown or black, the bud is damaged and will not produce fruit. If it's green or greenish white, it's okay. Calculate the percentage of damaged and undamaged buds in your random sample and you will have a good idea of the percentage of crop loss from winter damage.

If fully opened blossoms were frosted, examine them after the temperature warms. Because the most frost-sensitive part of a blossom is the central pistil, a flower with a brown or black center is damaged and won't produce fruit.

Pruning and Training

Prune plants to keep them consistently productive. Regular pruning controls plant growth and allows sunlight to penetrate the plant's canopy. This increases flower bud formation and photosynthesis near the interior of the plant. Opening up the canopy with regular pruning also increases air circulation and spray penetration and lessens damage from pests. Pruning removes some flower buds, thus decreasing the potential for stress and overbearing and indirectly increasing fruit size. It also removes dead, injured, and unproductive wood, making harvest easier.

Pruning reduces the overall size of a plant. Although some individual shoots may be stimulated to vigorous growth, the growth of the plant as a whole is reduced. Because total root growth is reduced, heavy pruning over several years is detrimental to the root system. Heavy pruning of young plants also delays the onset of the reproductive adult phase.

WHEN TO PRUNE

Pruning disturbs the internal water and nutrient balance of a plant, so its response to pruning varies slightly according to the time of year. Although you should remove dead, broken, and diseased branches as soon as you find them, regular pruning should be done in late winter and early spring. At this time of year, there are no leaves to obstruct your view, it's cool and pleasant to work outdoors, the buds are dormant and less apt to be knocked off during the pruning operations, wounds heal quickly with the warming weather, and much of the winter damage that has occurred will show by this time.

Conversely, if you prune in early autumn, before the leaves have

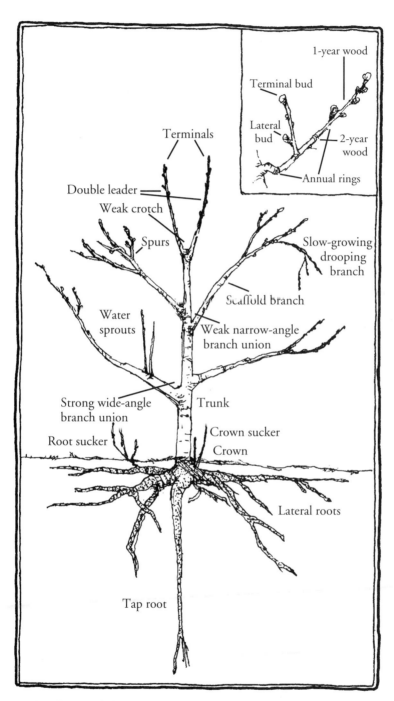

Study this figure of the gross structure of a tree and become familiar with all the terms—they'll be useful in learning proper pruning techniques.

fallen, it will be tough to see the plant's structure, the pruning could stimulate late growth that will not harden in time for winter, and you also may remove a lot of leaves at a time when flower bud formation for the following year is taking place. The decrease in photosynthesis can reduce the number and vigor of these flower buds.

Late-autumn pruning, after the leaves have fallen, won't stimulate late growth. But pruning late will leave open wounds that won't heal in time for winter. In severe-winter areas, the cambium may be damaged and the wound may rot. You'll probably have to reprune in the spring anyway to remove winter damage, and that will mean twice the work.

Summer pruning is recommended only for some summer-fruiting shrubs such as southern highbush blueberries, and only in areas of Florida and the Deep South where severe winter cold is not a problem.

HOW MUCH TO REMOVE

Severity of pruning depends upon the species, the plant's age, and the individual plant itself. For example, you need to remove about 90 percent of a grapevine each year, but many stone-fruit trees, such as cherries, are pruned only lightly once in bearing. The amount of pruning is a balancing act, and its severity can influence ripening. Most gardeners tend to prune too lightly. Light pruning delays and prolongs the ripening season, whereas heavy pruning hastens and concentrates it. Very heavy pruning substantially decreases the yield of fruit per plant but increases the size of individual fruits.

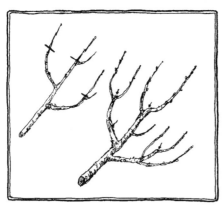

Some shoots grow long and leggy, are structurally weak, and have little bearing surface. Heading back, or cutting a portion off each long shoot forces the shoot to branch. The new branches are more rigid and have a greater bearing surface. The greater the portion of the original shoot you remove (strong heading cut), the more branches are formed.

Heading-back cuts reduce tall, spindly growth and stimulate the production of side shoots. The more you head back a branch, the stronger its

If your tree has been properly trained from the beginning, you should never have to remove large branches. The larger the cut, the more apt the tree is to form many adventitious shoots around the periphery of the wound. This causes weak, unattractive, bushy growth.

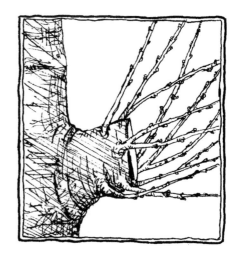

tendency to send out side shoots. In general, prune weak plants more severely to stimulate vigorous growth.

Many small cuts distribute the invigorating stimulus of pruning over the entire plant; a few large cuts cause overly vigorous growth near the site of the cut. Avoid large cuts, because the larger the cut, the more excessively vigorous growth will appear within a few inches of it.

PRUNING EQUIPMENT

Anvil shears have a cutting blade and flat plate that the blade strikes with each snip. Unless kept very sharp, anvil shears may crush rather than cleanly cut the wood, delaying healing. *Bypass shears* have a scissorslike action that produces a clean cut, provided the blade is kept sharp. Don't use shears to cut branches more than $1/2$ inch thick unless you have very strong hands. Turning your shears from side to side to force them through the branch can "spring" them and knock the two sides out of alignment. If a branch is too big for shears, use loppers.

Loppers are used with both hands. As with shears, there are anvil and bypass types, as well as offset-pivot types that provide enough leverage to cut branches up to an inch or so in diameter. For larger cuts, use a saw.

Saws come in various shapes and sizes. Those with coarse teeth cut faster but leave a ragged cut surface. Fine-toothed saws cut more slowly but leave a smooth cut surface that heals faster.

Keep your pruning tools sharp. Dull tools take longer to cut and the cuts take longer to heal. Disassemble and sharpen shears and loppers with a honing stone each year before you prune. Sharpen saws with a triangle file and set the teeth with a file-set gauge. Never use a bench grinder to sharpen your tools, because the heat generated may cause a blade to lose its temper or ability to keep an edge.

GENERAL PRUNING METHODS

Begin a pruning job by eliminating crossing branches, shoots growing back toward the center of the plant, major shoots arising within a few inches of each other, and all dead, weak, or damaged wood.

A tree or shrub forms branch and trunk *collars* to prevent pathogens from moving up a branch into the main system of the tree. Each lateral branch forms a collar around its base. A trunk collar forms at the junction of the branch and trunk. Always leave a short stub when pruning. A flush cut will remove the protective collar, damage the zone of protection, and prevent proper healing of the wound.

Where a fork or narrow crotch exists, there is no collar. Instead, there is a *bark inclusion* where the branches, called *codominant leaders*, join. This inclusion weakens the area and leads to splitting. Never allow codominant leaders to develop. If a tree has them, subordinate one leader or remove it completely.

Yes

No

At the base of each branch is a branch collar that aids in healing the wound left when the branch is removed. Never cut flush into the collar, but remove the branch to the outside of the swelling. The resulting wounds will heal faster.

Cutting off large limbs should be avoided, but if you must remove a major limb, make the cuts in stages. Undercut the branch first to reduce the chances of its tearing the bark as it falls.

It is unnecessary to dress pruning cuts or wounds. Treated wounds may be just as likely to develop infections as nontreated wounds. In any case, don't treat any wounds smaller than 2 inches in diameter. Never paint a wound with oil-based paint, tar, or creosote, which may damage the cambium and prevent proper healing. Use a commercial wound dressing if you must.

Pay particular attention to training and retaining branches that form wide crotch angles with the trunk or another branch. The wider the angle, the stronger the crotch. Narrow crotches are weak, and some bark is often buried as the branches grow together. Known as bark inclusion, this can lead to rot and a splitting out of the branch.

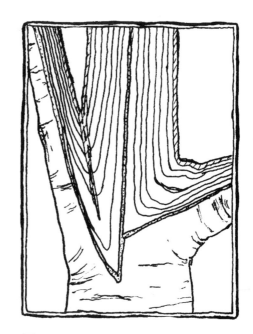

When removing a large branch, (A) make the first cut an undercut a few feet from the trunk. It should extend no more than a quarter to a third of the way through the branch. (B) Next cut at the top of the branch and continue until the branch splits and falls away. (C) Finish pruning by removing the stub, but don't cut through the branch collar.

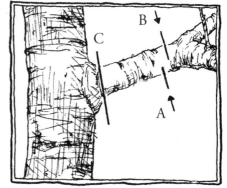

TRAINING

Besides pruning to remove damaged and excessive growth and to stimulate or control fruiting, you can also prune to train a plant to a particular shape and form that is most conducive to fruit production. There are many systems for training fruit trees. Here are a few that are commonly used.

Central Leader System

A well-developed *central leader* tree has a central trunk from which several scaffold branches arise. These branches should form wide-angled crotches where they leave the trunk, be spaced at least 8 inches apart, and not be directly above or opposite one another.

First pruning. At planting, cut back a one-year-old whip to about 30 inches (dwarf stock), 36 inches (semidwarf stock), or 40 inches (standard stock). This will stimulate lateral branching. Because early fruiting retards vegetative growth, remove all fruit buds. Begin pruning well-branched two-year-old trees with the method described for the second pruning.

Second pruning. One year after planting, save the most vigorous upright shoot for a leader and select two well-placed, wide-angled lateral branches for permanent scaffold limbs. Be sure these are at least 8 to 10 inches apart. Shorten them so that their length is about 6 inches less than that of the leader. Remove all others. For dwarf trees, cut back the leader to about 20 inches above the topmost scaffold branch. On semidwarf and full-size trees, cut it back to about 5 feet above the topmost scaffold.

There are three common training systems for fruit trees in the home garden. (A) The central leader system depends upon the strong vertical growth of a single shoot, or leader, with branches higher on the tree shorter than the ones below. (B) The open-center system allows several branches to arise at about the same spot on the trunk but removes the leader to keep the center open and allow good penetration of sunlight and air. This is often used for the trees of stone fruits. (C) The modified leader, or modified central leader system, maintains the strong leader to a point, then removes it. You can train just about any fruit tree to this system.

If the leader is not straight, tie a long pole along the trunk and up through it to hold it straight as it matures.

It's important to establish good branch angles at this time. Use spreaders or clothespins to hold the young branches away from the trunk to establish crotch angles of 45 to 60 degrees. Narrow crotch angles form weak unions, and the branches often split under a heavy snow or fruit load.

Third pruning. Two years after planting, keep as the new leader the topmost shoot that develops from the old leader. Select two or three lateral shoots from the older leader for new scaffold branches. Shorten them and remove all other new lateral shoots. The scaffold branches from the previous year will have developed a few branches of their own. These are secondary scaffolds. Select two or three of these that grow at least 8 to 10 inches from the trunk and remove the rest. Leave those closest to the trunk the longest and shorten the outer ones. Head back any that are longer than the scaffold to which they are attached, and treat each main scaffold as though it were a tree. Be sure lower scaffolds are longer than upper ones and lower secondary scaffolds are longer than outer secondary scaffolds.

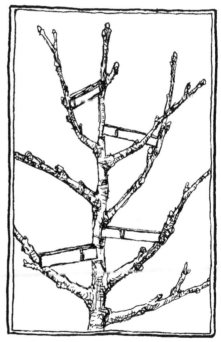

Fourth pruning. Three years after planting, select two or three more new main scaffold branches and keep the leader dominant, following the steps outlined for the third pruning. Let healthy trees produce a crop.

Fifth pruning. Four years after planting, the main framework, consisting of six to eight well-placed scaffold branches, should be well established. Further development of the

Wide crotch angles are strong, so spread young branches in their first year to force them to form wide angles. Clothespins work well.

leader need not be encouraged. Instead, cut it back to a well-placed lateral when the trees come into full bearing. Curtail the spread of the tree by heading scaffold branches. Some heading and thinning may be necessary to maintain proper tree balance.

Modified Central Leader System

This system is especially suited to apple and pear trees but can be used for any of the tree fruit. Training in a modified leader system is similar to that of a central leader system.

First pruning. Head one-year-old whips on dwarf stocks to 28 inches, stone fruits and those on semidwarf stocks to about 36 inches, and those on standard stocks to about 44 inches. Select four lateral branches spaced about 10 inches apart and remove the rest. Prune the leader to about twice the length of the scaffolds, and shorten the upper scaffolds more than the lower. Spread the scaffolds to create crotch angles of 45 to 60 degrees.

Second pruning. Select additional scaffolds as discussed under the central leader system. Keep scaffolds shorter than the leader, and the upper scaffolds shorter than lower ones.

Subsequent pruning. Continue to select scaffolds and to prune as described for the central leader system. Remove any crossed branches, water sprouts, and small branches near the tree's interior. When the tree is as large as you want it, head the leader to the uppermost scaffold. In later years, continue to head any scaffold that grows upright and tries to develop into a leader. This is the modification in the "modified" central leader system.

Open-Center System

In an open-center system, the tree develops two to four scaffold branches growing directly from the main trunk about 24 inches from the ground. This system is especially adaptable to stone fruits but can be used for all tree fruits. Because the scaffolds develop 60- to 90-degree crotch angles, there is little bark inclusion. The trunk develops a greater degree of winter hardiness, and branches are less apt to split out.

First pruning. At planting, head a one-year-old tree to 30 inches. Select branches that arise a couple of inches below the heading cut, and head these to a couple of buds each. Remove all other branches.

By June most buds will have formed rosettes or shoots, with the most vigorous growing from the top couple of buds. If these have narrow, undesirable crotch angles, head them to 2 to 3 inches to stimulate shoot development from lower buds. Lower buds often produce better crotch angles.

By the end of the first summer, you should have three wide-angled scaffolds, all headed to about the same length, and no leader.

Second pruning. Remove any shoots below the scaffolds, all water sprouts, and any shoots growing up from the scaffolds within 3 inches of the trunk. Head all scaffolds to the same length.

Subsequent pruning. Allow the tree to continue growing into the established form and do only enough pruning to maintain that form.

Espalier

Popular in England and Europe, espalier trains fruit trees to grow in picturesque shapes against walls or along fences. With this system you can grow trees in a very limited area. Espalier takes a lot of time and constant attention to detail.

First pruning. Begin with either a one- or two-year-old tree. Head back the central leader and the scaffold branches by cutting into one-year-old wood where you desire more branches.

Second pruning. Fasten new shoots in place as they develop and keep them fastened for at least two years. They'll remain in place after that without fasteners.

Third pruning. Regulate new growth by pinching out new shoots to eliminate them or pinching them back to dwarf them. If a shoot is too hard to pinch, you've let it develop too long.

Fourth pruning. Head back all branches each spring to suppress lateral growth and induce flower bud development close to the main scaffolds.

Fifth pruning. Thin out secondary branches as the tree grows older. This maintains the ornamental shape and productivity of the plant.

Pest Control

No matter where you garden, you'll have pests. By creating an unnatural system of plants growing side by side in rows in full sun, unhardened by drought or shade and untoughened by competition, you're inviting pests.

If you are philosophically against all artificial means of control, get used to cutting out worms and rotten spots in your fruit. If you want only absolutely perfect fruit, you may be better off buying fruit that's been graded and selected for perfection. Most gardeners stand on the middle ground.

Good pest control is a continuum of options. Use common sense and the least intrusive methods first. If these fail, move to more specific methods.

GENERAL PEST CONTROL: THE FIRST LINE OF DEFENSE
Sanitation
Cleanliness encourages health. Many pests overwinter in crop residue and debris. Remove all crop residues after harvest and compost them if they're not diseased. Bury or burn them if they are. Plants infected with a soil-borne pathogen like verticillium should be bagged and disposed of in a sanitary landfill. Keep the area around the planting free of weeds and tall grass that may harbor insects and diseases. Weeds and grass also compete directly with young trees and small fruit plants for water, nutrients, and light, so keep your plantings cultivated or mulched.

When you enter the garden, be sure your hands are clean. If you've handled a branch infected with fire blight or other viral disease, don't

Controlling insects and diseases is a year-round chore. Here are some common pests and the general control for them. Always check with your cooperative extension service for the latest recommendations on currently allowable pesticides and the timing for sprays in your area. Use a pesticide only in accordance with recommendations on the label.

PLANT	PEST	CONTROL
Apple	Aphids, scale, mites	Dormant oil, lime sulfur, sanitation
	Scab	Captan, sanitation
	Codling moth, leaf rollers, plum curculio, fruitworms	Malathion + methoxychlor, ryania, Dipel
	Apple maggot	Carbaryl, ryania
	Fire blight	8–8–100 Bordeaux, prune affected portion
	Powdery mildew, black rot	Captan
	Cedar apple rust	Remove junipers from the area
Pear	Blister mite, psylla, scale	Dormant oil
	Scab, leaf spot, sooty blotch	Captan
	Other pests—see apple	
Quince	Mites, scale	Dormant oil
	Plum curculio, oriental fruit moth, leaf roller	Carbaryl
Peach, cherry, and plum	Aphids, mites, peach leaf	
	Leaf curl, black knot	Lime sulfur, 6–6–100 Bordeaux
	Scale	Dormant oil
	Brown rot	Captan
	Plum curculio, eyespotted bud moth, prune moth, leaf rollers	Carbaryl, pyrethrins
	Bacterial spot	Lime sulfur
	Leaf spot	Captan, sulfur
	Cherry fruitworm	Carbaryl, rotenone
	Cherry fruit fly, fruit moth	Carbaryl, rotenone

PLANT	PEST	CONTROL
Blueberry	Scale	Dormant oil
	Anthracnose	Captan
	Mummyberry	Sanitation. Apply 2 inches of new mulch early every spring.
	Tipborer, fruitworms, maggot	Malathion
	Japanese beetle, flea beetle	Carbaryl
Grape	Black rot, cane canker	Captan
	Leafhoppers, rose chafer, flea beetle	Carbaryl, rotenone
	Downy mildew	Captan, fixed copper + hydrated lime
	Powdery mildew	Sulfur
	Berry moth, skeletonizer	Rotenone, Methoxychlor
Strawberry	Aphids, spittlebugs, plant bugs, spider mites, leaf rollers, weevils	Methoxychlor + malathion
	Leaf scorch, leaf spot, leather rot, gray mold, berry rot	Captan, basic copper
Ribes	Aphids, scale	Dormant oil
	Leaf spot, botrytis	Captan
	Currant aphid, fruitworms	Malathion
Rubus	Anthracnose, gray mold, spur blight	Captan
	Sap beetles, plant bugs, fruitworm	Malathion
	Japanese beetles, leaf rollers	Carbaryl
	Cane borer, stem girdler	Prune out and destroy infested canes
Other fruits	Generally, no regular spray schedules are recommended. Consult the package label and your cooperative extension service for further recommendations.	

Not all problems are caused by insect and disease pests, so be sure you have a real pest problem before you reach for the spray can. Here's a list of general symptoms you might find on your fruit plants.

Symptom	Possible Cause	Possible Control
WHOLE PLANT SYMPTOMS		
Wilt	Lack of water	Water
	Excess water	Stop watering; drain
	Disease	Plant resistant cultivars
	Insect damage to trunk, cane, and/or roots	Apply soil insecticide/protection
	Rodent damage	Pay attention next time
	Winter damage to roots or trunk	Mulch, protect trunk from sunscald
Weak/spindly growth	Not enough light	Remove shade; prune
	Excess water	Improve drainage
	Crowding	Remove every other plant
	Excess nitrogen	Reduce fertilizer
	Crown damage	Inspect and repair
	Root damage	Inspect and correct
	Winter damage	Inspect and repair
Abnormal twisted growth	Herbicide	Pay attention next time. Don't mulch with clippings from treated lawns.
	Virus	Remove; control insects; replant with virus-free plants
Shoot dieback	Fire blight	Bactericide; prune
Bark splitting	Winter damage	Repair
	Overloading	Corrective pruning; fruit thinning
Bark encrusted	Scale	Insecticides
Holes in bark	Birds	No correction necessary
	Borers	Insecticide and/or mechanical control; pay attention next time
Gumming	Borers	Insecticide and/or mechanical control; pay attention next time

Symptom	Possible Cause	Possible Control
	Gummosis	Inspect and correct problem. If canker, cut out; if borer, destroy; if no visible cause, leave it alone.
Abnormal growths on twigs	Black knot	Prune out
	Galls	Prune out

LEAF SYMPTOMS

Symptom	Possible Cause	Possible Control
Leaves/stems spotted	Fertilizer burn	Pay attention next time
	Pesticide burn	Pay attention next time
	Disease	Plant resistant cultivars; fungicide sprays
Leaves eaten or with holes	Caterpillars	Insecticide sprays; handpick
	Slugs	Bait
	Climbing cutworms	Insecticide sprays, mechanical protection
Leaves curl, may remain green	Wilt	Plant resistant cultivars; remove infected plants; fungicide sprays
	Virus	Control insects; remove infected plants and replant virus-free stock
	Aphids	Insecticide sprays; forceful stream of water
Leaves roll	Virus	Plant resistant cultivars; control insects; remove infected plants and replant virus-free stock
	Drought	Water
	Leaf rollers/tiers	Insecticide sprays
	Powdery mildew	Fungicide sprays; improve air circulation
Stunted/yellow leaves (not curled)	Excess water	Stop watering
	Poor drainage	Drain
	Compact soil	Add organic matter/sand
	Improper pH	Adjust soil pH (usually acidify)

Symptom	Possible Cause	Possible Control
	Insufficient iron	Add iron; adjust soil pH
	Insufficient fertility	Fertilize (especially with nitrogen)
	Disease	Plant resistant cultivars; apply fungicide sprays
	Virus	Remove infected plants; control insects; replant virus-free stock
	Nematodes	Replant in another area; use resistant stock
	Root damage	Examine and correct
	Rodent damage to trunk	Pay attention next time
	Rodent damage to roots	Pay attention next time
	Graft incompatibility	Pay attention next time
	Winter damage	Examine and repair
Spur leaves black but don't drop	Fire blight	Bacterial sprays; prune

FLOWER SYMPTOMS

Symptom	Possible Cause	Possible Control
Flowers black	Water imbalance	Adjust watering
	Compact soil	Add organic matter/sand
	Too-deep cultivation	Don't cultivate so deeply
	Frost damage	Pay attention next time
	Disease	Pay attention next time; fungicide sprays

FRUIT SYMPTOMS

Symptom	Possible Cause	Possible Control
Fruit does not set properly	Too hot	Water
	Excess nitrogen	Pay attention next time
	Nitrogen deficiency	Fertilize
	Poor pollination	Encourage bees; protect against frost next time; provide wind protection
	Immature plants	Wait
	Insect damage	Insecticides
	Imbalance in moisture	Inspect and correct
Fruit misshapen	Poor pollination	Encourage bees; protect against frost next time; provide wind

Symptom	Possible Cause	Possible Control
		protection; provide adequate nutrition
	Insect damage	Insecticides
	Cold	None
Fruit cracked	Russeting by sprays	Pay attention next time
	Boron deficiency	Test and correct
Fruit with surface blemishes	Nutrient deficiencies	Test and correct
	Insect damage	Insecticides; other controls
	Disease damage	Fungicides; other controls
	Limb rub	No action necessary
Premature fruit drop	Too dry	Water next time
	Too hot	Water next time
	Excessive fruit set	Thin next time
	Immature plants	Wait
	June drop	Nothing; it's natural
Fruit small	Too much competition	Thin next time
	Poor pollination	Encourage bees; protect against wind and frost; provide adequate nutrition.
	Too dry	Water
	Too wet	Improve drainage
Fruit with internal blemishes	Insects	Insecticides; pay attention next time
	Disease	Pay attention next time
	Nutrient deficiencies	Test and correct
	Senescence (old age)	Discard; pay attention next time

GENERAL

Symptom	Possible Cause	Possible Control
Poor transplant take	Insufficient time	Wait
	Too cold	Wait
	Too wet	Stop watering; wait
	Too hot	Water
	Too dry	Water
	Bird depredation	Control birds
Young plants die	Rot	Fungicide
	Fertilizer burn	Pay attention next time

touch any other potential host until you've washed your hands. Avoid handling wet plants. Brushing against the wet foliage of a diseased plant can cause the spores to cling to your clothing and brush off on a healthy plant you pass. A number of fungal diseases are spread in this way.

Crop Rotation

The buildup of insects, disease organisms, and toxins in heavily cultivated soils can adversely affect young fruit plantings.

If your selected planting site was in sod, don't plant strawberries for at least several years because of the potential for a high population of grubs that destroy strawberry roots.

Plants of the Solanaceae family, such as tomatoes, potatoes, eggplants, peppers, and petunias, as well as weeds like lamb's-quarters, pigweed, horse nettle, cocklebur, or groundcherry, can carry verticillium wilt. This disease can remain in the soil for up to five years, and it attacks strawberries and raspberries.

Because of the potential for nematode problems, don't follow peaches, nectarines, or tobacco with peaches or nectarines. If you must replant peaches or nectarines, use a cover crop of sudangrass or perennial or annual ryegrass for two years before planting. Nematodes won't feed on the roots of these grasses and will die out. Because annual ryegrass will not persist if kept mowed and not allowed to set seed, it may be the best choice for ease in later weed control.

Fall Plowing

Clean cultivation in the fall, after leaf fall, not only turns under orchard debris but also may turn up burrowing insects to be killed by winter cold. Because fall plowing leaves the soil surface bare and subject to wind erosion, plant a cover crop or mulch your plants both to reduce erosion and to insulate the roots from winter cold. (The United States loses about 80 tons of topsoil per acre per year due to wind erosion.) Don't cultivate too early in the fall or you may stimulate late-season growth that will fail to harden in time for winter.

Plant Quality

Plants are the cheapest investment in your orchard. Even at $20 apiece, quality trees are inexpensive considering the return you reap. Buy pest-resistant cultivars adapted to your area and grafted to the right rootstocks for your soil and climate. Buy only certified disease-free plants. And purchase plants that are the right age. Don't buy two hundred rooted blueberry cuttings if you have no nursery bed in which to pamper them for a year or two, and don't buy older plants thinking they'll produce a crop faster. Very immature and very mature plants suffer more from transplant shock and are apt to be more prone to pest attack.

Location
A sunny site with well-drained soil and good air circulation reduces the incidence of disease. Dead air pockets with high humidity increase the incidence of diseases, especially mildews. Poorly drained soil causes root rot and poor root growth, which leave a plant stressed and susceptible to pests.

Planting at the Right Time
Some gardeners get antsy and jump the gun, planting in spring soil that is too cold and wet, or in the autumn when the plant has little chance of hardening for winter. Plant at the right time for your area and your plants will be hardy and vigorously growing in time to resist most pest attacks.

Feeding and Watering Schedules
Well-fed, well-watered plants are better able to ward off pests and diseases. Fertilize your plants properly and keep the soil pH range properly adjusted. Water only in the morning to give the foliage a chance to dry before nightfall, or use drip irrigation to apply water directly to the soil without wetting the foliage.

Intercropping
Large blocks of identical species make it easy for insects and diseases to spread and thrive. By intercropping, or planting a mix of plants such as grapevines, apple trees, and raspberry shrubs together, you greatly reduce the chance of losing an entire crop to pests or disease.

BARRIERS AND TRAPS: THE SECOND LINE OF DEFENSE
Physical Barriers
Physical barriers like plastic or wire collars protect tree trunks from mice

and rabbits. Place them completely around the trunk to a height of 18 inches (higher if you have a lot of snow) and push them into the soil an inch or two. Apple trees are particularly susceptible to rodent damage.

Use floating row covers to protect newly set strawberry plants from insect pests. Use wood ashes or sharp sand placed in a wide ring around newly set strawberry plants to discourage slugs.

Traps
Beer attracts slugs. (Preliminary research indicates that they prefer premium beer to the cheap stuff, but when pushed into a corner, they'll drink any brand.) Sink tuna fish cans or other shallow pans to the rim in soil near your strawberry plants. Fill them with beer. Slugs will binge and drown. Remove the bodies in the morning.

Because soft-bodied slugs need a cool, moist, dark place to hide during sunny hours, boards placed on the ground make good slug traps. Lift the boards periodically and destroy slugs you find there.

Pheromone traps are used to help control certain insect pests. These traps use sex attractants to lure insects. Some traps are coated with a sticky substance that immobilizes and holds the insect until it dies; others, like Japanese beetle traps, catch insects in canisters. Hang pheromone traps in the plant canopy according to label instructions.

PHYSICAL REMOVAL: THE THIRD LINE OF DEFENSE
Although not useful for dealing with very tiny pests like aphids, handpicking is a very old and very effective method of controlling some insects. And it leaves no harmful residue! Spend time every day picking larger insects, such as Japanese beetles and curculios, from your plants. Look for many of these in the early morning or late afternoon when the weather is cool. Step on the pests or drop them into a can of kerosene or cooking oil for rapid disposal.

A strong water stream from a hose can be used to knock off some insects. Adding soap to the water makes it even more effective, because soap is toxic or repellent to many insects and fungi. You can use commercial insecticidal soaps or mix your own using a solution of a mild soap such as Ivory. Some soaps contain ingredients that may harm plants. Try your own preparations on only a few leaves to see if there is any damage. Never use detergent solutions.

PREDATORS, PARASITES, AND PATHOGENS:
THE FOURTH LINE OF DEFENSE

Predatory and parasitic insects feed on many fruit pests. Encouraging these beneficial insects to establish themselves in the orchard is always a good pest management practice. But except in the case of small, contained plantings, their effect on the overall population of insect pests may be small. Beneficial insects should certainly be a part of your line of defense against pests, but you should not expect them to entirely control the problem. The following are the most common and effective beneficial insects:

- Lacewing larvae, or aphis lions, feed on aphids, scale insects, insect eggs, spider mites, and other small insects.
- Damsel bugs eat aphids, caterpillars, leafhoppers, and mites.
- Lady beetles, or ladybugs, feed on aphids, insect eggs, scale insects, and mites. A single adult ladybug can lay one thousand seven hundred eggs in its lifetime and eat two thousand four hundred aphids.
- Pirate bugs eat many small insects, aphids, and mites.
- Praying mantids prefer grasshoppers, crickets, bees, wasps, and flies, which don't bother fruit plants. Because they hatch in mid to late summer, mantids have little effect on fruit pests. They also tend to eat each other!
- Syrphid flies look like wasps, and their maggots eat about one aphid per minute.
- Ichneumon wasps parasitize caterpillars.
- Tachinid flies glue their eggs to the skin of their host caterpillars or beetles or lay their eggs on leaves where the feeding host will ingest them. Once inside, the developing larvae eventually kill the host.
- Braconid wasps eat caterpillars and beetles.
- Trichogramma wasps lay their eggs in the eggs of more than two hundred species of caterpillars, including the armyworm, codling moth, eastern tent caterpillar, fall web worm, gypsy moth, oriental fruit moth, peach tree borer, and plum moth.

Birds are a mixed blessing. They'll eat a lot of bugs, but they'll also eat a lot of fruit. If you encourage them, be prepared to lose a certain percentage of your crop along with some bugs, or invest in bird netting to protect your fruit.

Geese feed on insects and weeds, and their rich eggs make great cakes. One old recommendation called for running four geese per acre of strawberries to control weeds. (I'll bet they'd work in the gooseberries, too.)

Box turtles and toads feast on hundreds of insects; bats eat a number of flying insects; and garden snakes are great predators of insects and mice.

PESTICIDES: THE FIFTH LINE OF DEFENSE

There comes a time in every orchardist's life when you know that your planting is overrun by pests. Handpicking, hosing, and traps are not enough. Insects and diseases have broken through the first four lines of defense and are threatening your food supply. It is time to call up the big guns.

Pesticides are classified as insecticides (insect killers), miticides (mite killers), herbicides (plant killers), and fungicides (fungus killers). Nontoxic pesticides do not exist. All pesticides are toxic to the pests they are intended to kill, but some are relatively nontoxic to nontargeted organisms, such as pets and children. I say "relatively" because everything is toxic if you eat enough of it. Try eating 25 pounds of pancake flour all at once and see if you don't get sick.

We express the relative toxicity of a material with an LD_{50} number. This stands for the number of milligrams of the pesticide that must be ingested all at once for every kilogram of body weight to cause half the test population to die. The smaller the number, the more poisonous the compound. For example, the botanical insecticide nicotine has an oral LD_{50} of 10. It's highly toxic to bugs and people. Rotenone has an LD_{50} that varies from 80 to 400, depending upon age and formulation. *Bacillus thuringiensis* (BT) has an LD_{50} of 1,200. Carbaryl (Sevin) has an LD_{50} of 700, and malathion, 1,200. All are classed as having low toxicity to nontarget organisms.

As a class, most fungicides and herbicides are less acutely toxic to humans than insecticides, although some of these compounds may have debilitating effects upon the orchardist with long exposure. The common fungicide captan is relatively nontoxic, with an LD_{50} of about 12,000.

Pesticides with low LD_{50} numbers, such as parathion, are very toxic and do not belong in the home fruit planting. Carbaryl, malathion,

Diazinon, and captan, which are synthetic pesticides, are considered relatively safe (at the moment). BT is relatively safe and works for certain foliage-feeding insects. Sulfur, mineral oil, and botanical compounds are relatively safe also but may not be very effective. Whatever pesticide you decide to use, follow the label directions carefully.

Pesticides can be divided into several categories: the biologicals, botanicals, organic compounds, and inorganic compounds.

When using pesticides, start with those that have the least toxicity to nontarget organisms: the biologicals. If they don't do the job, try the botanicals before resorting to the organic or inorganic compounds.

Biologicals

A very effective biological control is *Bacillus thuringiensis.*. Marketed as Thuricide, Dipel, or BT, this bacterium attacks more than four hundred species of caterpillars, while leaving other insects and animals unharmed. It's one of the safest pesticides for the home planting and worth every cent you'll pay for it.

Botanicals

The botanicals are derived from plants and generally are relatively nontoxic to humans and pets when used as directed. Nicotine, however, is highly toxic.

Rotenone is made from either the derris root of East Asia or the cube root from South America. It is a broad-spectrum, slow-acting insecticide that may not effectively control some rapid-feeding insects like caterpillars. It degrades in about a week. It has low toxicity to mammals and birds but is extremely toxic to fish.

Pyrethrum is derived from the dried and ground flowers of a form of tropical chrysanthemum. Because it knocks down insects rapidly but kills them slowly, it's usually mixed with another insecticide like rotenone or with an activator such as piperonyl butoxide that increases its potency. It breaks down rapidly. It is nonhazardous to birds and mammals but slightly toxic to fish.

Sabadilla, marketed as Red Devil, is made from the ground seeds of the tropical sabadilla bush. It gets stronger with age if kept in the dark but breaks down rapidly in sunlight. It controls many bugs, beetles, and caterpillars.

Organics

Organic pesticides are the most commonly used today. These fall into two groups—synthetics and botanicals. The synthetic organics contain organic phosphates (malathion and Diazinon), carbamates (carbaryl), and pyrethroids. All are broad-spectrum, meaning that they kill a wide variety of pests. They are relatively nontoxic to mammals but can be deadly to birds, fish, and beneficial insects like bees.

Captan is a broad-spectrum carbamate fungicide that has been used in home gardens for more than forty years. It is often used as an ingredient in "all-purpose" sprays. It is not highly toxic to mammals and birds, and it breaks down rapidly in the environment.

Malathion is an organic phosphate that degrades quickly and has broad-spectrum action. It has low toxicity to birds and mammals but is highly toxic to fish and bees. Malathion is one of the safest synthetic home pesticides we have, when used properly.

Carbaryl (Sevin) is a broad-spectrum insecticide with low toxicity to birds and mammals. It is slightly toxic to fish and extremely toxic to bees. Never apply this compound to plants that are in bloom because of its danger to bees and other nectar-foraging insects. About half the compound degrades in three days, and it is entirely degraded after two weeks.

Diazinon is an organic phosphate that is moderately toxic to humans and animals. Use this to control insects only when all else fails.

Inorganics

Among inorganics, the once-common arsenic, lead, and mercury compounds are out, and for good reason: The highly toxic lead-arsenate sprays once commonly used on apple trees persist for decades in the soil and make replanting old orchard sites highly questionable. Copper compounds control some diseases, and sulfur is still used for disease, mite, and insect control. Baking soda provides some control of powdery mildew in small fruits. Bordeaux mixture and lime-sulfur sprays are making a comeback for the control of certain fruit diseases. Used improperly, however, these compounds can damage sensitive foliage and fruit. The following inorganic compounds are safe to use in the home garden or orchard:

Sulfur controls mites, newly hatched scale, some caterpillars, and many fungus diseases. Ask for garden sulfur, sulfur dust, or wettable sulfur and follow directions carefully. If used in too high a concentration or under hot, humid conditions, it can russet fruit or burn leaves. Used over time, it will also lower the soil pH.

Lime-sulfur, a combination of hydrated lime and sulfur, controls many fruit insects. You can buy it or make it at home with 1 pound of quicklime, 2 pounds of sulfur, and 1 gallon of water. Working outdoors, make a paste of sulfur and a little water. Heat the remaining water and add lime, mixing until the lime dissolves. Add the sulfur paste. Bring the mix to a boil and simmer for half an hour, adding water when necessary to maintain the original level. The brew will turn dark amber, and when all the free sulfur has dissolved, it's done. Strain this concentrated mixture and store it in glass jars. For a dormant spray, dilute one part concentrate to nine parts of water. For a summer foliage spray, dilute one part concentrate to forty-nine parts water. Never apply lime-sulfur to fruit that is to be canned, because the sulfur may cause the can to explode. Never use undiluted concentrate, and remember that the mix will stain your hands and clothing.

Copper is a traditional fungicide that can be used alone as a dust or in combination with other minerals. Bordeaux mixture, a combination of copper sulfate and dehydrated lime, is an effective fungicide and has insecticidal properties as well. You can buy Bordeaux mixture or make it yourself by dissolving 3 ounces of copper sulfate in 3 gallons of water. Add 5 ounces of hydrated lime, mix everything completely, and it's ready to spray. Store it in a plastic container, as the compound corrodes metal. Bordeaux spray recommendations sometimes vary in strength. A 4–4–50 mix means 4 pounds of copper sulfate, 4 pounds of hydrated lime, and 50 gallons of water.

Cautions

Pesticides are useful tools when used responsibly. They can help you control pests in the orchard, but they must be handled carefully. Don't be afraid of them, but educate yourself about every one, respect it for what it can and can't do, and weigh the risks and benefits. If the relatively safe pesticides mentioned here don't work for you, resist the temptation to try something more lethal. Be sure to follow the label directions religiously whenever you use a pesticide, and check to make sure that the compound you use is legal for use in home orchards.

MAMMAL AND BIRD PESTS
Deer Control
Growing fruit in deer country is challenging. You may think deer are cute at first, but after they've browsed all the fruit buds from your plants during the winter, you'll soon think unkind thoughts of them.

There are a number of commercial deer repellent products on the market that are fairly effective for a short time. But deer quickly get used to them, or their effectiveness is mitigated by the weather. You'll have to either constantly replace the product or change products frequently to baffle the creatures. Other materials, such as bags of human hair, bars of soap, sweaty T-shirts, and lion manure are all supposed to scare deer. I haven't found any of these effective for any length of time. If deer are hungry—and they usually are in winter—they'll eat your fruit plants.

The only surefire way to keep deer out (other than using a gun) is to put up a fence. It must be at least 8 feet high, or slightly shorter, with the top flared toward the outside. Some fruit growers have reported success with electrified wire or strand fencing. Attach strips of aluminum foil smeared with peanut butter to the electrified strands. The deer smell the peanut butter, lick the strips, get zapped a few times, and leave the trees inside the fence alone. If deer are really hungry, however, and the fence is low enough to jump—electrified or not—they will get inside and eat with a vengeance. And there's not much you can do about it.

Rabbit and Rodent Control
Because rabbits nibble bark in winter, you should always place plastic or wire hardware cloth collars around your newly planted fruit tree trunks up to the lowest branch. If the snow is deep, rabbits will sometimes nibble the bark on the lower scaffolds or drooping canes. Painting these with white latex paint, particularly if it contains the ingredient thiram, is sometimes effective. Paint the trunk too if you don't use a collar.

Mice hide beneath the snow and nibble the bark of canes, trunks, and roots. This can seriously weaken or kill the plant by shutting off the flow of nutrients between the top and the roots. Plants damaged this way often leaf out and even bloom the next spring, only to die suddenly in early summer. Wire guards will help, especially if they're sunk below the ground or mulch line. Keep the grass mown near trees and bushes to discourage mice from nesting in it.

Birds are terrible pests to some fruit crops, particularly cherries, mulberries, and blueberries. Netting is the only protection against them that is almost totally effective. Cover the entire plant, bringing the net down to the trunk or ground, and tie it off. Simply draping it over the foliage will allow birds to fly up from the bottom.

Bird Control

Birds are a real nuisance to cherry and berry crops. Visual or auditory deterrents such as flashing reflective tape, owl and snake decoys, and loud noises may be effective for a short time, but some of these can become a nuisance to neighbors.

The most effective way to control birds is to net your plants. The $1/2$-inch plastic mesh bird netting sold in hardware stores will keep most birds out. Put the netting on as soon as the first fruits begin to ripen. Remove it when harvest is over. If you choose to cover individual plants, cover the plant completely, down to the base. Tie the netting tightly around the base of the plant to prevent birds from getting in from beneath. Each time you harvest, you'll have to untie and remove the netting, then replace and retie it when you're done. If you don't want this nuisance, or if you have many plants to protect, build a cage over the entire planting. Use 1-inch wire mesh poultry fencing for permanent protection, or $1/2$-inch plastic bird netting if you plan to remove the net at the end of each season.

Put in permanent posts of steel or decay-resistant wood, string heavy (11-gauge) wire from post to post to form a gridwork, then drape the netting over this, leaving a few extra inches at the bottom. Anchor the bottom edge securely to the ground with boards or bricks. Install a gate or doorway, and you're all set.

15

Harvest

Pick your fruit as soon as it is ripe, at the peak of flavor and tenderness. Waiting just a couple days too long may mean the difference between a prime harvest and a poor one—or none at all. Exceptions to this rule are pears, gooseberries, and medlars, which should be picked when slightly immature and allowed to ripen in a spare room.

Harvest during the cool of the evening and early morning after the dew has dried. After you've picked the fruit, cool or refrigerate it immediately. If you have to keep picked fruit in the garden for any length of time, say until you've finished harvesting for the day, put it into a cooler with ice, or cover it with a damp cloth. Water evaporating from the cloth's surface will cool the fruit. Once most fruit is harvested, the sugar it contains begins to convert to starch and its moisture content begins to drop. The higher the temperature, the faster the crop loses its quality. Sugar is converted into starch two to three times faster with every 18 degree F rise in temperature. A blueberry stored at 68 degrees F (room temperature) will lose sugar twice as fast as a blueberry stored at 50 degrees F and four to six times faster than one stored at 32 degrees F.

STORAGE

All fruit to be stored should be sound and free from bruises and injury and at the proper stage of ripeness to keep well. Most fruits should be slightly immature if you plan to store them for any length of time.

Soft fruits, like berries and peaches, will not keep as long as harder

If harvested too soon, some underripe fruits will continue to ripen off the plant but won't be as sweet and flavorful as those ripened fully on the plant. Other fruits won't ripen further once they're picked.

Fruit	Indicators of Maturity	Improve in Quality off the Plant?
Apple	Full size and color; ground color turns yellow in red cultivars, golden in yellow cultivars. Easy separation from spur with upward twist.	Yes, if mature before harvest
Blackberry	Berries turn dull black, soften, and sweeten.	No
Blueberry	Berries turn dark blue; separate easily from stem. No pink circle around the scar.	No
Cherry, sour	Full size and color; juicy, full flavor.	No
Cherry, sweet	Full size and color; juicy, full flavor.	No
Currant	Fully ripe fruit: full size and color and slightly soft. For jelly, harvest slightly underripe.	No
Elderberry	Fruit plump, full color, and starting to soften.	No
Gooseberry	Pick when firm.	No
Grape	Taste before harvest. Stem shriveled, seeds brown to black, full aroma and taste. Clip cluster from the shoot.	No
Peach	Ground color changing from green to yellow or white. Taste before harvest.	Yes
Pear	Pick before tree-ripe. Lenticels brown; fruit rounded, plump, waxy, and separates easily from the spur with upward twist.	Yes (ripen at 65°F)
Plum	Begins to soften.	Yes
Raspberry	Full color and separates easily from receptacle. Gently lift with thumb and forefinger.	No
Strawberry	Uniformly red, firm, but softening slightly. Pick with the calyx (cap) on to reduce rotting. Pinch the stem off about 1/4 inch above the cap.	No

Some fruits store better than others. Fruits not on this list should be processed as quickly as possible after harvest. Store only sound fruit.

Fruit	Best Temperature (°F)	Approximate Length of Storage Period
Apples	30–40	3–8 months
Apricots	31–32	1–2 weeks
Blackberries	31–32	2–3 days
Blueberries	31–32	2 weeks
Cherries, sour	32	3–7 days
Cherries, sweet	30–31	2–3 weeks
Cranberries	36–40	2–4 months
Currants	31–32	1–2 weeks
Dewberries	31–32	2–3 days
Elderberries	31–32	1–2 weeks
Figs (fresh)	31–32	7–10 days
Gooseberries	31–32	2–4 weeks
Grapes, *V. vinifera*	30–31	3–6 months
Grapes, American	31–32	2–8 weeks
Kiwifruit	31–32	3–5 months
Peaches	31–32	2–4 weeks
Pears	29–31	2– 7 months
Persimmons, Japanese	30	3–4 months
Plums and prunes	31–32	2–4 weeks
Quinces	31–32	2–3 months

fruits, like apples and pears. Fleshy fruits, like cherries, will not keep as long as dry fruits, like nuts. Late-ripening cultivars usually store better than early-ripening cultivars of the same fruit. Choosing the right cultivar is very important if you plan to store the crop for any length of time.

Most of us don't have elaborate storage facilities—the household refrigerator, kept at about 40 degrees F, serves as common storage for everything. There are other areas around the house, however, that are great for storing some fruits. An unheated, dry, well-ventilated basement

Apples are commonly stored for long periods, but some cultivars store better than others. In general, the later a cultivar ripens its fruits, the better they'll keep in storage. Apples begin to break down near the end of their storage life, resulting in pitting and/or breakdown and browning of the flesh and skin. For maximum storage, harvest at optimum maturity and store under ideal temperature and humidity conditions.

Cultivar	Normal Storage Period	Maximum Storage Period
Baldwin	4–5 months	6–7 months
Cortland	3–4 months	5–6 months
Delicious	3–4 months	8 months
Golden Delicious	3–4 months	6–8 months
Grimes Golden	2–3 months	4 months
Jonathan	2–3 months	5–6 months
McIntosh	2–4 months	6–8 months
Northern Spy	4–5 months	8 months
Rhode Island Greening	3–4 months	6– 7 months
Rome Beauty	4–5 months	6–8 months
Stayman	4–5 months	6–8 months
Wealthy	0–2 months	3 months
Winesap	5–6 months	8 months
Yellow Newtown	5–6 months	8 months
York Imperial	4–5 months	6–7 months

or root cellar is fine for the storage of apples, pears, and quinces. The key to successfully storing your harvest is to maintain steady temperatures and relative humidity and to provide adequate ventilation.

Temperature

Most crops store best at temperatures between 32 and 35 degrees F. Lower temperatures freeze tissue and cause it to break down; higher temperatures increase the likelihood of rotting. Some warmer-season crops, like figs, are exceptions, storing better at about 50 degrees F. Keeping them at lower temperatures for any length of time causes chill injury. Because lighting also raises air temperature, store your fruits in a dark place.

Nuts are less perishable than most other fruits but still maintain their best quality under refrigeration. Nuts lose their texture, color, and flavor and become stale, rancid, or moldy unless stored properly. Store sound nuts in a cool place or in the refrigerator as soon as possible after harvest. Nuts freeze well. Most will keep well for several years at 0 degrees F. With the exception of chestnuts, most nuts store best at low (60 to 80 percent) relative humidity. Chestnuts dry out easily, so store them in poly bags in the refrigerator. Storage below 45 degrees F controls most insect infestations. Store all nuts away from products with pronounced strong odors, such as onions, fresh fruit, and turnips, since they will often absorb those aromas and become off-flavored.

NUT	IN SHELL AT			SHELLED AT		
	32°F	50°F	70°F	32°F	50°F	70°F
		Months			Months	
Almonds	15–20	6–12	6	6–12	6	6
Chestnuts	4–6	—	—	—	—	—
Filberts	15–30	15–30	12	6–10	6	2–3
Pecans	12–18	6	2	5–12	4–6	1
Persian walnuts	10–20	6–12	2–4	6–12	6	1
Black walnuts	—	—	—	15	8	8

Relative Humidity

Relative humidity is also important. Most fruits are between 80 and 90 percent water, so storing them in air with less than about 90 percent relative humidity will cause the water in the fruit to evaporate and the fruit to shrivel. The drier the air, the faster the fruit will shrivel. On the other hand, very high relative humidity can cause rot. It is important to maintain a steady relative humidity throughout the storage life of your fruits.

Ventilation

Ventilation is another important and often overlooked consideration to successful fruit storage. All fruits give off heat—called the heat of respiration—as they sit in storage. This can be considerable. A ton of apples stored at 40 degrees F produces about 1,100 Btu every day. If this heat is not removed, the fruit will respire faster, liberating more heat, which in turn makes it respire even faster, and your fruit will turn to mush in no time. The heat buildup is worsened by an increase in humidity caused by the water given off by the fruit. If this is not vented, relative humidity will approach 100 percent and this, along with the increasing temperature, will hasten rotting and loss of quality. If you're storing fruit in the cellar, open a window and run a fan near the fruit to circulate fresh air.

Ethylene Gas

Ethylene is a colorless, odorless gas released by ripening fruit. The higher the temperature, the faster it's released, and the faster fruit continues to ripen. The less ethylene in the air, the longer the produce will keep. Lowering the temperature and increasing ventilation reduce the amount of ethylene. Store high ethylene producers such as apples, pears, plums, and peaches away from other fruit. Considerable quantities of ethylene also are emitted from cigarette smoke, engines, and fluorescent light ballasts. The old saying that one rotten apple ruins the barrel is true, since damaged and rotting fruit also gives off large quantities of ethylene. Store only sound fruit. Keep the fruit picked over and get rid of any that are rotting.

16

Tree Fruits and Nuts

APPLES

Apples are the most commonly grown deciduous fruit in the world. Cultivated apples originated in Asia Minor and spread quickly to Iran and Turkey, then into Europe. Carbonized apples were found in ancient Swiss lake dwellings. The Phoenicians raised them, and the ancient Greek poets Sappho and Theocritus mention them. Apple seeds were brought into the New World in 1629 and disseminated quickly among colonists and native tribes. Many of the trees planted by the Pilgrims were still producing fruit in 1900. The first named apple to originate in the United States was 'Blaxton's Yellow Sweeting', which sprang up in an orchard planted by William Blackstone near Pawtucket, Rhode Island, in 1635.

Apples were grown mostly for cider in Colonial New England, so there was little reason to select fine-tasting fruit; seedling orchards predominated. Some named cultivars, however, were sold by Henry Wolcott, Jr., a Connecticut nurseryman, as early as 1650. These cultivars—among them 'Summer Pippin', 'Holland Pippin', 'London Pippin', 'Pearmain', and 'Bellybond' ('Belle et Bonne')—were so valued that they were sometimes exchanged for land. In 1648, Governor Endicott of Massachusetts exchanged five hundred three-year-old trees with William Trask for 250 acres of land.

Grafting selected cultivars was common in Holland and England during Colonial times, and the practice spread slowly to the Colonies. Many cultivars popular today arose as chance seedlings along abandoned fencerows. During the nineteenth century, more than three thousand cultivars were selected, named, and described in the United States alone. Most have since vanished, but some, like 'Northern Spy', 'McIntosh', 'Granny Smith', and 'Delicious', are still pleasing palates. By 1868 apple orchards had been planted from the Atlantic to the Pacific, and by 1900 thousands of cultivars were grown by American farmers.

Apples grow best in the temperate, cold-winter regions of the Northeast and the Pacific Northwest. They're not well suited to areas where chilling is often inadequate and summer temperatures average above 75 degrees F, because under these warm, humid conditions, diseases are more severe and it's hard to get a good apple crop without fungicide sprays. Neither will apples do well in the Great Plains, where winters are severe and water is sometimes lacking. If rainfall is less than 20 inches a year, you'll have to irrigate your trees.

If you garden in northern areas, select cold-hardy cultivars that mature their fruit in 140 to 150 days. In southern New England, 155- to 160-day cultivars usually mature adequately. The Ohio Basin and northern areas of the Mid-Atlantic states are fine for cultivars that require up to 165 days. You can grow longer-season apples in more southerly regions provided you garden in the cool mountains.

Apples tolerate a wide range of soil conditions, as long as the soil is well drained and not compacted. They're not fussy about pH, either, although 6.5 to 6.8 is optimal. Because apple trees have deep roots, the subsoil is even more important than the topsoil. If your topsoil is good but the subsoil is not, the tree might make good growth for several years, then die in a dry year. A combination of 6 feet of topsoil and gravelly loam subsoil is ideal for apple trees.

Soil preparation for apple trees is the same as for all other species. Do not replant on old orchard sites, which can harbor pests and pesticide residues that can affect your new trees. If you must replant on an old site, try to determine where the old rows were and plant between them.

If you live in a windy area, plant your apple trees on a slope facing away from prevailing winds or establish a windbreak before you plant your apple orchard. Don't plant your windbreak with crab apple, hawthorn, mountain ash, or other apple relatives because they may harbor pests that will attack your orchard.

Order trees at least six months before your spring planting date to get

It's helpful to know how long your apples will take to mature and ripen after bloom. Harvest dates fluctuate according to temperature and rainfall.

Cultivar	Days to Harvest after Bloom	Cultivar	Days to Harvest after Bloom
Yellow Transparent	70–100	Jonagold	140–160
Duchess of Oldenburg	90–95	Melrose	140–160
Tydeman Early	90–95	Fuji	140–160
Jerseymac	90–95	Empire	140–160
Paulared	105–115	Delicious	140–160
Anna	110–120	Golden Delicious	140–160
Dorsett Golden	110–120	Baldwin	140–150
Summerred	110–130	Esopus Spitzenburg	145–150
Gravenstein	110–130	Mutsu	145–165
Wealthy	120–125	Northern Spy	145–170
Winter Banana	120–125	Braeburn	150–170
Cortland	125–140	York Imperial	155–175
McIntosh	125–145	Rome Beauty	160–175
Macoun	130–150	Yellow Newtown	160–165
Rhode Island Greening	130–155	Winesap	160–180
Spartan	135–150	Stayman	160–175
Jonathan	135–150	Black Twig (Paragon)	165–170
Grimes Golden	140–145	Granny Smith	180–210
Idared	140–155	Pink Lady	200–220

the cultivars and rootstocks you want. Purchase one- or two-year-old trees on the rootstocks that best fit your conditions.

Apple trees are grafted to either seedling or clonal rootstocks. Seedling stocks were used almost exclusively until about thirty years ago. They're cheap and produce strong trees that tolerate a wide range of soil conditions. But they produce tall trees that need at least 1,600 square feet of space. Clonal stocks are vegetatively propagated. All generations are identical and produce trees that are uniform in height and pest resistance. Clonal stocks produce trees that range from dwarf to standard heights.

Clonal stocks developed at the East Malling Research Station in England are designated by an *M* followed by a series number, such as M9.

Clonal stocks have different characteristics that you must understand to choose those that are right for you. The ultimate height of a tree is governed by the stock, the scion cultivar, and the soil type. For example, a 'Delicious' on M9 is a slightly larger tree than a 'Macoun' on the same stock. Trees growing in poorer soil are smaller than those in fertile soil. Heights given below are after ten years of growth. The most popular stocks for homeowners are M9, M7, and MM109.

Stock	Height	Soil Requirements	Characteristics	Notes
M27	4–6 feet	Fertile, well drained	Brittle roots; needs support	Use as interstem
M8	4–6 feet	Fertile, well drained	Early bearing and ripening; needs support	Use as interstem
M9	6 feet	Fertile, well drained	Early bearing and ripening; stock overgrows scion	Detailed pruning required
M26	6–8 feet	Fertile, well drained	Early bearing; needs support; stock overgrows scion	Hardier than M9
M7	8–10 feet	No special soil	Well anchored; suckers badly; tolerates heavy soil	
M2	10 feet	No special soil	Early bearing; well anchored; cold tender; susceptible to nematodes	Leans in heavy soil; use with weak scions
M1	15 feet	Fertile, well drained	Early bearing; well anchored; cold tender; collar rot	Dwarfing on sandy soils
M13	15 feet	Tolerates wet soil	Well anchored; poor in dry soil; no early bearing	Use in wet areas only
M16	15 feet	Fertile, well drained	Well anchored; collar rot	

MM106	10 feet	Fertile, well drained	Well anchored; early bearing; collar rot	Use on well-drained sites; wood matures late
MM111	12 feet	Fertile, well drained	Well anchored; drought tolerant; heavy bearing; suckers	Don't use with shy bearers
MM109	15 feet	Well drained	Well anchored; heavy bearing; few suckers; intolerant of heavy soil	
Alnap 2	12 feet	Fertile	Hardy; well anchored	Use as interstem
Robusta 5	15 feet	Fertile	Hardy	Use as interstem

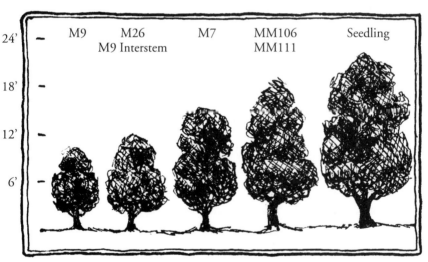

This is a visual example of the relative sizes of apple trees on different rootstocks. In general, the smaller the tree, the easier it is to care for.

Stocks in the Malling series produce full dwarf to nearly standard-size trees. East Malling stocks lack resistance to woolly apple aphids. Crossing Malling stocks with 'Northern Spy' trees produced a line of aphid-resistant clones. The work was done at the Malling Merton Research station, and these stocks are designated by MM followed by a number—for example, MM106 or MM109. (The numbers in both the Malling and the Malling-Merton series have no relation to the degree of dwarfing.)

Other clonal stocks, such as 'Robusta 5' (a selection of *Malus robusta*) and NS 'Novole' impart other valuable characteristics to the tree, such as extreme cold hardiness or resistance to pine voles.

The term *dwarf* only means that the tree is less than the height of a tree on a seedling stock. The term is useless in purchasing stock unless you know what rootstock the scion has been grafted to.

Certain apple cultivars do better in some areas than in others. Not all cultivars do well in all parts of a region or state. Plant those that require a longer season in the more southerly areas of the region.

NORTHEASTERN UNITED STATES
    McIntosh, Cortland, Empire, Delicious, Idared, Jerseymac, Paulared, Spartan, Northern Spy, Golden Delicious

CENTRAL ATLANTIC
    Delicious, Golden Delicious, Stayman, Jonathan, Rome, Winesap, Dorsett Golden, Anna

OHIO BASIN
    Golden Delicious, Delicious, Rome, Grimes Golden, Jonathan, Stayman, Yellow Transparent

SOUTHWESTERN UNITED STATES
    Jonathan, Golden Delicious, York Imperial, Stayman, Grimes Golden, Wealthy

NORTH-CENTRAL UNITED STATES
    McIntosh, Wealthy, Cortland, Oldenburg, Yellow Transparent, Jonathan, Stayman, Harlson, Honeygold, Red Baron, Regent, Joan, Sector, Anoka

PACIFIC NORTHWEST
    Delicious, Golden Delicious, Rome, Jonathan, Gravenstein

CALIFORNIA
    Gravenstein, Delicious, Yellow Newtown, Rome, Jonathan, Golden Delicious

UTAH, NEW MEXICO, AND WESTERN COLORADO
    Delicious, Golden Delicious, Jonathan, Rome

MONTANA
    McIntosh, Harlson, Anoka

The most common type of apple tree is one in which the scion has been grafted directly to the rootstock. This is a single-worked tree. A double-worked tree has an interstock, where the scion is grafted to an interstem piece that is in turn grafted to a rootstock. The three pieces of wood require two grafts, making the tree double-worked. The single-worked tree is best in most situations, because most gardeners have good locations and soil and are concerned only about obtaining some degree of dwarfing. Double-worked trees are used primarily to overcome some special conditions, such as lack of cold hardiness or very poor soil drainage.

There are thousands of apple cultivars available. Your county extension service office will be able to tell which are best suited for your area.

In most cases, newer cultivars are better than old or antique cultivars. Older cultivars are often biennial bearers, produce fruit with poor color or poor keeping characteristics, or are highly susceptible to pests. The flavor of antique varieties, however, is often unique, and including a few of these nostalgic cultivars in the small home orchard keeps a bit of living history alive. Original cultivar selection often depended upon where the orchard was located, when it was planted, and the social status of the owner. Wealthy owners were likely to plant named cultivars, sometimes imported from Europe. Orchards before the mid-twentieth century were planted on seedling rootstocks.

Over the past quarter century, a number of scab-resistant cultivars have been introduced through the joint breeding efforts of Purdue, Rutgers, and Illinois Universities. The names of these cultivars begin with *PRI* to reflect that association. 'Priam', 'Priscilla', 'Prima', and 'Sir Prize' are the results of their efforts to cross-named cultivars with crab apples such as the Siberian crab apple (*Malus baccata*) to impart scab resistance to the offspring. Although these trees have good scab resistance, they are still susceptible to other apple diseases and pests. They are best used where scab is a serious problem.

Color strains are another important group of cultivars. These generally emerge as bud sports and have better color than the parent type. Use them in poor-coloring areas of the country, but not in areas where you normally have good color development, or the red color will become too intense and turn to an unattractive maroon or purplish black.

Spur-type strains produce more spurs per foot of branch than standard types. Because of the heavier fruit load, the trees also tend to be

Antique apples are popular for period orchards. Here are some cultivars that were grown in days gone by.

		TIME PERIOD	
REGION	COLONIAL	LATE 18TH CENTURY	MID-19TH CENTURY
NEW ENGLAND	Summer Pippin	Pearmain	Baldwin
	Holland Pippin	Hightop Sweeting	Pome Grise
	London Pippin	Pig Nose	Jonathan
	Bellybond	Foxwell	Lady
	Pearmain	Longred	Maiden Blush
	Hunt Russet	Russetin	Early Harvest
	Orange Sweeting	Black Gilliflower	Fall Pippin
	Seedling trees	Roxbury Russet	Sweet Bough
		Westfield	York Imperial
			Tompkins King
NEW YORK	Seedling trees	Esopus Spitzenburg	Similar to
		Green Newtown	New England
		Hawley	
		Newtown Spitzenburg	
		Swaar	
		Titus Pippin	
MID-ATLANTIC	Mains	Green Newtown	June
	Pippins	Cathead	Summer Rose
	Costards	English Redstreak	English Codling
	Marigolds	Priest	Large White
	Kings	Bell Catlin	Bellflower
	Magitems	Robeson	Albemarle Pippin
	Bachelors		Early Harvest
	Seedling trees		Summer Queen
			Red Astrachan
WEST	Seedling trees	Seedling trees	Roxbury Russet
			Esopus
			Spitzenburg

Apple cultivars have different degrees of susceptibility to diseases. The more susceptible a cultivar is, the more you'll have to spray. 1 = very resistant, no control necessary; 2 = resistant, control sometimes necessary; 3 = susceptible, control usually necessary ; 4 = very susceptible, control always necessary

CULTIVAR	APPLE SCAB	CEDAR APPLE RUST	FIRE BLIGHT	POWDERY MILDEW
Baldwin	3	1	3	4
Britemac	3	2	2	3
Burgundy	3	3	4	–
Cortland	4	3	3	4
Delicious	3	1	2	2
Empire	4	2	2	3
Golden Delicious	3	4	3	3
Granny Smith	3	2	4	4
Gravenstein	3	2	3	3
Idared	3	3	4	3
Jerseymac	4	1	3	–
Jonagold	4	3	4	3
Jonamac	3	2	3	3
Jonathan	3	4	4	4
Liberty	1	1	2	2
Lodi	3	4	4	2
Macfree	1	3	2	–
Macoun	4	2	3	3
McIntosh	4	1	3	3
Monroe	3	3	3	3
Mutsu	4	3	4	4
Northern Spy	3	3	2	3
Nova Easygro	1	1	2	3
Paulared	3	2	3	3
Prima	1	4	2	2
Priscilla	1	1	2	3
Puritan	3	2	3	3
R.I. Greening	3	3	4	3
Rome Beauty	4	4	4	3

Sir Prize	1	3	4	2
Spartan	3	2	3	2
Spigold	4	4	4	3
Spijon	3	3	3	3
Stark Bounty	3	3	2	–
Stark Splendor	3	3	2	–
Stayman	4	3	2	3
Twenty Ounce	3	4	4	3
Tydeman	3	1	3	2
Viking	3	2	2	–
Wealthy	3	3	3	3
York Imperial	3	4	4	3

There are many color strains of common apple cultivars. Consider those listed here if you don't live in a good color area. The fruit of color strains grown in good color areas can get very dark and appear almost purple or black. In additions to those listed here, 'Northern Spy', 'Gravenstein', 'McIntosh', and 'York Imperial' also have color strains.

PARENT CULTIVAR

DELICIOUS	ROME BEAUTY	STAYMAN	JONATHAN
Richared	Gallia	Stamared	Blackjon
Red King	Cox Red Rome	C + O Stayman	Jonard
Redspur			Jonee
Starkrimson			Jonamac
Starking			Jonagold

more dwarfed and require less pruning than those with a normal standard bearing habit. 'McIntosh', 'Golden Delicious', 'Delicious', and 'Rome Beauty' are available as spur-type strains.

Low-chill apples were developed for growers in subtropical climates such as Florida, which don't have the chilling hours necessary to break dormancy in standard cultivars. 'Anna', 'Ein Schemer', and 'Dorsett Golden' should be planted only in such areas. These lack cold hardiness and are not for northern gardens.

Apples are usually self-unfruitful. To get a good crop, you need good cross-pollination, so plant at least two or three different cultivars. Lopsided fruits are the result of incomplete pollination. The weather may have been bad during bloom or there may not have been enough bees. Fruit set can also be influenced by cultural conditions. To ensure a good crop, keep the following tips in mind:

- Plant early-, midseason-, and late-ripening cultivars so that their bloom times will overlap.
- Interplant trees so that pollinating cultivars are no farther than 50 feet apart.
- Parent cultivars will not effectively pollinate their strains. For example, 'Delicious' will not pollinate its color strain 'Richard Delicious'.

Some apple cultivars will set a partial crop by their own pollen; others are pollen sterile. To be on the safe side, plant at least two cultivars for good cross-pollination. If one is pollen sterile, plant at least three.

PARTIALLY SELF-FRUITFUL	POLLEN STERILE (TRIPLOID)
Jonathan	Rhode Island Greening
York Imperial	Arkansas
Rome	Hibernal
Duchess of Oldenburg	Winesap
Wealthy	Paragon
Golden Delicious	Summer Rambo
Yellow Newtown	Mutsu
Grimes Golden	Spigold
Yellow Transparent	Tompkins
	Jonagold
	Baldwin
	Gravenstein
	Stark
	Blenheim
	Boskoop
	Bramley's Seedling

Space your apple trees according to rootstock. This table gives recommended planting distances in average soils. You can space them slightly closer on poor soil and slightly farther apart on rich soil.

	SPACING (FEET)	
ROOTSTOCK	IN ROW	BETWEEN ROWS
M9	5	10
M26	5	10
M7	8	16
MM106	8	16
M2	8	16
MM104	14	22
MM111	14	22
Robusta 5	18	26
M16	18	26
MM109	18	26
Seedling	20	28

- Some crab apples are a good pollen source for apples. Check with your county extension agent for cultivars to use as pollinators.

Mulch young trees to a depth of at least 6 to 8 inches or cultivate the soil to keep weed competition down. Mulching not only conserves soil moisture, but also softens the impact of windfalls, so that they will not bruise and can be used for applesauce or cider. Place collars around young trunks; where there is mulch, there will be mice.

Determine your fertilizer needs by the amount of new growth produced. Apple trees less than ten years old should make about 10 to 14 inches of new growth per year; older trees in full bearing should make about 6 to 10 inches. If new growth is sparse, give apple trees 1 pound of 10 percent nitrogen fertilizer per year per inch of trunk. Don't apply too much. Excessive growth can lead to increased susceptibility to fire blight, winter damage, and poorly colored, soft fruit. You can use manure provided you apply it early in the spring and don't apply too much.

Bitter pit, caused by a calcium imbalance or deficiency, shows up as sunken brown spots in the fruit's flesh. It can be caused by an actual deficiency in soil calcium or by excessive nitrogen fertilization, heavy thinning, and heavy shade. Some cultivars, such as 'Northern Spy', 'Gravenstein', 'Grimes Golden', 'Rhode Island Greening', 'Delicious', 'York Imperial', and 'Rome', are especially susceptible.

Boron deficiency causes sunken corky spots near the skin and core of the fruit. Affected fruits drop prematurely. If you see these symptoms, have your soil tested for boron and closely follow the recommendations for adding the element.

Measles, or rough, pimply bark, is caused by excess manganese in the soil and is most common on acid soils. To correct it, raise the pH to an acceptable level.

Rosette is caused by a zinc deficiency. The leaves are small and seem to grow from one spot along the stem. Add zinc according to recommendations based on a soil test.

If your apples look good but have no taste, this may be caused by lack of nutrients; environmental stresses such as drought, high temperatures, or rapid temperature changes; or untimely harvest.

Apple trees can be pruned and trained to a number of different systems, but the modified leader is probably best for the home gardener. Because apples bear mostly on spurs produced on wood two years old and older, don't prune away too much older wood. Be very careful you don't break off the spurs when pruning or harvesting.

Apple trees will begin to blossom and bear fruit several years after planting, depending upon cultivar and rootstock. Only 5 percent of the blossoms need to set fruit to have a good crop. Apple trees shed excessive fruit in two drops, one in June, when the young fruits

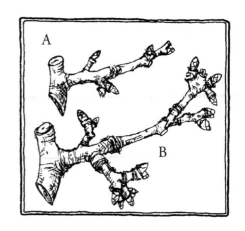

Apples, pears, and some of the stone fruits are borne on spurs. (A) In this case a two-year-old apple shoot is headed to induce the small spurs to form (B) larger, stronger ones and the new growth to be heavily spurred. Never remove all new growth completely.

are marble sized, and one in late summer just before ripening. This pre-harvest drop can be characteristic of the cultivar or might be caused by the stress of drought, pest damage, or storms.

Some apple trees are notorious for biennial bearing. They produce a heavy crop one year and a light crop, or no crop, the following year. This trait is inherent in some cultivars and is the reason why many of the old cultivars are no longer commercially grown. 'Lodi', 'York Imperial', 'Northern Spy', and 'Yellow Transparent' have this trait, as well as the newer 'Puritan' and 'Delicious'. Prune a bit more heavily during off years; water your trees well, give them a bit more nitrogen, and thin the fruit during on years. If you do this faithfully, you might be able to even out the bearing habit of the tree.

Harvest apples when they are fully colored, seeds are dark brown or black, and the fruit is juicy and has a strong, aromatic flavor with no trace of sourness. Pick apples by cupping the fruit in your hand, twisting gently, and pulling away from the spur. If it separates easily, it's ripe. If you pull the spur off, wait a few more days to begin harvesting.

PEARS

Pears are native to Europe and the countries bordering the Caucasus mountains. Like apples, pears have been grown since prehistoric times. The ancient Romans truly domesticated the fruit and developed several named cultivars. Interest in pear culture peaked in Europe in eighteenth-century Belgium and France. Pear seeds were brought to America in 1629. Here, as in Europe, the pear was used to produce perry, or pear cider. The oldest pear tree in this country is thought to be the Endicott pear tree, planted near Salem, Massachusetts, in 1630. Although pears were more popular than apples in Colonial New England, they now take second place to apples in the American diet.

Many commercial American cultivars like 'Bartlett', 'Bosc', and 'Anjou' are European cultivars. Of the old standard pear cultivars, only 'Seckel' originated in this country, near Philadelphia.

The common pear is *Pyrus communis*, but several other species are also grown in the United States. The sand or Asian pear (*P. serotina*) originated in China; the fruit resembles an apple. 'Kieffer' is a hybrid of this species and 'Bartlett'. Other species grown for rootstocks or ornamentals include *P. ussuriensis*, *P. calleryana* (resistant to fire blight), *P. betulaefolia* (useful as a rootstock in alkaline and sandy soils), and *P. nivalis*, which is primarily grown for perry.

Pears tolerate a wide range of climatic conditions but need adequate chilling to break rest. Using low-chill pears from India, plant breeders have introduced cultivars like 'Pineapple', 'Hood', 'Flordahome', and 'Orient' that require only 100 to 150 hours of chilling and can be grown in northern Florida. Standard cultivars withstand -30 degrees F if well hardened, which makes them only slightly less hardy than apples and gooseberries. 'Flemish Beauty', 'Anjou', and 'Clapp Favorite' are among the most hardy and are perfect for planting on the northern fringe of pear regions. 'Bartlett' is one of the least hardy.

Quality in some cultivars is strongly affected by climate. 'Bartlett' and 'Bosc' grow best where the temperatures are high for two months preceding harvest. If a spell of cool weather sets in, the core of each pear begins to break down and the flesh becomes mealy. Other cultivars are less temperature sensitive but may undergo core breakdown if cool temperature occur about a month before normal harvest.

Pears tolerate higher temperatures than apples and do best where average summer temperatures are 75 to 80 degrees F. Pears bloom several days earlier than apples, so good air drainage is a must to avoid frost damage.

Order your pear trees early from a reputable nursery. They should be certified disease-free, one- or two-year-old plants on appropriate rootstocks. *Pear decline* is a disease that has devastated trees on the West Coast. It is caused by a mycoplasma spread by the pear psylla. A tree with slow decline may take a year or two to die; those with quick decline die suddenly in a single season. The disease clogs the phloem vessels just above the graft union, starving the root system. A brown line around the cambium just above the union identifies the disease. Nongrafted trees are immune, but since all modern pear cultivars must be grafted, you must use resistant rootstocks to reduce the spread of the disease.

Seedlings of *Pyrus communis* (hardy to -30 degrees F) are most commonly used as rootstocks, with those of 'Winter Nellis' preferred in California. 'Old Home' and 'Old Home' x 'Farmingdale' are also acceptable and resistant to pear decline, fire blight, and suckering. Seedlings of *P. calleryana* (hardy to -10 degrees F) and *P. betulaefolia* (hardy to -5 degrees F) are also decline resistant and are especially good for marginal soils.

Pear cultivars are almost as numerous as those of apple. Except in Florida, if you're in doubt about a suitable cultivar, plant 'Bartlett', which makes up about 75 percent of U.S. pear production. 'Anjou' is great for the home pear planting, and 'Winter Nellis' is a wonderful keeper. 'Kieffer' is tough, hardy, resistant to fire blight, and a heavy bearer, but its fruit is poor. 'Magness' is also resistant to fire blight and produces respectable fruit. For a delightful experience, try 'Sheldon' if you can find it. Cultivars recommended for Florida are all low-chill. 'Hood' makes a particularly good pollinator for 'Flordahome'.

EUROPEAN TYPE

CALIFORNIA
Bartlett, Hardy, Comice, Bosc, Winter Nellis
WASHINGTON AND OREGON
Bartlett, Anjou, Bosc, Comice, Seckel
EASTERN STATES
Kieffer, Bartlett, Clapps, Maxine, Comice, Flemish Beauty, Bosc, Seckel, Duchess, Anjou, Magness
SOUTHERN STATES
Kieffer, Bartlett, Garber, Baldwin, Carrick, Morgan
FLORIDA
Hood, Carnes, Orient, Pineapple, Kieffer, Ayers, Flordahome.

ASIAN TYPE

CALIFORNIA AND THE PACIFIC NORTHWEST
Twentieth Century, Shinseiki, Shinko, Seigyoku, Niitaka, Hosui

---

Stocks of Asian pears—*P. serotina* and *P. ussuriensis*—are very susceptible to decline. All produce trees of standard size.

Dwarf pears by grafting them to quince stocks, but plant dwarf trees only on the best soils. Cultivars grafted to 'Angers Quince A' produce early-bearing trees about 30 to 60 percent of standard size. Those on 'Angers Quince C' produce trees about half the size of those on 'Angers Quince A' stocks. Both rootstocks produce trees with very brittle root systems that must be supported throughout their entire lives, making them particularly good choices for espalier plantings. Some cultivars are incompatible with quince roots, and this may not show up for a few years. A tree may grow well for two or three years, and then suddenly break at the graft union. Be sure that your scion cultivar is compatible with quince roots. If not, buy a double-worked tree with an interstock of 'Old Home' or 'Hardy' pear between the scion and the quince roots.

Pears have few problems with pollination if you remember that most cultivars, most of the time, are self-unfruitful. You'll need at least two cultivars for good pollination. 'Magness' and 'Waite' are pollen sterile, and some, like 'Bartlett' and 'Seckel', are incompatible. If you choose any of these, plant another cultivar for adequate cross-pollination.

Prepare the soil as you would for other fruit crops and plant in the early spring. Set trees on standard stocks a couple of inches deeper than they grew in the nursery, with the graft union below the soil line to encourage scion rooting. Plant dwarf trees with the graft union a few inches above the soil line to keep the tree dwarf. Space standard-size trees about 25 by 25 feet apart; trees on 'Angers Quince A' stocks can be spaced 6 by 8 feet apart. Give the trees slightly more room on richer soils.

As long as the soil is well drained but moisture retentive, pears will tolerate a wide range of soil types. They do best on deep loams but toler-

---

Quince makes a good dwarfing rootstock for pear trees. Some pear cultivars are not compatible with quince stock, however, and need an interstock to bridge the incompatibility.

Cultivars that make good graft unions with quince stocks and need no interstock:
Anjou, Dumont, Gifford, Hardy, Buffum, Colmar, Covert, Comice, Early Seckel, Elizabeth, Flemish Beauty, Gorham, Howell, Kieffer, Maxine, Old Home, Tyson, White Doyenne, Winter Bartlett

Cultivars that unite with quince, grow several years, then fail; double-work these:
Bartlett, Cayuga, Clapp, Madeleine, Max Red Bartlett, Onondaga, Winter Nellis

Cultivars that either fail to unite with quince or grow poorly on quince roots; these must be double-worked:
Bosc, Early Seckel, Farmingdale, Illinois Bartlett, Seckel, Sheldon, Waite, Worden Seckel

---

ate heavier soils. They'll even tolerate wet feet and thin soil a little better than almost any other fruit but may produce only light crops. The best crops are produced in 4 to 6 feet of rich soils.

Pears are particularly sensitive to salts, so both the soil and the irrigation water must be free of salinity and alkali. This is an important consideration in some western states.

The pear flower produces little nectar and is unattractive to bees, which will go to nearly anything else in bloom first. So keep the dandelions mown and have no other blooms nearby when your pear trees flower. As with other fruits, keep the soil weed-free at least for the first several years. Organic mulch is great for pears, but put rodent guards in place before you mulch.

Pears are very light feeders. Young trees making 16 to 20 inches of new growth each season and mature trees producing about 8 inches of new growth do not need fertilizer. I've seen home pear orchards produce great crops year after year with no fertilizer whatsoever. Too much nitrogen, whether from commercial fertilizers or manure, stimulates excessive vegetative growth that is highly susceptible to fire blight.

If the blossom ends of your pears are black and cracked, have your soil tested for boron deficiency and add the nutrient if necessary, following the recommendations of the soil test lab or your local cooperative extension service.

Pears on standard stocks come into bearing in about six to eight years. Trees on dwarf stocks come into bearing in about half that time. Flower buds are formed at the ends of short spurs on wood two years old or older. Train trees to the modified leader system and don't overprune, because excessive pruning may delay bearing by several years and make the trees more susceptible to fire blight. Restrict pruning to heading back new growth to give the spurs on older wood enough light to form healthy flower buds. Very old spurs should be removed. Keep fire blight under control by doing nothing to stimulate vigorous growth, because young, tender shoots are most frequently attacked. Blighted shoots look as though they've been singed (hence the name); the blackened leaves don't drop but fold back along the blackened shoot tip, which itself will bend over to form a crook. Infected tissue oozes. Blighted blossoms turn brown and remain on the tree. The disease is caused by a bacterium and is transmitted by bees, aphids, and infected pruning equipment.

Pears tend to grow upright, with new shoots having very narrow crotch angles. Spread these during their first year, forcing them to develop wider angles for stronger branches that bear at a younger age.

If you're pruning out tissue infected by fire blight, make the cut at least 6 inches below all visible signs of the disease and disinfect the saw or shears after each cut. Rubbing alcohol works well. A 1:9 mixture of household bleach and water also makes a good disinfectant but may corrode your tools.

Pears tolerate both drought and floods but make their best growth when they get adequate water throughout the season. Too much water, like fertilizer and pruning, stimulates excessive soft new growth and makes the tree more susceptible to fire blight. If you had a good pollination year, you may have to thin the fruits to increase their size, because pears need about twenty to thirty leaves to fully develop each fruit.

Harvesting pears is tricky because you must pick them a little before they're ripe. Pick them too soon and they won't ripen properly; pick them too late and they'll break down at the core. The easiest way to determine harvest time is to wait for the first fruit to fall to begin picking. A mature fruit ready for picking has lenticels that have turned from white to brown, a noticeably waxy skin, and a light green-yellow undercolor, and separates fairly easily from the spur. If too many spurs are coming off with the fruit, wait a little longer.

After picking, store pears at 32 degrees F. About a week before you wish to use them, move them to a room at 65 degrees F. This temperature is critical: At temperatures below 60 degrees F, the pears won't ripen; above 70 degrees F, they'll rot. Fall and winter cultivars, like 'Anjou', 'Hardy', 'Comice', 'Bosc', and 'Winter Nellis' store best. Delayed harvest or storage will cause the cores to break down.

Asian Pears

The Asian pear, also known as the sand pear, apple pear, pear apple, and Japanese pear, has been cultivated for centuries in Asia. It was introduced into this country in the nineteenth century, when Chinese gold miners brought Asian pears to California during the gold rush. These early cultivars were gritty and attracted little attention. Modern-day breeders have removed most of the grit, and today's cultivars are crisp and juicy.

Most Asian pears are grown in California, Oregon, and Washington.

They are not as easily grown as other pears. They require more thinning and multiple harvests and are susceptible to fire blight and other diseases. Asian pears tend to bear very early, and trees are stunted as a consequence.

Asian pears need about four hundred to eight hundred hours of chilling and can be grown farther south than European pears. They're grafted onto the same stocks as other pears, though with slightly different effects. They are all incompatible with quince. *P. communis* stocks dwarf most Asian pears by about 50 percent and cause them to lack vigor and develop small fruit. However, some hybrids developed by the University of California, as well as cultivars such as 'Yali', 'Seuri', and 'Ishiiwsase', grow well on *P. communis* stocks. *P. betulaefolia* is the best stock and produces good fruit on a vigorous tree tolerant of wet soil, although these trees are not as cold hardy as *P. communis*. Insects and diseases are similar to those of European pears.

Most cultivars are partially self-fruitful, but for the best crops, you should plant at least two cultivars. Some cultivars, such as '20th Century' and 'Kikusui', and 'Kosui' and 'Shinsui', are cross-incompatible.

Train your trees to a central leader or an open-center form. Asian pears need full sunlight. Don't crowd trees or neglect pruning. Thin your crop to one fruit per spur, with fruit no closer than 6 inches apart.

Determine harvest time by the ground color: Russet types turn from green to gold; yellow types from green to light yellow; and green types from green to light green. When you think it's time, taste a couple. If they're sweet, crisp, and juicy, it's time to pick. Handle them gently. Asian pears are very susceptible to bruising, chafing, stem punctures, and finger marks, and they turn brown-black a few hours after injury.

QUINCES

Highly esteemed by the ancients and dedicated to the Greek goddess of love, quince (*Cydonia oblonga*) was brought to Italy from Kydron, Crete. It was introduced into England by the late Middle Ages, where Chaucer mentions it as "coine," and by 1446 baked quinces were being served in England. Seeds were shipped to Massachusetts in 1629, and the trees were grown in Virginia by 1648. Quinces grew abundantly in the colonies by 1720. The fruit was eaten primarily cooked or as a jelly, but in Mexico, quinces were eaten fresh, like apples. Quinces' popularity peaked in this country by the Civil War; now they are little grown and relatively unknown.

Quince culture is similar to that of pears. They are adapted to a similar climate, do well on a similar soil and planting site, and are planted the same way. Because it's a smaller tree, however, space quinces only about 15 feet apart. On lighter soils, you can space them even closer.

Buy two- or three-year-old disease-free trees grafted to 'Angers' quince stocks. Because they're self-fruitful, you'll need to plant only a single cultivar. 'Van Deman', 'Orange', and 'Pineapple' are popular and make terrific jelly.

Quinces are extremely susceptible to fire blight. Because fire blight first attacks tender new growth, limit the amount of nitrogen the trees receive so that new growth is held to about 16 inches a year for young trees and 8 inches for mature trees. A sod cover planted around young but established trees will use up extra nutrients and keep quince shoot growth in check.

Limit pruning to the removal of dead wood and a few thinning cuts each year. Train quinces to a small open-center tree or to a bushlike tree. If you prefer the latter, head trees at planting to a foot above the soil to stimulate the formation of bushy side shoots. My preference is for the tree form, since it's easier to maintain the good air circulation that also deters fire blight.

Harvest begins in the third or fourth year after planting; the tree will be in maximum production by the tenth year. Expect about a bushel of fruit per tree. Wait until the fruit is dead ripe. Fully ripe quinces are yellow, highly aromatic, and sweet. But don't bite into them. I had a student break a tooth doing that.

The quince flowers at the end of new shoots that arise from buds formed the previous season. Quince flowers are large, pink, and very attractive.

Process them into jelly or use them to flavor applesauce. One quince to about a dozen apples is about right. (Grandma used to stick cloves into a quince fruit and put it in her bureau draw for a sachet. It lasts a long time if you use sound fruit.)

MEDLARS

The medlar is an intriguing, little-known fruit that looks like a small russet apple with a wide-open bottom end and a mushy, brown, aromatic flesh when ripe.

It's difficult to trace the history of this ancient fruit, since the name medlar was also given to hawthorn, cornelian cherry, loquat, cotoneaster, and some stone fruits. It probably originated in western Europe. It may have been cultivated as long ago as 1000 B.C. The Greeks grew it about 300 B.C., and though there is no direct evidence for it, the Romans may have introduced it into Britain, where it is now naturalized and grows in thickets. Charlemagne had it planted in his royal gardens in the ninth century, and it was commonly cultivated by monks in medieval monasteries.

The medlar is an odd-looking fruit. The resemblance of the calyx, or bottom end of the fruit, to the bottom end of something more human gave rise to the unappetizing name "open-arse." Despite its appearance, the medlar remained in common cultivation up to the nineteenth century, then faded in popularity. But because it's so long-lived—trees four hundred years old still survive in England—it hangs on in gardens where it might no longer be appreciated.

The medlar is fairly hardy to Zone 5; it may tolerate Zone 4 conditions with protection. Medlars are not fussy about soil, so long as it's well drained, but they must have full sun. Spring frost is not usually a problem since the medlar blooms fairly late in the season.

Purchase one-year-old trees. You may find them offered on medlar, *Amelanchier*, hawthorn, quince, or pear roots. They do best on pear roots, particularly on heavy soil. If your soil is dry, buy them on hawthorn roots; if moist, on quince roots. Quince roots also dwarf the tree, which doesn't reach much above 20 feet in height on its own roots anyway. Those on medlar roots make slow-growing, crooked trees. Pear roots will get the tree off to a fast, straight start.

Medlar has shown a number of delayed graft union incompatibilities. The graft union might look fine for a few years, but then breaks

The medlar is an unusual fruit with a large, open area near its blossom end.

suddenly. If you aren't planting in soil where you need a special-purpose rootstock, plant grafted medlars with the graft union a couple of inches below the soil line to encourage the scion to root before the union breaks.

There are few cultivars from which to choose, and some of those are hundreds of years old. 'Dutch', 'Royal', and 'Nottingham' bear good crops and are all self-fruitful. Some nurseries offer medlar-hawthorn crosses (designated 'x *Crataegomespilus*') and hawmedlars, which are graft chimeras of hawthorn and medlar. They develop sometimes when medlar is grafted to hawthorn roots. A bud arises near the graft union that contains genetic material from both parents. This bud produces a shoot that develops into a tree with characteristics intermediate between the two parents. Both medlar-hawthorne crosses and haw medlars are ornamental, not fruit-producing, trees.

Train medlars to a modified leader system. Mature trees need only a little thinning out each year to produce good crops.

Medlars are members of the Rosaceae family and so are susceptible to the same pests as apples. But pest problems are usually not severe with these plants, however, and you'll rarely have to worry about them.

The plants begin to bear after a few years. Large flowers up to 2 inches in diameter are borne singly at the tips of shoots that arise from lateral buds on one-year-old wood or small spurs. Nearly all the flowers set fruit, some even without pollination (parthenocarpic fertilization).

Keep medlars on the tree as long as possible before harvesting, even after the first couple of light frosts. They don't need the frosts to ripen, but they do need the extra days at the end of the season. Pick the fruits when the first leaves have fallen. They should be hard and astringent but separate easily from the tree. The fruits are not ripe when you pick them but are allowed to ripen off the tree. Place them in a cool room with good air circulation, bottom end down and not touching each other. They'll ripen slowly in a process called *bletting*. The firm flesh softens from a whitish color to a fragrant, mushy brown, custardlike consistency, and the skin darkens. Touch them only when you are ready to eat them. Bletted medlars keep a couple of weeks if you don't handle them.

APRICOTS

Apricots contain nine times more vitamin A than most other fruits and have more protein, carbohydrates, phosphorus, and niacin as well.

The fruit originated in the mountains of Afghanistan and spread to China, the Caucasus, and Siberia. Alexander the Great brought the fruit into Greece, where it was mentioned by later writers like Dioscorides. It was introduced to Italy and brought directly into England in the early sixteenth century. By 1720, apricots were growing well in Virginia. Twenty-six cultivars were grown during the Civil War.

Apricot blossoms are as hardy as those of peach, but because apricots bloom earlier, they're more susceptible to late-spring frosts. There are few fruits that do well on north-facing slopes, but apricot is one of them; the cooler conditions delay bloom and help the trees escape late frosts. Siberian bush apricots are hardier in the wood than regular apricots, but their flowers are just as susceptible to frosts. This susceptibility and disease limit their planting to only the best sites with good air and soil drainage.

Purchase one- or two-year-old, certified trees budded to apricot roots, which have inherent nematode resistance. Sometimes you'll find apricots budded to myrobalan plum or peach rootstocks. These generally produce inferior trees, although peach stocks will cause apricots to ripen a few days earlier. To determine the type of rootstock used, scratch the root bark with your thumbnail. Apricot roots have a blood red color; plum and peach roots don't.

Cultivar selection is important. In western states, 'Chinese', 'Blenheim', 'Tilton', and 'Sunglo' are great producers. 'Goldcot', 'Farmingdale', and 'Veecot' are better for eastern areas. If you live on the northern fringe of apricot country, try 'Sungold' or 'Moongold', both cold-hardy cultivars developed in Minnesota. 'Sunshine', 'Tola', and 'Manchu', all from South Dakota, and 'Scout' and 'Robust', from Manitoba, are Siberian apricots that survive Zone 3 winters. Apricots are usually self-fruitful, so you can plant a single variety.

Build soil organic matter and set plants in the early spring, 1 to 2 inches deeper than they grew in the nursery and 20 feet apart. Be sure you can see the bud union above the soil line.

Apricots are shallow rooted and suffer from weed competition and drought more than most other fruit plants. Right after planting, mulch with strawy manure or wood chips to conserve moisture and control weeds. If you use chips, side dress with a handful of 5–10–10 fertilizer after the foliage has fully developed. You can continue to mulch throughout the life of the tree, or discontinue after a few years and put the soil into mown sod. If you irrigate, apply water only to the roots. Wetting developing fruit will cause cracks and rot.

Composted manure applied at the rate of about 200 pounds per tree, supplemented with $1/2$ pound of 10–10–10 fertilizer per inch of trunk diameter, is excellent for apricots. If you can't find manure, then fertilize with a pound of 10–10–10 per inch of trunk diameter per tree per year, applied in early spring. Measure the trunk diameter at the tree's base just above the bud union.

Train the trees to a modified leader system. Apricot limbs tend to get willowy; head them back to strong laterals and make thinning cuts if the tree head gets too thick. Older trees may become overgrown; increase pruning to stimulate new wood and to increase fruit size. Remove branches with old spurs and replace them with younger ones.

A young tree should make about 15 to 30 inches of new shoot growth per year; older trees, about 10 to 15 inches. If your trees are not putting out that much, increase the severity of pruning to stimulate them. If they're putting out too much new growth, decrease the amount of pruning. Apricots bear on one-year-old shoots and on short spurs that live only a couple of seasons.

Apricots are susceptible to the same pests as peaches, as well as to plum curculio and brown rot.

Your trees will be in good production in a few years. Pick the fruits when they're fully ripe, soft, and have developed a blush on the outside cheek.

CHERRIES

Cherries have always been popular in home gardens, but they were not planted extensively in large commercial orchards until the 1920s and 1930s.

Prunus cerasus is the tart, or sour, cherry used for pie fillings and cooking. It is native to the Middle East. This species is easier to grow than the sweet cherry.

P. avium is the sweet, or Mazzard, cherry native to central and southern Europe. Its fruits are mainly eaten out of hand.

The *Duke cherry* is a hybrid of the sweet and sour cherries and has characteristics intermediate between its parents, although it resembles the sweet cherry slightly more than the sour.

P. mahaleb, the mahaleb, or St. Lucie, cherry, originated in Asia Minor and is used mostly as a rootstock for sweet and sour cherries.

P. tomentosa is also used as a rootstock. It grows wild in the Upper Mississippi River Valley where temperatures are too cold for other cherries.

P. besseyi, the western wild cherry, or sand cherry, is sometimes used as a rootstock for plums, prunes, and peaches, but never for cherries. It's native to central North America.

Cherry-plums are crosses of plums and *P. besseyi*. They are popular in the northern Great Plains where other fruits do not thrive. These hybrids bear at an early age, are prolific, and hold their fruit firmly against strong prairie winds. They bloom late, escaping late frosts, and usually ripen their fruit early in the season. The plants are drought-resistant and relatively free of insects, and the fruit is better than the native plums of the region. Unfortunately, cherry-plums are short-lived and the small fruit keeps poorly. Cherry-plums are usually grown to a bush form.

Both sweet and sour cherries grow best in the Pacific Northwest, coastal California, and the East above the Mason-Dixon line. Both are sensitive to high temperatures, humidity, and drought, and don't do well in the southern United States. They also need about twelve hundred chilling hours, so they don't produce in the Deep South.

The sweet cherry can be grown in Zones 5 to 7. It recovers slowly from winter damage and blooms early, so late spring frosts are a problem. It is more sensitive to both heat and cold than the sour cherry.

The sour cherry is hardy in Zones 4 to 6. It doesn't bloom as early in the spring as the sweet cherry, but late frosts can still be a problem. Even on a good site you can expect to harvest a crop of either sour or sweet cherries only once in four years. Sour cherries do best north of the Potomac and Ohio rivers where temperatures in May, June, and July average about 60 degrees F.

Cherries are very moisture sensitive. With any cherry species, excessive rain during bloom will cause blossom rot, during fruiting will cause fruit rot, and during ripening will cause the fruit to crack. Excessive dryness during the season will cause cherries to shrivel.

Plant on an elevated site with good air circulation and good air and soil drainage; cherries will not tolerate poorly drained soil. Select a site with a well-drained, warm, deep, friable sandy loam.

Plant cherries either in late autumn or as early in the spring as possible. A delay in planting could mean disaster because cherries leaf out early, and cherry roots grow slowly and take time to become established. If the new leaves transpire faster than the young roots can replace the moisture lost, the tree shrivels and dies. Fall planting is best if you live in a milder climate where frost heaving and severe winter cold are not a problem.

Plant the trees as deeply as they grew in the nursery, with the bud union above the soil line. Morellos produce small trees, so space them 15 feet apart. Plant sour and Duke cherry trees about 20 feet apart, and sweet cherry trees about 25 feet apart.

Lay a 6- to 10-inch-deep organic mulch beneath cherry trees to keep the soil moist and cool enough to delay bloom a couple of days—maybe just long enough to escape a frost. Mature trees can be grown in sod, but only if you keep them well supplied with water. The thousands of small fruits on a cherry tree create a tremendous demand for water, and sod often outcompetes the tree for the available moisture.

Young, nonbearing sour cherry trees should make about 12 to 24 inches of new growth per year; sweet cherry trees, about 22 to 26 inches per year. Mature trees of both types should make about 8 to 12 inches of new growth per year. Apply fertilizer only if new growth is sparse. A well-balanced general-purpose fertilizer or composted manure should be applied in the spring, before blossoming.

Because cherry trees mature their fruit early in the summer, soil water from spring rains is usually adequate. During a dry spring, however, and especially if the trees are in sod, cherry trees will suffer injury more quickly than most fruits because of the drying effect of the huge number of fruits on the tree. Water deeply if necessary.

Many cherry trees are infected with a variety of viruses. Purchase only certified disease-free trees. One-year-old sweet cherry trees and two-year-old sour cherry trees are best. Cherry buds are large and rather brittle so be careful not to rub them off when you handle the plants. Mazzard seedling rootstocks produce big trees that are highly resistant to nematodes and have some resistance to gophers, mice, trunk borers, and oak root rot fungus. The trees usually outproduce those on mahaleb stocks. Mahaleb stocks are more cold-resistant, however, and better adapted to areas with severe winters. If you live on the northern fringe of cherry country, use mahaleb rootstocks for all types of cherries.

You can tell what rootstocks your trees were grafted to by slicing into a root and looking at the color of the tissue inside. After a few minutes, mazzard root tissue turns orange; mahaleb turns cinnamon. After a few hours, the color in mazzard will have turned to a burnt sienna, while that of mahaleb will remain unchanged.

There are no good dwarf rootstocks for cherries, but 'Meteor' and 'North Star', both sour cherries, produce genetically dwarf trees.

Although there are as many as one thousand cherry cultivars available, the differences among cultivars are so slight that all cultivars are grouped into categories or types such as Montmorency-type cherries or Morello-type cherries. And because cherries are very regionally adapted, you should purchase your trees only from local sources, or from nurseries in a similar climatic zone.

All sour cherry cultivars are self-fruitful. All Duke cultivars (there are only a few) are self-unfruitful. Because Duke cherries bloom in a period between the sweet and the sour cherries, use late-blooming sweet cherries to pollinate early-blooming Dukes, and early-blooming sour cherries to pollinate late-blooming Dukes.

All sweet cherry cultivars are self-unfruitful, and there is a lot of cross-incompatibility among them. Look at the table of cross-incompatible groups on page 169 before you choose your cultivars. Furthermore, sour cherries won't pollinate sweet cherries because their bloom periods don't overlap. And although the bloom period of some Duke cherries overlaps the bloom period of some sweet cherries, Duke is not a reliable pollinator for sweet cherries.

Sour cherries form flower buds laterally on one-year-old terminal shoots and on spurs. The terminal buds on shoots and spurs are usually leaf buds. If the terminal growth is less than 7 inches, then all buds on it will be flower buds. If it's longer than 7 inches and at least pencil thick, some of the lateral buds will become leaf buds and develop spurs and lateral shoots, increasing productivity of the tree. Prune mature trees only enough to thin the dense tops for better light penetration. Neglecting this will cause spurs and lower branches to die back. Sour cherries are particularly weak wooded, so strap or brace long limbs to prevent them from splitting out.

Sweet cherries fruit mostly on spurs and produce less lateral growth than sour cherries. They are less prone to limb breakage than sour cherries but are more susceptible to crotch splitting, so spread the main branches to develop wide crotch angles.

Duke cherries need a lot of heading to keep the trees from growing too tall and too wide. Dukes produce long limbs with whorls of side limbs located at long intervals on the leader. Reduce the number of these side limbs to no more than two to three to a whorl during the first pruning after they form. The bearing habit of Duke cherries is similar to that of sweet cherries.

It is best to train young cherry trees to a modified leader system. Young cherry trees commonly have one vigorous limb that outgrows the others. Keep it subordinated.

After three to four years, your sour cherry trees should come into bearing. Sweet cherry trees take about five to six years. All types should be in full production by the tenth year after planting.

Although commercially grown sweet cherries are sometimes thinned to allow them to develop better size, it is unnecessary for home growers to thin their crops.

Expect some premature fruit drop, usually due to competition for available water or nutrients, severe defoliation from diseases or storms, poor nutrition, or poor weather conditions, especially within a week or two of bloom. Cracked or deformed fruits are usually the result of drought or nutrient shortage and are primarily a problem with sweet cherries grown in dry areas.

There is no standard maturity index for cherries. When the cherries taste good, have developed good overall coloring, and separate easily from the tree, it's time to harvest. Delay harvest as long as you can; cherries will increase in size up to 35 percent after the first day they could be picked, and those that are not ripe will not ripen off the tree. Grasp a

Cherry cultivars have strong regional adaptations, but there are a few that are widely grown. Cherries are divided into types that closely resemble the parent for which the type was named. The Bigarreau-type sweet cherry, a round fruit with crisp flesh, is commercially more important than the heart-shaped, soft fleshed Heart-type. Both sweet types come in dark and light colors. The Morello-type is highly susceptible to foliar diseases. 'Meteor' is a genetic semidwarf and 'North Star' is a genetic full dwarf. 'Stella' and 'Bing' are also available as genetic dwarfs but have not been widely tested. All are very good for home fruit gardens.

SWEET CHERRIES

	HEART-TYPE	BIGARREAU-TYPE
Light	Coe	Napoleon
	Ida	Emperor Francis
	Elton	Ranier
	Governor Wood	Gold
Dark	Black Tartarian	Windsor
	Early Purple	Hedelfingen
	Stella	Bing
		Lambert
		Schmidt

SOUR CHERRY

AMARELLE-TYPE	MORELLO-TYPE
Montmorency	English Morello
Early Richmond	
North Star	
Meteor	

DUKE CHERRY

May Duke, Royal Duke, Late Duke

Sweet cherries can have pollination problems if you don't choose the right combination of cultivars for planting. Here's a list of cross-incompatibility groups. Plant cultivars from different groups; cultivars in the same group will not cross-pollinate each other.

Group #	Cultivars
1	Bing, Lambert, Napoleon, Emperor Francis, Ohio Beauty
2	Windsor, Abundance
3	Black Tartarian, Black Eagle, Knight's Early Black, Bedford Prolific, Early Rivers
4	Centennial, Napoleon
5	Advance, Rockport
6	Elton, Governor Wood, Stark's Gold
7	Early Purple, Rockport
8	Black Tartarian, Early Rivers
9	Sodus, Van, Venus, Windsor
10	Bing, Emperor Francis, Lambert, Napoleon, Vernon
11	Velvet, Victor, Gold, Merton Heart
12	Hedelfingen, Vic
13	Hudson, Giant, Schmidt, Ursula
14	Seneca, Vega, Viota
15	Royal Purple, Lambert, Ironside, Woodring Bing
16	Schmidt, Oreland

cluster of ripe cherries by their stems and pull them from the tree. Don't handle the fruit and don't pull the stems off until you're ready to eat or process the fruit.

Cherries are prey to a host of pests. Viral and fungal leaf diseases are particularly bad in hot weather. Your county extension agent can recommend a good preventive spray program to control most diseases. The worst pest of cherries—particularly sweet cherries—is birds. You'll have to protect the entire tree with $1/2$-inch plastic mesh netting to keep them at bay.

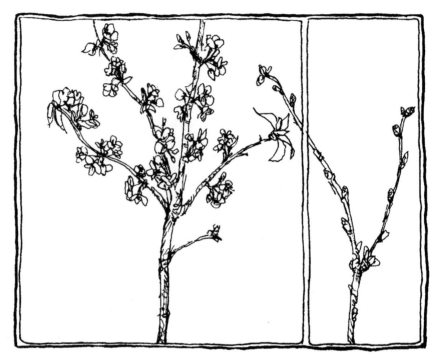

The sour cherry forms axillary flower buds (formed in the axils of leaves) but terminal leaf buds. This results in almost bare twigs the year after flowering.

There are several winter-related problems you also may encounter. One is *blackheart,* the biggest killer of cherry trees. It occurs when the sapwood of the trunk and main branches is injured by early winter cold. The cambium layer is not injured. Injured wood turns orange or light brown and interferes with conduction of nutrients. Tree growth is checked. If the problem is not too severe, cultivation and a good application of nitrogen fertilizer will sometimes lead to a recovery.

Bark splitting is caused by a rapid temperature drop in immature tissues, usually occurring in late fall or early winter before the tree has hardened off sufficiently. The splitting itself is not a big problem, but it can serve as an entrance for diseases and the formation of blackheart because the sapwood is exposed to the cold.

Crotch damage is caused by the effect of cold on weak crotches. Remove the dead tissue, prop up the branch to relieve strain on the crotch angle, paint it with wound dressing, and hope for the best.

The sweet cherry forms a spur system on which it flowers and fruits. It also forms axillary flower buds on newer wood.

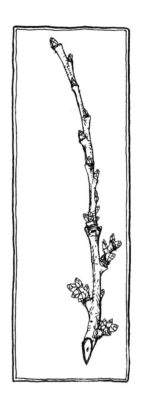

Crown injury is caused by a rapid drop in temperature in the fall before the tree has hardened sufficiently, and tender new growth dies back.

Sunscald, sometimes called *southwest injury*, is caused by the rapid temperature fluctuations of late winter. This rapid heating and cooling may cause bark to split and flake. Painting the entire trunk with interior white latex paint effectively reduces the problem by reflecting the sun's rays away from the bark and eliminating the heating. Use only interior latex paint; oil-based paints may damage the bark.

PEACHES

Georgians would like to claim peaches as their own, but, although Georgia produces arguably the best peaches in the world, the peach didn't originate there. It originated in China, where it has been cultivated for at least four thousand years, and from there it was carried by caravans into Iran. It was introduced into Greece early in the fourth century B.C. Columbus carried it to Florida on his second and third voyages, and from there it quickly spread among the Native Americans. It was introduced into England in the middle of the sixteenth century, and peach stones were among the seeds ordered by the Massachusetts Bay Colony in 1629. By 1648, great crops of peaches were being used as hog feed in the colonies and the fruit was plentiful in Florida by 1664. They were so popular among the native tribes, and so widely distributed, that some early naturalists thought them native to this country.

Peaches grow well throughout much of the United States, from Zones 5 through 10. Because peach buds respond quickly to a few days of warmth, lose hardiness, and are killed by subsequent cold temperatures, cold-winter areas with fluctuating temperatures may not produce reliable peach harvests. High-chill cultivars are available that don't react rapidly to midwinter warm spells. They also bloom later in the spring, thus reducing the chances of frost damage. Conversely, areas with mild winters may not provide enough chilling hours; spring bud break will be poor and shoot growth delayed. Low-chill cultivars, developed for the Deep South, satisfy their chilling requirements with only a few hundred hours of chilling. They will bloom and grow normally after a mild winter.

Purchase certified one-year-old trees. They will be larger and transplant better than June-budded trees, which are usually small whips. June-budded trees will do well only for late-fall or late-winter planting in the warm southern states.

Peach trees are usually budded onto seedlings of 'Lovell', 'Elberta', or another peach cultivar. These are not nematode-resistant rootstocks. Where soil nematodes are a problem, particularly in the southeastern United States, buy peaches budded to resistant stocks such as 'Nemaguard' and 'Okinawa'. These stocks are not cold-hardy; for cold northern gardens, use 'Harrow Blood' or 'Siberian' peach stocks.

Peach cultivars are very regionally adapted. Exceptions are the widely adapted 'Elberta', 'Rio Oso Gem', and 'Redhaven'.

CALIFORNIA
    Springgold, Junegold, Redtop, Suncrest
CENTRAL UNITED STATES
    Harbinger, Stark Earliglo, Harbelle, Harken, Reliance, Rio Oso Gem, Loring, Redhaven
NORTHEAST
    Harbinger, Early Redhaven, Newhaven, Early Rio Oso Gem, Reliance, Sunhaven, Redskin
SOUTHEAST
    Springgold, Early Coronet, Maygold, Redhaven, Redglobe, Summergold
NORTHERN FLORIDA
    Flordadawn, Flordaglobe, Flordaking, Flordacrest, FlordaRio
NORTHWEST
    Cardinal, Garnet Beauty, Regina, Ranger, Rosa, Suncrest
SOUTHWEST
    Dixired, Maravilha, Rio Grande

Dwarf peach trees are either genetic dwarfs or standard tops grafted onto a dwarfing rootstock. Peaches grafted to *Prunus tomentosa* or *P. besseyi* stocks produce dwarf trees. 'St. Julien A' plum rootstocks produce mid-size peach trees. These peach-plum grafts produce weak unions and often break after a few years. If you lose your young peach tree to drought in the first summer or to damage during the first winter, a vigorous shoot may grow from the base of the dead tree. If it arises from above the graft union, train this shoot into a new tree. If it arises from below the graft union, it is the rootstock sprouting, not the cultivar grafted to it. Remove the tree and start again with a new one. Genetic dwarf peaches are available for small gardens. 'Bonanza' is one I'm familiar with. Twenty years after planting, it's only 3 feet tall. The peaches are edible but not the greatest. If you must grow peaches in pots, plant the genetic dwarfs. If you have the space, plant regular trees.

With the exception of 'J. H. Hale', most peach cultivars are self-fruitful, so you don't have to worry about cross-pollination.

Well-drained soil is essential to peaches. Wet, compacted soil and lack of soil oxygen causes peach roots to produce hydrogen cyanide; the tree self-destructs. A cool northeastern exposure is generally a good peach planting site because the area is protected from prevailing winter winds and may remain cool enough in the spring to delay bloom and decrease chances of spring frost damage.

Don't plant on old orchard sites because of the possibility of arsenic residues from pesticides, and don't replant peaches to sites where they grew before because of the possible presence of diseases in the soil. Avoid sites where oak trees recently grew, because the mushroom root rot fungus that lives on oak tree roots also can attack peach trees.

Plant during the late fall in warm southern areas, during early spring elsewhere. Set peach trees a couple of inches deeper than they were grown in the nursery, making sure the bud union is above ground. Tree spacing varies depending upon cultivar, soil, and climate; 24 feet apart is standard spacing.

Mulch or cultivate young trees to keep weed growth down. Mature trees can be grown in sod. Corncobs or wood chips make great peach tree mulches, but add enough nitrogen to compensate for that used by the decomposing mulch or sod.

Young trees should make no more than 18 to 24 inches of growth each season; mature, bearing trees, about 10 to 15 inches of new growth. If your trees are growing well, don't fertilize. If they're not, add just enough fertilizer to get them growing. One pound of 10–10–10 per inch of trunk diameter near the base of the tree but above the bud union is adequate to stimulate proper growth. Excessive new growth causes poor crops and an increased susceptibility to disease. Feed in the early spring, applying half the recommended fertilizer as soon as the ground thaws and the other half when shoot growth begins.

Because peaches are so sensitive to cold, winter protection is important. Paint trunks with white latex interior paint to decrease sunscald, and prop the scaffolds against heavy snow loads. In the fall, mound soil about a foot high against the crown of the tree. Reduce damage from late-spring frosts by not cultivating during bloom.

Train young peach trees to an open-center form. At planting, cut back the whips of June-budded trees to 24 to 30 inches. If the tree is less than 24 inches high, don't head it. Select three to four strong, well-spaced laterals and head them to two to three buds each. Remove the rest. If you have no strong laterals, head poor laterals back to two buds. Allow no lateral to develop less than 18 inches from the ground; you'll need this amount of trunk for good borer control. If you planted strong one-year-old trees, head the strong laterals to two buds. Remove all suckers during the first season.

After one year in the field, select three strong laterals and remove the others. Head them lightly, and head the leader above the top scaffold.

After three years, you should have a well-formed framework. You will need to do only light thinning to keep the center open. In fact, heavy pruning, especially in the third, fourth, and fifth years, delays bearing, overstimulates shoot growth, causes poor color development in the fruit, and increases winter damage. Head back vertical shoots to keep the tree height at about 10 feet, and do enough pruning to keep shoot growth within limits. Prune every year. Otherwise, the bearing wood will grow too far from the trunk and the tree will be unproductive.

There are special things to consider when pruning peaches. Oriental fruit moth damage causes shoot tips to die back, stimulating lateral branching. Trees with this type of damage require a lot of thinning. Severely winter-damaged trees should not be dehorned in the spring. This old practice involved cutting trees back severely so that the main scaffolds were just stubs. This seriously weakened the trees and they often died. A badly winter-damaged tree should be removed.

Watering is critical during fruit growth, especially during the last month of the season, when peaches develop two-thirds of their size. Don't let the trees dry out, because this increases winter damage and decreases shoot and fruit size. Overwatering when the fruit is about the size of a half dollar may cause the pits to split. An inch or two of water per week is adequate for good peach production.

Peaches bear fruit on one-year-old wood. Most of the fruits—and the best fruits—are borne on the upper third of the tree. The average mature peach tree produces more than twenty-five thousand blossoms, but you need only about 5 percent fruit set to produce a good crop. Although pruning removes many flower buds, you may have to thin both blossoms and developing fruits to ensure a crop of large, well-formed peaches.

Your tree will produce light crops in the third or fourth year and should be in full production by the sixth year. Harvest peaches when the ground color has turned to a deep orange-yellow on yellow-fleshed fruit and to a creamy white on white-fleshed fruit. Red overcolor does not indicate maturity because it develops long before the fruit is ripe. Taste a few to be sure they're ripe before harvesting the whole crop.

NECTARINES

Nectarines are fuzzless peaches. Contrary to popular belief, nectarines are not crosses between peaches and plums, but are the result of a bud sport or mutation to the common peach.

The fuzzless character is governed by a single recessive gene, so a peach seed may produce a nectarine tree, and a nectarine seed may produce a peach tree. Buds on either tree can mutate also, and a peach tree might bear a branch that produces nectarines, and vice versa.

Like peaches, nectarines originated in China many centuries ago. First mention of nectarines in Europe was by Cieza de Leon in about 1540. They grew abundantly in Virginia in 1720.

Nectarine fruit is a little smaller than the peach, has a distinctive flavor, and is more susceptible to brown rot, curculio, and cracking than the peach. They are grown exactly the same way as peaches, on the same soil and site, and harvested the same way. They are a little softer than a peach when ripe, so handle them gently.

Nectarine cultivars are highly regionally adapted.

CALIFORNIA
Early Sun Grand, Sun Grand, Grand River
NORTHEAST
Nectarose, Nectacrest, Nectared #1–9, Morton, Hunter
MID ATLANTIC
Cavalier, Pocahontas, Red Chief
GULF STATES
Stark Early Flame
FLORIDA
Sunred, Sungold, Sundollar, Suncoast
PACIFIC NORTHWEST
RedGold, EarliBlaze, SunGlo

PLUMS

There are a number of different plum species grown for their fruit. They all have similar cultural requirements and growth habits.

European plum (*Prunus domestica*) trees have smooth, gray bark and thick, glossy, dark green leaves. They are hardy to Zone 5. European plums are divided into five groups: *prunes,* which are small, oval-shaped fruits that can be dried successfully without removing the pits; *greengage,* or Reine Claude, plums, which are round and have green, yellow, or slightly red skin; *yellow egg* canning plums; *Imperatrice* dessert plums, which have thick blue skin; and *Lombard* plums, which are similar to Imperatrice but have red skin.

Japanese plums (*Prunus salicina*) were brought to the United States by Luther Burbank about 1870. They are hardy from Zones 5 to 9. These rough-barked trees bloom very early, which makes them susceptible to spring frosts. The fruits are large and heart shaped with yellow, red, or purple-red, but never blue, skin. The flesh is yellow, amber, or red.

A number of plum species are native to the United States. Fruit quality has been improved by cross-breeding with European plums, and many American plums have been used to impart cold hardiness to European plums.

Prunus americana is a cold-resistant plum native from southern New England to Montana and south to Florida, Texas, and Colorado. It was widely planted by Native Americans in the New England area. Called the goose plum, red plum, sloe, or hog plum, it is sometimes cultivated for its fruit. *Prunus americana* var. *nigra* is the related Canadian plum, one of the most cold-hardy plums in North America. *P. americana* var. *mollis*, the wolf plum, is also highly cold resistant. Its fruit has good flesh but astringent skin.

P. angustifolia, the Chickasaw plum, has thick, thorny trees native to the Deep South and west to southern Oklahoma. The fruit is grown locally and the plant has been used in breeding.

P. besseyi, the Hanson bush cherry, is a plum that is native from Kansas to Manitoba. It is mainly used in breeding and as a dwarfing rootstock for stone fruits.

P. hortulana, the Wayland plum, is native to the southern Mississippi River Valley. It is resistant to brown rot and its fruit is good for jelly.

P. maritima, the beach plum, grows wild on sand dunes and coastal plains from New Brunswick to Virginia. It resists most pests (except red mite) and makes excellent jelly.

P. munsoniana, the wild goose plum or Downing plum, is native to the lower Mississippi River Valley. It's highly resistant to spring frosts and brown rot.

P. subcordata, the Pacific plum, is native to southwest Oregon and northwest California. It is highly esteemed for jelly making.

Minor Plums

P. cerasifera, the myrobalan or cherry plum, is native to Turkey and is used primarily as a rootstock for Japanese and European plums, though its fruit is delicious.

The 'Damson' (purple-fruited) and the 'Mirabelle' (yellow-fruited) plums belong to the species *P. insititia*. The fruits are small, up to an inch in diameter, and those of 'Damson' are highly acidic. The trees are hardy, productive, disease-resistant, and require little care. 'St. Julien', also of this group, is used as a dwarfing rootstock for other plums.

P. simonii, the Simon or apricot plum, was introduced from China via France. It has served an important role in the breeding of high-quality Japanese plums such as 'Shiro', but its own fruit has little merit.

Order one-year-old whips of European and American plums and either one- or two-year-old trees of Japanese plums. More important than age, however, is making sure they are certified disease-free stock, as viruses plague the plum family.

Most plum trees are grafted to myrobalan plum roots, although peach, apricot, and almond roots are sometimes used for plum stocks. Myrobalan roots tolerate poor soil aeration and are widely adapted throughout the United States. You can tell the difference between myrobalan roots and those of other plums because the former show a brown color when the bark is scratched.

There are no good dwarfing rootstocks for plums, although 'Pixie', introduced from England, shows some promise. European plums grafted to *P. besseyi* produce dwarf trees that seem to do well under optimal conditions. Japanese plums on *P. besseyi* produce very dwarf trees that may be useful in a small yard where space is at a premium. If you think your soil

When you choose a plum cultivar, consider not only fruit use and species cold hardiness, but also pollination requirements.

EUROPEAN

Prune: French, Sugar, Stanley, Italian, German, Robe de Sargeant
Greengage: Reine Claude, Jefferson, Washington
Yellow Egg: Yellow Egg
Imperatrice: Grand Duke, Diamond, Tragedy, President
Lombard: Lombard, Bradshaw, Pond

JAPANESE

Wickson, Eldorado, Queen Ann, Formosa, Redheart, Burbank

AMERICAN AND MINOR

P. americana: Hawkeye, Wyant, DeSota, Weaver, Terry
P. hortulana: Golden Beauty, Wayland, Miner, Surprise
P. munsoniana: Wild Goose, Newman
P. insititia: Frogmore, Shropshire
P. besseyi: Oka, Saca, Zumbra, Compass

*When choosing plums, stick with self-fruitful cultivars if possible. If the culti-
vars you've chosen are self-unfruitful, interplant at least three of them for
cross-pollination. There are a few cross-incompatibilities, as listed below.
'Italian Prune', 'Agen', 'Reine Claude', and 'German Prune' are self-fruitful
only in some areas.*

SELF-FRUITFUL	SELF-UNFRUITFUL
Agen	Anita
Bavary	Arch Duke
California Blue	Belgian Purple
Coates 1418	Blue Rock
Czar	Bradshaw
Drap d'Or	Burton
Early Mirabelle	Cambridge Gage
French Damson	DeMontfort
German Prune	Golden Drop
Monarc	Italian Prune
Mayer	President
Pershore	Reine Claude
Sannoir	Sergeant
Stanley	Sultan
Sugar	Tragedy
Yellow Egg	Washington

CROSS-INCOMPATIBLES

Golden Drop, Coe's Violet, and Allgroves Superb are cross-incompatible.
Cambridge Gage, Late Orange, and President are cross-incompatible.

may be infested with nematodes, especially in California, purchase trees
on a resistant rootstock such as 'Myro 29C' or 'Marianna 2624'. The latter also resists oak root rot. Grafts of Japanese plums onto European
plum rootstocks will work, but the reverse is not true.

Because there is such a close relationship among species and because
some cultivars may originate from more than one species, there is a good
deal of cross-incompatibility and unfruitfulness among plums. To ensure

good pollination, regardless of the cultivar or species you plant, always plant at least two different cultivars whose blossom times overlap.

Select a site with good, well-drained soil and plenty of air circulation. Plant in the early spring. Set the trees an inch or so deeper than they grew in the nursery, but make sure the bud union is visible above the soil. Spacings depend upon cultivar and soil conditions, but 18 feet by 24 feet is about right.

Because they are so rugged, plum trees need little fertilizer, especially in heavier soils. If you cultivate beneath the trees, apply about 2 pounds of 10–10–10 per tree per year for young trees two to five years old. Increase this to 8 to 10 pounds per mature bearing tree per year. If you grow your trees in sod, you may have to double the rate of application. Apply all fertilizer in the early spring before growth begins. Always adjust the amount of fertilizer by looking at the shoot growth. Young trees should make about 16 to 20 inches of new growth per year; mature trees should put out about 8 inches.

The plum bears fruit laterally on one-year-old wood and on spurs on older wood. Train the trees to the open-center or, preferably, the modified leader system.

Prune European plum trees more lightly than Japanese plum trees, but never prune plums very heavily because it will throw them into

In the East, most plum cultivars bloom at about the same time, but in the West they don't. Be sure bloom times of your cultivars overlap for good cross-pollination. Here's the sequence of plum bloom in California.

EARLY	MIDSEASON	LATE
Reine Claude	Sugar	California Blue
Lombard	Grand Duke	Hungarian
	French	Pond
	Robe	Giant
	Burton	Italian Prune
	Imperial	Yellow Egg
	Agen	Washington
	President	

vigorous vegetative growth at the expense of fruit. Remove dead, diseased, or damaged wood annually.

Thin plums to increase the size and quality of the fruit. The first natural fruit drop in plums occurs early, when the small fruits drop with their stems attached. After the June drop, in which fruits drop without their stems, check the pits of those that are left on the tree by cutting open a few fruits. When the pits begin to harden, pick off excess fruit so that those that remain are spaced about 2 inches apart for European plums or 3 inches apart for Japanese plums. American plums are not usually thinned. Some Japanese cultivars, such as 'Burbank', set large quantities of fruit and need heavy thinning; others, such as 'Santa Rosa', do a good job of self-thinning and need only a little attention.

Plums get many of the same diseases and insects as peaches. They are especially susceptible to black knot, which causes large, knotty, black growths on branches. Prune out affected areas, and remove all wild plum and cherry trees from the area surrounding your planting to help control this disease. Another common problem is the adult plum curculio, whose egg-laying punctures cause small, half-moon-shaped blemishes on fruits.

Harvest plums for fresh eating when the fruit is well colored, ripe, and slightly firm. For jelly, wait until the fruit begins to soften. If you wait too long to pick, the fruit will form gas pockets, dark flesh, and look puffy. In either case, the undercolor will have gone from yellow-green to yellow or red, or from green to blue. Slightly immature plums will ripen after picking at 55 to 60 degrees F.

Because not all plums on a tree ripen at once, make two or three pickings. Harvests usually begin in the second or third year for European plums and in the third to fifth year for Japanese plums. Most plum cultivars produce about 1 to 1½ bushels of fruit per tree per year. Prunes bear up to 2 to 3 bushels per tree.

MULBERRIES

Mulberries are best known for their role in silk production. The white mulberry (*Morus alba*), the red mulberry (*M. rubra*), and the black mulberry (*M. nigra*) produce leaves that are the exclusive diet of the silkworm.

Mulberry trees begin growth in late spring and are rarely damaged by spring frosts. White mulberries tolerate cold between 25 and -25 degrees F.

A hybrid of white and red mulberries, however, is extremely cold tolerant. The red mulberry is native to the eastern United States, growing from New York west to Nebraska and south to the Gulf Coast. The black mulberry is the least cold hardy, surviving winters only as far north as Zone 6. For this reason, it's grown primarily on the West Coast.

There are not many mulberry cultivars to choose from. Of the white, 'New American' is probably the best, followed by 'Wellington' and 'Trowbridge'. 'Travis', 'Wiseman', and 'Cooke' are fine red cultivars. Of the red x white hybrids, 'Hicks' and 'Illinois Everbearing' are common, the latter being an excellent choice. 'Black Persian' is the best black cultivar.

Mulberries are wind pollinated, and some cultivars, including 'Illinois Everbearing' and 'Hicks', are parthenocarpic. You should plant several trees, however, because they can be either dioecious or monoecious and can change sex any time after reaching adulthood. Your female tree might bear fruit this year and become a nonfruiting male next year.

Purchase one- or two-year-old trees, preferably grafted to Russian mulberry stocks for cold hardiness. Mulberries are not fussy about soil, but they do need full sun. Plant them in the spring, 15 feet apart. Only corrective or maintenance pruning is required. Propagate the trees by hardwood, softwood, or root cuttings.

Mulberry trees begin to bear after about ten years. Mulberries ripen over an extended season and fall when ripe, to be collected in a sheet placed beneath the tree. Don't park your car beneath a mulberry tree; the fruit stains anything it lands on and makes a mess of drives and walks.

NORTHERN PAWPAW

The pawpaw is a member of the Annonaceae family, which includes the tropical soursop, sweetsop, and cherimoya. The northern pawpaw, *Asimina triloba*, looks and tastes like a banana. Native Americans used and cultivated the fruit, and one of De Soto's party, exploring the southern United States over four hundred years ago, remarked on its fine flavor. Before 1900, the wild fruits were harvested and sold in large quantities in cities throughout the United States.

Pawpaws are native from the East Coast to Nebraska, exclusive of New England and Florida. They are hardy to -25 degrees F but need at least 150 days to ripen, making them Zone 5 to 8 plants. They do not grow well along the coasts because the cool summers delay ripening.

In the wild, the northern pawpaw is an understory plant growing where the soil is well drained with a pH between 5 and 7. Young plants grow tall in the shade of their elders. Duplicate these conditions and you won't go wrong. Shade your young plants with evergreen boughs or lath for the first three years, then remove the shade, because a mature tree requires full sun for good production. Mulch well with leaves after planting and maintain until the plants mature. Don't feed pawpaws, and don't bother to prune except to mow or pull the suckers that develop.

Most pawpaws are grown from seed, but a few cultivars, such as 'Overleese' and 'Mitchell', have been developed for interested growers.

If you want to propagate pawpaw, take root cuttings or suckers, or graft the trees. Seeds germinate very slowly, and seedling trees take a long time to produce. If you do decide to plant pawpaw seeds, do so late in the spring.

The pawpaw has a long taproot, so you must dig an especially deep planting hole to accommodate it. The roots are brittle and require careful handling. Purchase only potted or container-grown nursery plants.

The pawpaw is self-unfruitful and dichogamous, meaning that the male and female parts of the flower don't ripen at the same time. Pawpaws are pollinated by beetles and flies, rather than bees.

Pawpaws bear after five to seven years, eventually yielding up to a bushel of fruit per tree in good years. Although the flowers are produced singly, each has a multiple ovary and fruits are borne in clusters. Ripe fruit has a green to yellow skin that soon turns to a deep brown. Large fruits drop from the tree when ripe. You may pick the fruit as it's just beginning to turn color and ripen it indoors. Firm fruit will keep for several months in the refrigerator.

PERSIMMONS

The oriental persimmon (*Diospyros kaki*) is native to China, where it has been cultivated for hundreds of years. The trees are very long-lived, with some recorded as being more than six hundred years old.

The American persimmon (*D. virginiana*) was used as a dried fruit by Native Americans and, when mixed with honey locust pods, made into a fermented drink. In the South, a beer is made of cornmeal and persimmons.

Oriental persimmons are hardy to 0 degrees F (Zones 7 to 10), although some Chinese cultivars tolerate -15 degrees F. The fruit loses its astringency in hot summers but retains it in cool summers. American persimmons are hardy to Zone 5 but require a fairly long season to mature fruit.

Some cold-hardy *D. kaki* cultivars include 'Eureka', 'Saijo', 'Giombo', 'Great Wall', and 'Peiping'. The first cultivars of American persimmons were introduced in 1880; some popular ones are 'Garretson', 'Killen', and 'Earlybolden'. Those especially adapted to northern conditions include 'Meader', 'Pieper', and 'Hicks'.

Persimmon trees are usually either male or female, but they can change sex from year to year. Oriental persimmons usually have few pollination problems, but American persimmons need good cross-pollination, either by wind or insects. Oriental and American persimmons will not cross-pollinate each other.

All persimmons need well-drained soil and full sun. They have a long taproot and need a deep planting hole. Plant in the early spring. The taproot is naturally black, so don't be alarmed at the color—it's not dead.

Train your trees to a modified central leader system. The wood is brittle, so head back one-year-old wood each year to decrease the fruit load. Don't worry if you see a lot of twigs on the ground beneath the tree—the American persimmon sheds these small branches naturally.

Oriental persimmons can be grafted onto American persimmon roots to produce cold-hardy trees. Propagate persimmons by hardwood cuttings, suckers, and seeds. Stratify the seeds for at least three months.

Persimmon trees bear after several years, always on one-year-old wood. A mature oriental persimmon will bear over 400 pounds of fruit; a mature American persimmon will yield 50 to 100 pounds of fruit. You must snip off oriental persimmons at harvest, but American persimmons often drop when ripe.

Unripe, astringent persimmons contain leucodelphinidin, a compound that causes your mouth to pucker and can give you indigestion. The calyx of a ripe persimmon separates easily and the pulp is so mushy that it bulges the fruit. If your persimmons are nearly ripe when you harvest them, they'll ripen further on the kitchen counter or in a plastic bag with an apple to speed the process. Oriental persimmons take about three to four days to ripen; American persimmons, about a week.

ALMONDS

Almonds originated in western Asia and have been cultivated since ancient times. Almonds are related to the peach, and their cultural requirements are very similar. Although some cultivars are hardy as far north as New York, almonds thrive only in a limited area of the country, mainly California. Because of its early blooming period, its grown where there's little or no frost.

Purchase only trees budded to almond roots. Bitter almond rootstocks make better trees than do sweet almond rootstocks. Some nurseries graft almond to peach stocks, but such trees have proven short-lived in some areas. If you suspect nematodes, plant trees on Nemaguard stocks.

'Nonpareil' is the most widely grown cultivar, but 'Mission', 'Merced', and 'Ne Plus Altra' are also fine. Many cultivars are self-sterile, and some are cross-incompatible. You must plant at least two different cultivars whose bloom times overlap to ensure good pollination. 'Ne Plus Altra', 'Peerless', and 'Milow' are early bloomers; 'Mission', 'Mono', 'Yosemite', and 'Planada' are late bloomers; the rest are intermediate.

Interplant cultivars 22 by 26 feet apart. Plant almonds on light, sandy soil where air drainage is good. Soil preparation, watering, pests, and fertilization are similar to those for the peach.

Train the trees to a modified leader system, and prune them lightly every couple of years. Remove dead wood, and where the wood is greater than an inch in diameter, head it back to a strong lateral.

Harvest begins in the third or fourth year after planting. By their eighth year, almond trees will be in full production, bearing about 20 pounds of fruit per tree. Begin harvesting when the hulls of fruits in the shadiest part of the tree have begun to shrivel and crack. Pick them one at a time or knock them from the tree with a length of rubber hose attached to a long pole. Hull the fruits and air dry. Almonds keep in dry, cool storage for several months.

CHESTNUTS

Chestnuts are a close relative of beech and oak, and the trees and their nuts have been used for food, fuel, and timber for more than four thousand years.

The European chestnut originated near Asia Minor and was introduced early into Greek and Roman culture. This species is slightly susceptible to chestnut blight and is dying out throughout its native range. The American chestnut, smaller and sweeter than its European cousin, once grew wild from Maine to Florida and west to Michigan. The tasty fruits were eaten by Native Americans, and early colonists used them to fatten hogs. Chestnut blight, a viral disease, decimated native stands earlier in this century; although stumps of the decay-resistant wood still sprout, there are no sizable mature trees left. Researchers in Connecticut have introduced nine strains that may be resistant to the blight. They have not been widely tested, but they may work in your area. It's still a gamble, however, so don't plant them if you are unwilling to risk losing them.

The Japanese chestnut produces the largest nuts of all but is less hardy and more susceptible to blight than the Chinese chestnut. Its nuts are also poorer in quality than those of the Chinese chestnut.

The Chinese chestnut is the only surefire chestnut to grow. It's highly resistant to chestnut blight, and it produces good-quality nuts. Chinese chestnuts are cold hardy to Zone 5 and will survive -20 degrees F when fully dormant. They have a short chilling requirement and the buds respond rapidly to early warm spells, making them highly subject to damage from late spring frosts. For this reason, choose a site with especially good air drainage. A sandy loam soil with a pH of 6 to 6.5 is best. Although chestnuts will tolerate moderate drought once established, they will not tolerate poor soil drainage.

Plant seedling trees. Although some grafted trees are available, most suffer from incompatibility problems and are short lived. If you do plant grafted trees, 'Crane' and 'Nanking' are good choices for most areas of the United States. 'Orrin' is a bit better for northern gardens.

Plant trees in the early spring, about 50 feet apart. Prune them back to about half their size at planting and paint the trunks white to reduce sunscald. Keep white paint on the trunks throughout the lives of the trees. Plant at least two seedling trees or two grafted cultivars to ensure good pollination.

Keep chestnuts weed-free while the trees are young. Don't apply any fertilizer to new trees, but begin applications early in the spring of the second year, applying about 1 pound of 5–10–10 per inch of trunk diameter (measured chest high) per year.

Let the tree come into bearing before your first pruning, then remove all branches within 6 feet of the soil line. Remove and burn any blighted, damaged, dead, or discolored shoots to keep the tree healthy.

Seedling trees begin to bear about six to eight years after planting; grafted trees, two years. The fruit is very perishable and you'll have to harvest it every day or two. Gather the fallen burrs or handpick the fruit when the burrs begin to split. Deburr the fruit as soon as possible. Store chestnuts in the refrigerator or hang them in a mesh bag in a room at 40 degrees F with good air circulation. Never let the nuts' surface become damp or moist.

FILBERTS

The filbert, hazelnut, or cobnut *(Corylus* spp.) is native to both Europe and the Americas. The American hazelnut bears good-flavored nuts, but they're smaller and their shells are harder than the European species. The European species has been grown in China and was cultivated by both the Greeks and the Romans for culinary and medicinal use.

The filbert is hardy to about 0 degrees F and requires four hundred to eight hundred hours of chilling. Although the open flowers tolerate 16 degrees F with no wind, they often open very early in the spring and are injured by frosty temperatures, so plant filberts on cooler northeastern slopes to delay bloom.

The beaked hazelnut, native to the eastern United States, is the hardiest species but produces inferior nuts. The choice of most growers is a hybrid of *Corylus americana* and the European filbert. This cross has produced some of the most cold-hardy filberts available. Most gardeners plant readily available seedling trees, but layered plants produce better crops. 'Winkler', 'Bixby', and 'Potomac' are fine cultivars. 'Barcelona' does well in the Pacific Northwest, and 'Cosford' produces fine crops in New York and southern New England. Although 'Winkler' may be partially self-fruitful in some areas, don't take a chance—plant at least two cultivars for good cross-pollination.

Plant the trees about 15 feet apart in deep, fertile soil. Shallow planting reduces the amount of suckering and is best if you wish to train the plants to tree form. After planting, head the trees to about 24 inches in height, mulch heavily with wood chips, and paint the trunks white for protection against sunscald. Fertilize your filberts as you would peaches, and propagate them by mounding or seeds.

Although you'll get better fruit if you train the plants to a tree form, most gardeners train them to a bush habit. For a tree form, remove all suckers as they appear. To grow a bush, let all the suckers develop and prune the plant as you would a lilac or mock orange by removing all

Flowering in nuts is a little different from that of other fruit species. (A) The hanging male flower (catkin) sheds pollen that falls on smaller female flowers. (B) The mature fruit is enclosed in a husk, or involucre, which is peeled away to expose the nut.

weak canes at the soil line. Thin the center of the bush to admit light. Because the plant bears its fruit terminally and laterally on one-year-old wood, prune the remaining branches lightly.

Filberts get a number of pests, including blight, aphids, and mealybugs. Squirrels are your worst competition for the tasty nuts. Remove any native filberts near your planting to reduce the possibility of eastern filbert blight infection.

Filberts will begin to bear several years after planting and reach maximum production after fifteen to twenty years. Harvest the nuts after they fall, but don't be upset if you find some hollow husks. Up to a quarter of the nuts may be "blanks." The cause for this is unknown. Dry the nuts and store them in a dry room. If you hold them too long in low humidity, they'll lose their flavor; moving them to a humid area for a week or so will restore that flavor.

PECANS

Pecans (*Carya illinoensis*) are native to eastern North America. Native tribes selectively bred the largest and thinnest-shelled nuts for pecan oil to flavor their foods. The pecan is the most widely distributed American nut, ranging from Mexico to southern Iowa to Kentucky and west into the arid states. It is commercially important in the South. George Washington planted pecans in 1775, and Thomas Jefferson followed suit, planting a grove in 1778. Most early trees were seedlings, but there are records of pecans being grafted to hickory roots as early as 1800.

The pecan is closely related to the hickory. A hybrid of the hickory and the pecan, called the *hican,* bears thick-shelled nuts longer and larger than those of hickory.

Pecans tolerate 120 degrees F but do best at around 80 degrees F. Southern cultivars, such as the paper-shell strains, require a 210-day growing season to fill, while northern cultivars must have 180 days. In the cooler Northeast, the trees flower and produce fine shade but will not develop fruit. Cultivars developed for western conditions contract scab when planted in the East. Widely adapted cultivars include 'Comanche', 'Choctaw', 'Wichita', 'Sioux', 'Apache', and 'Mohawk'.

Although pecans are wind pollinated, they are dichogamous, meaning that the male and the female flowers don't open at the same time on

Pecans are generally adapted to Southern areas. Here are a few good cultivars and the areas to which they are best suited.

FLORIDA
Desirable, Stuart
NEW MEXICO
Clark, Barton, Desirable
TEXAS
Barton, Desirable, Sioux
OKLAHOMA
Barton, Squirrel, Mahan
MISSISSIPPI
Stuart, Lewis, Stevens
LOUISIANA
Stuart, Sabine, Magenta
CAROLINAS
Stuart, Farley, Mahan
GEORGIA AND ALABAMA
Stuart, Desirable, Farley
KANSAS
Squirrel, Giles, Buice
MISSOURI TO KENTUCKY (NORTHERN REGIONS)
Busseron, Indiana, Butterick

Pecan, hickory, and walnut have similar habits of flowering and fruiting. (A) The catkins are borne axillary on previous season's growth; (B) the female flowers are borne terminally on current season's growth. The female flower is often brightly colored.

the same tree. Plant several cultivars or seedlings to assure that there is enough pollen around when the female flowers open.

Plant pecan trees about 50 feet apart in deep, fertile, well-drained soil. They leaf out and bloom late, so there's little danger from late frosts. To accommodate their long taproots, dig planting holes about 3 feet deep. Purchase one- or two-year-old trees from 3 to 10 feet high and head them to half their height. Rub off the buds and paint the trunks white for sunscald protection. As the tree develops limbs, let the first scaffold form about 6 feet from the soil line. Mulch the trees and keep them well watered. Pecan trees are slow to take hold, so pamper them a bit.

Do not fertilize pecans the first year. For the second through the sixth year, apply about 2 pounds of 10–10–10 fertilizer or equivalent per year per inch of trunk diameter measured chest high. For mature trees, about 100 pounds per tree per year is sufficient. Fertilize each year in the early spring as growth begins. Prune pecans so that you can walk beneath the tree. Except for the removal of dead or damaged wood, no other pruning is necessary.

The pecan has a couple of drops each season. The first drop occurs at pollination and is made up of poorly developed female flowers. The second drop occurs soon after bloom and is made up of small, insufficiently pollinated nuts. The third drop occurs in late summer or early fall and is composed of weak, inferior nuts.

This fruit is injured by several insects, but the greatest pests are raccoons, deer, and squirrels. Crows and blue jays will eat paper-shell pecans. If Spanish moss grows thickly on the branches, it will shade the tree and reduce the crop; control the moss with 6–2–100 Bordeaux.

Harvest the pecans when the hulls split. Pick them by hand, beat the branches with a long pole, or shake the tree to knock down ripe nuts.

WALNUTS

The black walnut (*Juglans nigra*) is native to the United States and is grown mostly for its timber from Massachusetts to Florida and west to Minnesota and Texas. Native tribes and colonists used the nuts for food and fattened their swine on the wild nuts. The kernels are used in ice cream, candy, and breads. Although the meat is the best flavored of all the walnuts, the husks are tough, thick, and secrete a black juice that stains hands and nut meats. The shells are difficult to crack and the kernels tough to separate from the shells. Further, the trees are difficult to propagate and transplant and come into bearing very slowly. Black walnuts emit a chemical called *juglone,* which stunts the growth of many plants, including tomato, potato, blackberry, alfalfa, and heaths.

There are not many walnut cultivars from which to choose. Here are some that will do well in your area. Most black walnut trees are seedlings, but a few superior cultivars have been developed.

PERSIAN WALNUT

CALIFORNIA
      Serr (for the San Joaquin–Sacramento Valley and hot areas)
      Chico, Amigo, Vina (for Vina–Red Bluff areas)
      Hartley, Placentia (southern California)
      Franquette (central and northern California)
PACIFIC NORTHWEST
      Franquette
NORTHEAST
      Clinton, Gratiot, Greenhaven, Somers

BLACK WALNUT

Thomas, Ohio, Stabler

The English, or Persian, walnut grows in the eastern United States as far north as Niagara Falls. In the West, it is grown in California and eastern Oregon. Carpathian walnuts are cold-hardy selections of the Persian walnut introduced from the Carpathian mountains of Poland.

Although walnuts can be found through a wide geographic range, they won't survive in areas where temperatures regularly fall below 0 degrees F. If you live in a marginal area, plant the hardy Carpathian selections. Walnuts sunburn if temperatures exceed 100 degrees F and the humidity is low. If high temperatures occur during the growing season, many of the nuts will be "blanks." If high temperatures occur just before harvest, nut meats may blacken and shrivel. Places like southern California are near the southern limit of walnut range because of inadequate chilling.

California gardeners prefer Persian walnuts grafted to rootstocks of the northern California black walnut (*Juglans hindsii*); in Oregon seedlings of 'Manregian' walnut are preferred for stocks. Hybrid stocks called 'Paradox' (Persian walnut x black walnut) and 'Royal' (Eastern black walnut x California black walnut) are also available. You can also purchase trees on Persian seedling stocks. Most black walnuts are seedling trees.

Like the other nuts, walnuts are wind-pollinated. Plant at least two to three cultivars for good cross-pollination. Well-drained silt loams several feet deep, high in organic matter, and nearly neutral in pH are best for walnut production. Walnuts won't tolerate wet feet or alkali soils. Dig the planting holes deep and narrow to accommodate the long taproots. Set the trees at the same depth they grew in the nursery. Paint the trunk white or wrap it to reduce sunscald. Head back the top half of the tree at planting, leaving several good buds along the trunk. This drastic pruning helps bring the top of the tree into better balance with the partial root system and is absolutely essential.

Persian walnut trees should be set 50 feet apart. Black walnut trees should be spaced about 60 feet apart. Mulch the plants heavily to reduce competition from weeds, and keep them well watered.

Trees in the arid Southwest often need no fertilizer. In the Pacific Northwest, increase the amount of fertilizer each year, beginning in the second year, until a mature tree is receiving about 60 pounds of 10–10–10 fertilizer or equivalent each spring. In the East, give young trees less than 6 inches in diameter about 2 pounds of 10–10–10 for each inch of trunk diameter measured chest high. Trees 7 to 12 inches in diameter need about 4 pounds of 10–10–10 per inch of trunk diameter chest high; those over 12 inches in diameter require about 6 pounds of 10–10–10 per inch of trunk diameter chest high. Apply all the fertilizer in one early-spring application.

Propagate walnut trees by seed. Plant them in the ground about 2 inches deep in the fall. Protect them from marauding squirrels by cutting a 1-inch hole in the bottom of a tin can and pushing the can down over the nut. By the time the seedling has made substantial growth, the can will have rusted away. (Don't use aluminum cans, as they will not rust and can restrict tree growth.) You also can patch bud or graft superior clones to your seedling trees.

Pruning is simple. In the season of planting, when the new shoots are 8 to 12 inches long, select the best for a leader and pinch the tips of all competing ones. Early each spring, shorten the lower branches or pinch the growing points. As the tree grows, remove all branches lower than 6 feet from the ground. It's important to leave these branches on young trees because they supply carbohydrates to the tree and shade the trunk to reduce sunscald. Once the tree is mature and has a strong framework, you shouldn't have to prune at all.

Squirrels and deer are some of the biggest pests of walnuts. Canker, crown gall, aphids, and blight also take their toll.

Ripe walnuts drop naturally over a two-month period. In cooler regions, hull cracking coincides with kernel maturity. In warm areas, kernels mature before the hulls crack. If the temperature is very high during ripening and the nuts sunburn, the hulls will adhere tightly to the shells, giving them the name of "sticktights." If this occurs, you'll have to remove the shells by hand.

After shucking, cure walnuts in a warm (90 to 100 degree F) area with good air circulation for a few weeks until the kernel snaps between the fingers. Don't let the temperature rise above 110 degrees F or the nut oil will turn rancid. After this curing process, store them in a cool area.

Small Fruits and Grapes

BLUEBERRIES

Blueberries (*Vaccinium* spp.) are native to North America. Native Americans and early settlers added the fresh fruit to puddings, cakes, and pemmican, or dried them in the sun or campfire smoke for winter use. The strong, flexible wood makes ideal tool handles.

The fresh fruits of two species—highbush and rabbiteye—are grown in home gardens. A third species, the lowbush blueberry, is useful as a ground cover and produces fruits that are best in syrups and preserves.

There are two subgroups of highbush blueberry: northern and southern. Grow northern highbush blueberries in acid-soil areas of the United States and southern Canada, such as those east of the Mississippi river from New England to North Carolina and in the Maritime Pacific Northwest. The southern highbush does best in South Carolina, Georgia, Florida, the Gulf states, and eastern Texas. Grow rabbiteye blueberries from Virginia south along the Atlantic and Gulf coasts to Texas, and inland to southern Arkansas, mid-Tennessee, and the mountains of northern Georgia.

Late cultivars of highbush need 160 days to mature their fruit, although early and midseason cultivars need only 120 to 140 days. Flower buds withstand temperatures of -15 to -20 degrees F. Half-high cultivars are hybrids of high- and lowbush blueberries that produce high-quality fruit on plants only a foot or two high. They are hardy to Zone 3, where insulating snow protects them against extreme cold.

Avoid planting sites with poor air circulation, but shelter the plants from strong winds. A snow fence gives protection from high winds, and extra mulch in the fall protects the shallow roots from extreme cold. Cool spring temperatures cause red or orange-yellow discoloration of new leaves, but this will disappear when temperatures warm.

Although they'll produce a little fruit with only a few hours of sunlight each day, plants in full sun with moist, acid soil will bear heavily. Soil pH should range from 4.5 to 5.2; a higher pH may cause iron deficiency in the plant and yellowing of the foliage (iron chlorosis). A high pH also causes nitrogen to become less available to blueberries. But although blueberries are acid-loving plants, don't get carried away with soil acidification. Soil pH lower than about 4 can cause aluminum and manganese toxicity, and buds and young shoots will die back.

Adjust the soil pH before planting by using a soil acidifier. Don't use aluminum sulfate. This adds no nutrients to the soil and may cause a buildup of toxic aluminum. Use ammonium sulfate instead; it both acidifies the soil and adds valuable nitrogen. Peat moss worked into the soil will make it slowly more acid over a period of years.

Build up soil organic matter before planting. Don't use the leaves of maple or elm for blueberry soil; they leave an alkaline residue when they rot. Rotted sawdust or peat moss uniformly mixed with good loam and used to fill the planting hole is fine. Soak the sawdust and peat moss before incorporating or it will act like a sponge and dry the root zone. The organic material must be mixed with the soil; filling the hole with plain peat moss or sawdust can damage plants.

Plant in the spring, setting the plants at the same depth as they were in the nursery. Space highbush blueberries 5 feet apart, in rows spaced about 10 feet apart, and rabbiteyes about 6 to 8 feet apart in rows spaced 12 to 14 feet apart. Remove all weak growth and flower buds at planting to encourage strong growth.

The hairlike roots of blueberry can't penetrate heavy soil, so plant only in porous soil with a high organic matter content. Don't plant blueberries where the water table is less than 20 inches below the surface; in addition to restricting root growth, many wet soils, particularly in the South, are infested with *Phytophthora* root rot fungus. If your yard is a swamp with no high ground, plant on small mounds of good soil or in raised beds that elevate the roots above the water table.

There are dozens of blueberry cultivars. Consult the table or check

Different blueberry cultivars are adapted to different areas of the country. Plant those best for your area.

AREA 1: NORTH FLORIDA, GULF COAST, EASTERN TEXAS, LOWER SOUTHWEST, CALIFORNIA (SOUTH OF SAN DIEGO)

Flordablue	Sharpblue	Avonblue	Woodard
Bluegem	Tifblue	Climax	Bluebelle

AREA 2: COASTAL PLAIN OF GEORGIA, SOUTH CAROLINA (SOUTH OF CHARLESTON), GULF STATES, EAST TEXAS, CALIFORNIA (SOUTH OF LOS ANGELES)

Flordablue	Sharpblue	Tifblue	Woodard
Southland	Delite	Briteblue	Climax
Bluebelle			

AREA 3: UPPER PIEDMONT AND MOUNTAINOUS REGIONS OF AREA 2

Bluetta	Patriot	Berkeley	Blue Ridge
Croatan	Bluecrop	Murphy	Cape Fear
Morrow	Bluechip	Lateblue	Tifblue
Woodward	Southland	Delite	Briteblue
Climax	Bluebelle		

AREA 4: SOUTHERN VIRGINIA SOUTH TO PIEDMONT AND COASTAL PLAIN CAROLINAS, TENNESSEE, LOWER OHIO VALLEY, SOUTHERN AND EASTERN ARKANSAS, LOWER SOUTHWEST, AND MID-CALIFORNIA

Morrow	Croatan	Bluecrop	Southland
Murphy	Tifblue	Woodard	Climax
Bluebelle	Patriot (not for coastal plain Carolinas)		

AREA 5: MID-ATLANTIC STATES, OZARK HIGHLANDS, MIDWESTERN STATES, MOUNTAINOUS REGIONS OF AREA 4, WASHINGTON, OREGON, NORTHERN CALIFORNIA.

Bluetta	Lateblue	Collins	Darrow

| Berkeley | Herbert | Bluecrop | Elliott |
| Blueray | Elizabeth | Patriot | Elizabeth |

AREA 6: NEW ENGLAND AND GREAT LAKES STATES

Earliblue	Berkeley	Bluetta	Darrow
Collins	Meader	Northland	Herbert
Patriot	Blueray	Bluecrop	Coville
Bluehaven	Spartan	Northblue	Northcountry
Northsky			

Some blueberry cultivars are hardier than others. If you live in a very cold area, choose the hardiest available. In general, the highbush cultivars are far more hardy than the rabbiteye cultivars

| HIGHBUSH | | |
HARDY	MEDIUM HARDY	TENDER
Patriot	Jersey	Collins
Northland	Burlington	Berkeley
Meader	Rubel	Coville
Bluecrop	Earliblue	Pemberton
Blueray	Rancocas	Dixi
Elliott	Weymouth	Stanley
Herbert	Atlantic	Concord
Bluetta		Southern Highbush
Northcountry		
Northsky		
Northblue		

RABBITEYE

Briteblue		Delite
Tifblue		Woodward
Climax		Homebell

with your county extension service office for those best adapted to your area. Select cultivars that ripen their fruit early, midseason, and late to spread out the harvest season over many weeks and provide for good cross-pollination. Purchase vigorous, disease-free, dormant two-year-old plants 12 to 18 inches high.

Most cultivars are self-fruitful, and a planting of a single cultivar usually produces well. But cross-pollination is always better, especially with rabbiteye blueberries. Plant different cultivars no more than 20 feet apart. Pollination must occur within about three days after the flowers open or you won't have much of a crop. Bumblebees are the best blueberry pollinators, because they fly in inclement weather, but they're scarce, so you'll have to rely on honeybees to do most of the work. You have good pollination activity if you see fifteen bee entries into the flowers within ten minutes. Pollinated flowers remain white and drop within a week of bloom; flowers that have not been pollinated stay on the bush for one to two weeks and turn a brilliant wine color. If you see a lot of purple flowers, you won't have much of a crop. Bees don't particularly like flowers of 'Earliblue', 'Coville', 'Berkeley', 'Jersey', and a few minor cultivars, so interplant these with other cultivars for cross-pollination.

Keep blueberries well weeded for at least the first two or three years. Because they're so shallow rooted, be careful when you cultivate; it is better to use a clean organic mulch around the base of the bush—about 5 bushels of sawdust or wood chips per mature plant.

Cottonseed meal or 10–10–10 fertilizers work well with blueberries. Don't use nitrate of soda, calcium nitrate, bone meal, or wood ashes because they reduce soil acidity. Rabbiteye blueberries respond well to azalea-camellia fertilizer or cottonseed meal. Don't use fertilizers containing muriate of potash (KCl), because blueberries are sensitive to the chlorine compound in this nutrient. Make sure at least half the nitrogen your blueberries receive is in slow-release organic form.

About two to three weeks after planting, fertilize highbush blueberries with the equivalent of about 1 ounce (2 tablespoons) of a 10–10–10 fertilizer per plant. Make a second application in early July in areas with moderate winters. Young rabbiteye plants are very sensitive to fertilizer, so don't fertilize them the first year.

Increase fertilizer applications each year until mature bushes are getting about 1 pound per plant, half applied as bloom begins and the rest six weeks later. Determine the right amount of fertilizer by watching for signs of good vigor or deficiency symptoms. Mature plants should produce several whips near ground level and laterals about 15 inches long. These will have fifteen to twenty leaves.

Highbush blueberries are most often propagated by hardwood cuttings, but semihardwood and softwood cuttings, mounding, layering, leaf-bud cuttings, clump division, and budding also work. Rabbiteye blueberries propagate best as softwood cuttings and sucker division.

Begin pruning immediately after setting your new plants into the ground. Prune each year in the early spring before the buds begin to swell. Some gardeners prefer to prune in the fall, because weak canes can be easily identified as their leaves turn color first; fall-pruned plants, however, may suffer greater winter injury in colder areas. Rabbiteye plants may need pruning only once every several years; highbush plants are pruned annually.

Because blueberries form their flower buds on the current year's wood and bloom on one-year-old wood only, each year's crop is borne farther from the root zone and the bush center. This means that each year nutrients must travel a longer distance to both the fruiting wood and the non-fruiting, "extra" wood. Canes older than five years are not highly productive, nor are bushes with more than about eight to ten

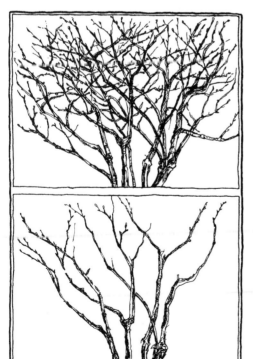

The highbush blueberry is not difficult to prune. Remove the oldest canes and dead or diseased wood, then thin out crossing stems and weak growth. (Top) The bush before pruning. (Bottom) How the bush should look after pruning. The harder the bush is pruned, the fewer fruits it produces, but the larger each fruit will be.

canes. Remove all dead, injured, and weak canes, canes older than five years, and crowded canes first.

After one growing season, vigorous bushes may bear twenty to thirty flower buds. Remove all weak growth and all flower buds on less vigorous plants. After two seasons, let most bushes bear a light crop. Heavy fruit production at this time will dwarf the plant. Remove weak growth. Follow a similar pruning procedure every year, allowing the plant to produce successively larger crops until the bush is mature.

With mature plants, remove dead and injured wood and cut back old and unthrifty canes to ground level. Don't cut back to stubs since these can harbor borers. Remove all soft and irregularly flat-sided basal growth. Next, remove all canes older than five years. These are usually about $1\frac{1}{2}$ inches in diameter at their base. Remove the oldest 20 percent of the canes each year. After most of the pruning is done, remove bushy growth clusters and weak lateral shoots.

Absence of new shoots frequently indicates that the bush is overcrowded with old canes or underfertilized. Proper pruning stimulates new growth; the plant should produce three to five new canes each year.

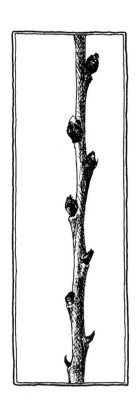

To restore an old blueberry bush, cut it back to the ground. Renewed bushes make substantial vegetative growth the first year and bear an ample crop the following summer. If you're slightly lopper shy, cut back half of each bush and allow the other half to bear fruit. The following year, cut back the unpruned half. This completely rejuvenates the bush in two years while providing a partial crop each year.

Blueberry plants need 1 to 2 inches of water per week during the growing season, or

Blueberries form their flower buds in leaf axils near the top part of the shoot. Buds formed at the lower end of the shoot are smaller, pointed leaf buds. This species forms flower buds only on the current season's growth.

Blueberries are highly ornamental. Use them as accent or specimen plants in your landscape or as beautiful hedges to define your property. 'November-Glow' and 'Ornablue' are strictly ornamental types; don't grow them for their fruit.

RATING	CULTIVAR	NOTES
		HIGHBUSH
Good	Berkeley	Gracefully spreading
Good	Bluechip	Stems amber-red in winter
Excellent	Bluecrop	Fiery red in autumn
Very good	Bluehaven	Half high, upright
Good	Bluejay	Yellow-orange in autumn
Excellent	Blueray	Burgundy red in autumn
Good	Bluetta	Low stature
Excellent	Burlington	Upright, bushy
Good	Collins	Leaves redden early, last long
Good	Coville	Yellow-orange in autumn
Good	Earliblue	Attractive bush shape
Very good	Elliott	Blue-green leaves turn orange-red
Excellent	Friendship	Long-lasting brilliant orange-red
Good	Herbert	Stems yellow in winter
Good	Jersey	Long-lasting yellow-orange in autumn
Very good	Northcountry	Fiery red in autumn; outstanding
Good	Northblue	Dark green leaves turn dark red
Very good	Northland	Orange-red in autumn, yellow stems
Good	Northsky	Bush 10–18 inches; leaves dark red in autumn
Excellent	NovemberGlow	Slender leaves turn bright red
Very good	Ornablue	Profuse bloom, long-lasting autumn color
Good	Rancocas	Slender leaves red in autumn
Very good	Rubel	Long, slender leaves turn bright red
Very good	Tophat	Dwarf, profuse bloom, bonsai-type
		RABBITEYE
Very good	Beckyblue	Powder blue foliage turns yellow-blue

		in autumn; stems red in winter
Very good	Bluegem	Light green foliage turns red
Very good	Bonitablue	Bright red foliage in autumn
Good	Chaucer	Profuse bloom
Excellent	Choice	Outstanding autumn color and winter
		stem appearance
Good	Climax	Round leaves turn fiery red
Very good	Sunshine Blue	Profuse bloom; very fine leaves

at least from fruit set through harvest. Typical drought symptoms include reddened foliage; weak, thin shoots; early defoliation; and decreased fruit set. Don't use overhead sprinklers during ripening, because wetting the berries will cause them to split.

Blueberries are relative pest-free—except for birds. Starlings, robins, and grackles are most destructive, but at least fifteen other types can cause damage. Forget the scarecrows; net your bushes.

Blueberries start producing in the second year after planting and continue in well-managed plantings for more than fifty years. Yields commonly average about 1 pint per bush in the third year, and possibly 20 pints per bush after eight to ten years. I know one gardener who gets 50 pints per bush!

A blue berry is not necessarily a ripe berry. Let the berries hang on the bush for another four days after they turn blue, and they'll accumulate up to 15 percent sugar and increase half again in size. Pick them when they're dead ripe—when the pink ring around the scar has turned blue. Berries harvested as soon as they show a slight pink coloration will ripen off the bush, but the fruit won't be as sweet or as large. Overripe berries shrivel and drop, so pick over the bushes once a week. Blueberries don't ripen simultaneously in the cluster. Roll ripe berries into the palm of the hand with your thumb. This prevents immature berries from detaching and reduces tearing and bruising of the fruit.

BLACKBERRIES

Both blackberries and raspberries belong to the *Rubus* genus and are commonly referred to as bramble fruits. When picked, the blackberry separates at the stem and the core remains inside the fruit. A raspberry separates from its torus, or core, and looks like a thimble in your hand.

Several species go by the name of blackberry. All the common cultivars originated in America. Most have biennial canes, perennial roots, and sharp prickles.

Early settlers considered the blackberry a noxious weed. It was a common wild fruit in both Europe and North America, where the vigorous, vicious canes threatened to take over yard and garden. Because they were so plentiful, there was little reason to cultivate them. The plants were domesticated in Europe by the seventeenth century, but the first American reference to their culture did not appear until 1829; by the late 1840s, the first cultivar, 'Lawton', had been introduced.

Common blackberries have upright, stiff canes and sharp thorns. They are very cold hardy and spread by suckering.

Trailing blackberries, of European origin, produce very long canes that grow at about a 45-degree angle from the base, then droop and run. They are not as hardy as the erect type and produce no suckers, reproducing from tip layering. Their fruit is black.

Dewberries are either black or red. The thin canes run along the ground and tip-layer. They do not sucker.

Thornless blackberries either are mutations of thorny types or are genetically thornless. In the mutant type, it is possible for a single cane or the entire plant to revert back to being thorny. If this happens, remove the entire plant. Genetically thornless cultivars, such as 'Thornfree', 'Smoothstem', and 'Black Satin', reproduce only thornless plants. All thornless blackberries are less hardy than thorny types.

Because blackberries and raspberries are in the same genus, there are a number of hybrids of the two, including 'Loganberry', 'Boysenberry', 'Tayberry', and 'Youngberry'. Grow these as you would blackberries.

Blackberries are adapted to temperate areas of North America but are not considered particularly hardy. They'll do well in Zones 5 to 9, provided you choose the correct type and cultivar. Some gardeners in Zone 4 depend upon insulating snow cover to protect plants from extreme cold.

All blackberries do well in poor soils but will not tolerate wet feet or extremely heavy soils. Root suffocation and rot run rampant where drainage is poor. They're not fussy about pH, as long as it's not extreme. Don't follow strawberry, potato, tomato, or eggplant with blackberries, and keep your plants isolated by at least 700 feet from wild brambles.

Choose the right type and cultivar for your area, and purchase disease-free one-year-old plants. Prepare the soil by working in compost,

Blackberry cultivars are not as numerous as raspberry cultivars, but you still have a good choice. Plant only those best suited to your area.

LOCATION	CULTIVAR
SOUTHERN AREAS OF MIDWEST AND NORTHEAST	Erect, thorny, hardy: Darrow, Illini Hardy, Hedrick Trailing, smooth, less hardy: Smoothstem, Thornfree, Black Satin
SOUTHERN STATES, ARKANSAS, OKLAHOMA	Erect, thorny: Shawnee, Cheyenne, Cherokee, Choctaw, Brazos Erect, smooth: Navaho, Arapaho Trailing: Boysenberry
CALIFORNIA	Trailing: Boysenberry, Olallie
PACIFIC NORTHWEST	Trailing: Thornless Evergreen, Marion, Loganberry, Boysenberry

rotted manure, and amendments the fall before you plant. Plant in the early spring. Space plants 10 feet between rows and 4 feet (erect types) to 7 feet (trailing types) between plants. Set plants as deep as they grew in the nursery, and orient the rows of upright types into the wind to help keep plants upright. If you're using root cuttings, plant them 4 inches deep. Set them so that the end that was closest to the mother plant is slightly raised above the other end.

Soil requirements are the same as for raspberries. Plant sod between rows and keep it mowed. Hand cultivate within rows. Don't use mulch, as it will encourage excess suckering and may keep the soil too damp. Since winter hardiness can be a big concern, don't mow the sod in late summer; the growing grass will compete for water and nutrients with the blackberries and encourage them to harden for winter.

Blackberries are light feeders. A small application of balanced fertilizers applied in early spring is sufficient. Overfeeding will result in rank growth, excessive suckering, and poor hardening of new growth.

If you live on the northern fringe of good blackberry country, give

Erect blackberry plants are often grown free-standing in hills and don't sucker like their cousins the red raspberries. (Right) The plant is properly pruned by heading back some of the lateral branches to force better fruiting.

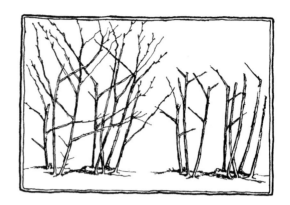

them a little winter protection. Cover trailing canes with leaves and let the snow insulate them. Use windbreaks to block cold, dry winds. Precondition the plants in the fall by withholding water and nutrients and letting the sod grow to harden them off.

Propagate erect blackberries by root cuttings less than ½ inch thick and 4 inches long or by suckering. Propagate trailing types by softwood stem cuttings or tip layering. For tip layering, use canes that have thickened and have small leaves near the tip, giving the cane a "rattail" appearance.

Each summer, prune erect blackberries by heading back the largest canes (primocanes) to about 3 feet when they reach 40 inches. This stimulates strong laterals. Remove unwanted suckers. In the fall, remove fruited canes. In spring, remove damaged canes. Thin the plants to five vigorous canes per running foot of row, and allow the row to spread to only 18 inches at its base. Because even erect blackberries tend to fall over, a support is needed to keep the berries off the ground.

For trailing blackberries, don't head the plants in summer, but allow the primocanes to run on the ground until after harvest. In the fall, remove canes that have borne fruit. In warm climates, tie primocanes to a trellis. In cold areas, leave them on the ground and cover them with several inches of straw. In the spring, select the ten most vigorous canes, cut them back to 8 feet in length, and tie them to the trellis. Remove all other canes.

Blackberries need only an inch of water a week. Too much will cause root rot. These plants have few pests. With good air drainage, isolation, and conscientious removal of diseased plants, you'll have few problems.

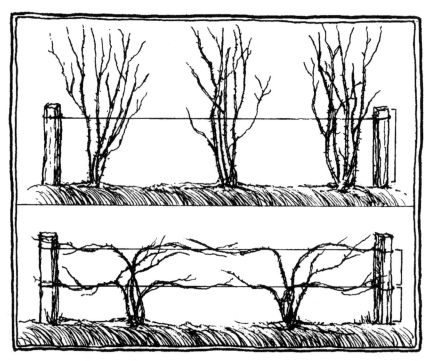

(Top) Vigorous erect blackberries sometimes need the support of a simple one-wire trellis. Fasten the wire 36 inches above the ground on stout posts. (Bottom) Trailing blackberries always need support. Use two wires, the lower fastened 40 inches above the ground and the upper one 20 inches higher. In either case, posts should be 15 feet apart.

Don't harvest blackberries as soon as they color. Wait until the fruit has become dull and separates easily from the stem. Blackberries ripen over a month or two, and you may have to pick every day in hot weather. Ripe blackberries are highly perishable. Don't leave the picked fruit in the sun, or it will turn red and bitter.

RASPBERRIES

Red raspberries were first recorded by Pliny as being harvested from the wild Greek countryside. By 1548, they were mentioned as garden plants in England, where the fruit and leaves were widely used for a soothing gargle, tea, and wine. The fruits were not used for dessert until well into the eighteenth century, probably because they were so perishable. The plants became widely popular by the time of the American Revolution, and the first everbearing types were described in 1778. The American black raspberry was not domesticated until sometime after 1850. As red and black raspberries grew side by side in the gardens of America, a natural cross occurred and the purple raspberry was domesticated.

There are dozens of species of raspberries worldwide, growing from the equator to the Arctic Circle. Domesticated raspberries do best in moderate climates with minimal fluctuating winter temperatures. They are primarily cooler-season plants, growing best when temperatures are between 60 and 70 degrees F. They do poorly when temperatures rise much above 80 degrees F. The red raspberry is generally more cold hardy than the black, but you can expect some damage to any raspberry where temperatures frequently fall below -10 degrees F, particularly in areas where there are strong winds and little snow cover.

Red and purple raspberries do best in Canada, New England, New York, the Dakotas and upper Midwest, and the Rocky Mountain states, even though some of these areas may not have a growing season long enough to ripen the fall crop of everbearers. Middle Atlantic, lower Midwest, and lower West Coast states are best for black raspberries.

Raspberries need plenty of moisture but don't tolerate wet feet; their roots will suffocate where water stands for more than a day. Light, well-drained sandy loam soils are best. Avoid clay soils. Because all bramble fruits are susceptible to soil-borne verticillium wilt, don't plant raspberries where tomatoes, potatoes, eggplants, strawberries, lamb's-quarters, redroot pigweed, or weedy nightshades have grown within several years. Sodded areas often are infested with grubs that destroy raspberry roots. Remove the sod at least a year before planting, and keep your patch away from wild brambles, which may be infected with viruses that will piggyback on aphids to your plants. Separate highly virus-susceptible black raspberries by 700 feet from plantings of red and purple raspberries, and separate all raspberries by 700 feet from wild brambles.

Raspberries contract many foliar diseases, so try to keep the humidity in the area down. Plant in full sun in an area with good air circulation and drainage. Consider northern, eastern, or northeastern slopes near the southern limit for these plants, and southern or southeastern slopes near the northern limit. Because the canes are thin, they are apt to suffer some winter damage in windy locations, so use a windbreak.

Don't transplant raspberries from a neighbor's patch; they are likely to be infected and will contaminate your area. Instead, purchase one-year-old certified disease-free stock. Red raspberry plants are sold as suckers (handles) and black and purple raspberries as tip-layered plants. Tissue-cultured plants are most apt to be disease-free and are often more vigorous growers than those propagated traditionally. To propagate, use suckering, tip layering, or 6-inch root cuttings that each contain a bud.

Superior raspberry cultivars are legion. Red raspberries are popular for all uses. Yellow raspberries are more delicate and fragrant than red but are soft and crumble easily. Purple raspberries are the best for preserves, since they retain their flavor during processing. Everbearing (primocane) types give you a summer and a fall crop each year, but gardeners in extreme northern areas may not have a season long enough to ripen the fall crop. If that's where you hold your hoe, stick to the June-bearing (floricane) types.

Adjust your soil pH to 5.5 to 6.5 and turn under about 500 pounds of rotted manure or compost per 1,000 square feet in the autumn before spring planting.

In the North, set dormant plants in the early spring. If your plants have begun growing, wait until danger of frost has passed before setting them to the field. In the South, set tissue-cultured plants and dormant plants in the spring and potted, mature plants in the fall. Mulch the fall-set plants to protect them against frost heaving.

Set plants of red and yellow raspberries to the same depth as they grew in the nursery, 3 feet apart in rows about 10 feet apart. Spread the roots laterally and head back the top to 5 inches. Set black and purple raspberries about 5 feet apart and positioned so that the center of the crown is about 3 inches below the soil line, with the crown buds pointing up. Remove the old portions of the cane when the plants begin to grow to decrease the incidence of anthracnose.

Tissue-cultured plants have shallow root systems and are more susceptible to drought, wind, and heaving. Mulch these right after planting. Remove the mulch by the end of the first year.

Keeping the suckering red raspberries in bounds may be a problem. Planting them in a trench 18 inches deep with the sides—but not the bottom—lined with a double thickness of plastic sheeting prevents the plants from spreading. You can mow any suckers that escape, but they'll keep coming back.

Once established, raspberries are strong growers. Young plants, however, don't compete well with weeds. Hand weeding and shallow

There are hundreds of raspberry cultivars, in four colors and two types. 'Goldie' and 'Kiwigold' are excellent mutations of 'Heritage'. Aphids will not feed on 'Royalty' and so it rarely succumbs to mosaic virus. E = everbearing .

LOCATION	RED	YELLOW	PURPLE	BLACK
NORTHERN STATES, MIDWEST, EASTERN CANADA	Latham Boyne Milton Newburg Taylor Killarney Nova Heritage (E) Autumn Bliss (E) Redwing (E)	Fallgold (E) Forever Amber (E) Goldie (E) Kiwigold (E)	Marion Brandywine Royalty	Cumberland Bristol Jewel Allen Blackhawk
PACIFIC NORTHWEST	Willamette Chilcotin Skeena Centennial Heritage (E) Amity (E) Autumn Bliss (E)	Goldie (E) Kiwigold (E)		Bristol
NORTHERN CALIFORNIA	Willamette Autumn Bliss (E)			
SOUTHERN STATES	Southland Dormanred			

cultivation are the best way to control weeds. Don't use mulch; it impedes the growth of new canes and may keep soil wet enough to promote rot.

The area between the rows is best planted to sod. Neatly mown grass keeps dust down, soaks up extra water, and helps to harden canes in the fall by providing some competition for available water and nutrients.

If you built up the soil's organic matter before planting and watered your plants with a water-soluble fertilizer, you won't have to fertilize until growth begins. At that time, apply 1 1/2 ounces of a high-nitrogen fertilizer, such as 15–15–15, to each plant. Three ounces of ammonium nitrate or equivalent per 3 feet of row is adequate for mature plants. Use slightly less on younger plants or plants in heavy soil and in areas with low rainfall. Use slightly more on older plants, particularly those in sandy soils and where rainfall is heavy. Apply in early spring before buds break.

Raspberry canes are biennial, although the roots are perennial. All raspberry canes die after two years and are replaced by new ones.

Red and most yellow raspberries have upright growth habits. Flower buds form on new canes in the summer. In June-bearing types, all flower buds overwinter and bloom at once the following spring, producing a single, early-summer crop. The canes then live out the season and die. Fall-bearing types form their flower buds in the summer of the first year, but those on the top foot or so of cane bloom right away to produce a crop in the fall of the first year. That portion of the cane dies back after fruiting. Buds formed on the lower part of the cane overwinter and produce fruit

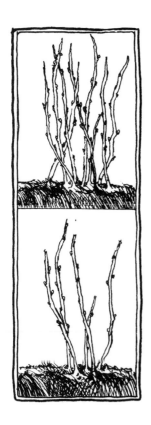

in the summer of their second year. The entire cane then dies at season's end.

To prune red and yellow raspberries, remove dead, weak, and injured canes in the spring. Thin the remaining canes to stand 3 to 4 feet apart. Remove any fruited tips of fall bearers. Keep the rows about 18 inches wide at the base.

In the summer, remove fruited canes after harvest. Head back the excessively tall first-year canes of June bearers to a quarter of their height to keep them from drooping into the aisles. In the fall, remove any remaining fruited canes of June bearers.

June-bearing red and most yellow raspberries are grown in hedgerows and pruned each spring by removing the old dead canes and thinning newer canes to stand about 6 inches apart. Do this for everbearing types too, in addition to removing the fruited tips of one-year-old canes.

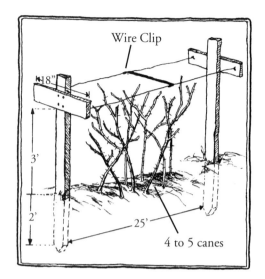

Wire Clip

18"

3'

2'

25'

4 to 5 canes

Red raspberry plants grown on highly fertile soil may become too large and droop to the ground; their berries will get dirty, rot, and be tough to pick in the tangle of canes. Support the plants with a simple trellis to prevent this.

Remove the fruited tips of fall bearers after harvest of the fall crop.

If you dislike the detailed spring pruning raspberries require, try growing fall-bearing raspberries for a single crop. After fall harvest, cut all the canes to the ground, but be careful not to injure the crowns. You won't get a summer crop the next year, but growth of the new canes will be rampant and the fall harvest luxurious. For those who garden in Zones 6 and 7, near the southern limit for raspberries, mow the canes in the fall and again the following summer when they're a foot high. This delays their fruiting until the brutal summer heat has passed.

Black and purple raspberries have a bushier habit. Most June-bearing black and purple raspberries form their flower buds in the summer of the first year, overwinter, and fruit the following summer. The entire cane then dies. You'll rarely encounter fall-bearing black or purple raspberries.

To prune black and purple raspberries, remove dead, injured, and weak canes and laterals in the spring. Head back laterals of black raspberries to 10 inches and those of purple raspberries to 20 inches. The least productive fruit buds on purple raspberries are those nearest the cane, so leave longer laterals to take advantage of the productive buds farther out. Leave at least six laterals per cane. Black raspberries don't have root buds, so new canes grow close to the original crown. Purple raspberries may have many root buds, depending upon the cultivar.

In the summer, remove old canes after harvest. When first-year canes reach a height of 3 feet, head them back to 30 inches. It's important to remove at least 4 to 6 inches of cane at one time; this constitutes a strong

Black and purple raspberries have a growth habit different from that of red raspberries. Top them in summer to force strong laterals upon which flower buds will form. In spring, head the laterals to remove excess buds and to aid in production of good-size fruit.

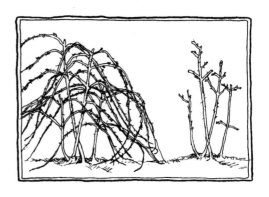

heading cut and forces vigorous laterals. If you let the cane get taller than 3 feet before topping, growth will be inferior. Because canes grow at different rates, the heading-back process may take several weeks. Complete the summer topping before fall, because late-emerging laterals often winter kill. In the fall, if you have fall-bearing black or purple raspberries, remove the fruited lateral tip. Remove canes that have borne fruit when the leaves begin to fade.

Because raspberry canes tend to flop over, most gardeners train them to some support. The simplest are the T-trellis and the hill systems. For the T-trellis, set 5-foot posts 2 feet into the ground and 25 feet apart. Nail a 20-inch crosspiece near the top of each post, fasten a 12-gauge wire to each end, and run the wire between posts along each side of the row. Canes are contained between the wires. Run short lengths of wire between the rows to reduce wire spreading. Loosen the wires in the fall because winter cold contracts the metal and may pull the posts out of the ground.

Black and purple raspberries are usually maintained as original crowns in the hill system. They are not allowed to spread like the red and yellow raspberries. You can grow them as free-standing plants or, less commonly, drive a post into the ground and tie the canes to it. This is particularly helpful in windy locations.

Raspberries are delicate plants, susceptible to foliar diseases caused by both high humidity and drought. They need an inch or two of water per week during summer, but don't wet the foliage. Use drip irrigation.

Pests are a problem. Deal with insects as outlined earlier in the book. If you suspect a plant is infected with a virus, remove it immediately.

Summer-top black and purple raspberries by snapping off the top 3 or 4 inches of the main shoot when the plants reach about 3 feet. You can summer-top overly vigorous erect blackberries as well. Topping encourages the formation of vigorous laterals.

Raspberries are very perishable fruits. Pick them at their peak color, before you notice darker hues. They'll separate easily from the core at that time but won't crumble. Cool immediately. Red raspberries keep for a few days in the refrigerator; black and purple raspberries keep slightly longer. No raspberry will ripen after harvest. At the peak of the summer season, you may have to harvest every morning at about 9, after the dew has dried but before the air temperatures rise. Pack the berries only in $1/2$-pint baskets and never more than four berries deep to prevent crushing.

ELDERBERRIES

Although American elderberries (*Sambucus* spp.) were first domesticated in this country about 1760, Native Americans and early settlers used the ripe purple fruits from wild bushes for dyes, preserves, and wine. The pickled, unopened flower buds were sometimes used as a substitute for capers. With the soft pith removed, the hollow stem was widely used for tapping sugar maple trees, and the tannin-rich shoots were ground and used to tan leather.

The American elderberry grows well from Nova Scotia to Minnesota and south to Florida and Texas. It can be grown in gardens farther west, but other species may be better adapted to arid or Mediterranean conditions. Elderberries rarely suffer winter injury.

Because there are a number of viruses that infect elder, purchase virus-free one-year-old plants from a reputable nursery. 'Adams 1', 'Adams 2', 'Johns', and 'Ezyoff' are good cultivars. The plants are only partially self-fruitful, so plant at least two cultivars.

Elderberries are not fussy about soil conditions, so long as the soil is well-drained. Plant on a gentle slope and in full sun to reduce the incidence of diseases. Set the plants in the early spring at the same depth as they grew in the nursery, 5 feet apart in rows spaced 10 feet apart. You generally won't have to turn under any fertilizer before planting.

Fertilizer requirements are modest. Beginning in the second year after planting, side dress the plants with $\frac{1}{2}$ pound of 10–10–10 or equivalent per plant per year of age up to a maximum of 5 pounds per plant. Plants showing vigorous growth and good flower and fruit production do not need feeding.

Propagate elderberries by softwood cuttings, tip layering, or suckering. Because some plants may become virus-ridden, be sure you have clean plant stock before you propagate. Thin out older canes early each spring, leaving about a half dozen vigorous one-, two-, and three-year-old canes per bush. These produce the best fruit.

Birds are the biggest pests, and nothing but netting will keep them away from the berries.

You'll harvest a limited crop the second year and be in full production by late summer of the third or fourth year—about 12 to 15 pounds of fruit per bush. Harvest the entire cluster when the fruits are plump, brightly colored, and just beginning to soften. Strip the fruits from the cluster and refrigerate immediately. Elderberries deteriorate rapidly—within a couple hours at room temperature—and they will not ripen further off the bush.

FIGS

The fig (*Ficus carica*) is an ancient fruit, revered by the Egyptians and praised in the Bible and the Greek classics of Homer and Plato. Probably introduced into England by the Romans, its culture there was nearly forgotten until Thomas Becket set out fig gardens in Sussex in the twelfth century. Figs were used as laxatives and cold and cough cures in the early sixteenth century. Spanish missionaries introduced fig trees into California around 1750; the U.S. industry has been centered there since.

There are four kinds of figs grown for their fruit: Smyrna, White San Pedro, Caprifig, and Adriatic. The first three require pollination by the blastophaga fig wasp, which will not tolerate northern climates. Their cultivation is limited to California and warmer areas of the southern United States. The discussion here will focus on the Adriatic fig, which produces fruit parthenocarpically and can be grown in a much wider area of this country. Popular hardy cultivars of the Adriatic fig include 'Brown Turkey', 'Celeste', and 'Brunswick'. Order one-year-old plants.

A well-hardened Adriatic fig tree will tolerate 10 degrees F but is easily killed by a sudden drop to 20 degrees F in early autumn. It can be grown with reasonable care in the Maritime Pacific Northwest and from Virginia south—anywhere winter temperatures remain above 20 degrees F. With winter protection, it can be grown as far north as Zone 6.

A good, rich, well-drained heavy loam soil high in organic matter produces the best crops. With a soil pH of 7 or slightly higher, the plants remain fairly small but produce abundant, sweet fruit. Higher soil pH causes leaf drop. Figs are fairly salt-tolerant, which makes them great for planting in coastal gardens.

Because many gardens are borderline for figs, give them as much shelter and sun as possible. Gardeners in southern Rhode Island and New Jersey plant them on southern or southwestern exposures to maximize the amount of heat they receive. If possible, plant figs against a south-facing masonry wall to take advantage of the collected solar warmth.

Prepare the soil by working in abundant compost and adjusting the pH to 7 to 7.5. Set out figs in the spring, about 12 feet apart and 2 inches deeper than they grew in the nursery. When they have been watered in, cut them back to a height of 2 feet to force strong laterals.

Keep your plants mulched heavily with an organic mulch. This will help to keep weeds under control. If you've planted in very rich soil, you'll need little fertilizer. If the soil is less than ideal, apply 1 pound of 10–10–10 or equivalent per foot of tree height per year. Apply a third of the fertilizer in late winter, a third in early June, and a third in late July. If you garden on the fig borderline, omit the July application. In all cases, avoid excessive fertilizer.

Train your figs to either tree or bush form. The bush form is more popular among borderline gardeners because it produces a plant with multiple stems; if one or two are damaged by winter cold, there are others to take their place. A strong heading back at planting initiates the bush form. Early the following spring, select about a half dozen strong branches, spaced about 8 inches apart, for scaffolds and remove the rest.

Shoots begin to grow in the spring and set flower buds along their upper parts. These flower and produce a late-summer crop right away. Flower buds formed farther down on the new shoots overwinter and produce a crop the following year. Meanwhile, new shoots are setting buds for the late-summer crop.

Figs don't bear fruit on older wood. Prune early every spring, cutting back to buds on old shoots that have borne a crop. Head back vigorous scaffolds and lanky shoots to force new laterals, and remove dead and crowded shoots to open the bush.

Figs have few pests. If ants are attracted to the sweet fruit, just brush them off.

Figs begin to bear the second year. They are one of the most difficult fruits to harvest. If picked too soon, they won't ripen; if left too long, they'll sour on the bush. When they're soft, twist or cut them from the stem at the neck. Wear gloves, because the latex that leaks from the wound can irritate the skin. Figs keep for a week or so in the refrigerator.

Winter protection is necessary for borderline gardeners. Planting on a southern or southwestern exposure or against a south-facing wall is a good place to start. You can also bank soil around the trunk to a height of 18 inches in the late fall to protect the collar. Some northern gardeners bend the plants to the ground, peg them, and cover them with a foot of soil, then cover the mound with several inches of leaves. If your plants are too large to bury, wrap the tops with heavy burlap and surround them with cornstalks for insulation. (I built a movable box frame with rake and eave ventilation under a removable roof. When placed over the figs and filled with leaves for insulation, it provides excellent winter protection.) Wait until leaf fall before you bury or cover your fig plants.

You can plant figs in movable shrub tubs or 12-inch pots and move them into an unheated basement during winter. Fill the tubs or pots with a mixture of seven parts loam, three parts sharp sand, and three parts peat, and adjust the pH to 7. Add a handful of 10–10–10 fertilizer or equivalent to get growth off to a good start. To propagate figs, use straight hardwood cuttings, mallet cuttings, or tip layering.

KIWIFRUITS

Kiwifruits are the edible members of the *Actinidia* genus. These Chinese natives were introduced into New Zealand in 1904 and, until 1959, were known as Chinese gooseberries. They were valued for food and medicine in their native land, but the name was not appealing and few people outside China bothered with the fruit. Smart New Zealand growers changed the name to the more appealing kiwifruit, and demand skyrocketed.

Actinidia deliciosa var. *deliciosa*, the common supermarket kiwi, is hardy only in the warmer areas of the United States, notably California, the Maritime Pacific Northwest, and the Gulf Coast. Other species, including *A. kolomikta* and *A. arguta*, are hardier farther north and produce abundant crops of small, green, fuzzless fruit. Fruit of *A. kolomikta* is about the size of a grape and that of *A. arguta* slightly larger. Although both tolerate extreme cold, they need a 140-day season to ripen their crop. Plants of *A. deliciosa* survive temperatures of 10 to 15 degrees F but require a growing season of at least 220 days. Kiwis are heavy feeders and do best on rich, moist, slightly acid soil, although they will grow in poorer soil if it is well drained. Plant kiwis where air drainage is good and where they will be protected from strong winds.

Kiwifruit plants are woody vines that are either male or female (dioecious). They require good cross-pollination. Purchase one-year-old plants in the proportion of one male to every six females.

A. kolomikta has a popular cultivar known as 'Arctic Beauty'. Through overuse of the name, 'Arctic Beauty' has become a nickname for the species. Many plants sold as cultivars under that name are actually the Russian cultivar 'Krupnoplodnaya'. *A. kolomikta* is hardy to Zone 3 and produces the smallest plants of the fruit-bearing kiwis (8 to 10 feet). It has reddish foliage, blooms early, and is susceptible to late frosts. The sweet fruits drop when ripe. Fruit of this species is extremely high in vitamin C, which may make up 1 percent of its fresh weight.

A. arguta, better known as the hardy kiwi, bowerberry, or Siberian gooseberry, reliably survives winters in Zone 4. It is a rampant grower and requires heavy annual pruning. Its fruit contains about 30 times more vitamin C than an orange, pound for pound, and is slightly smaller than, but has flavor superior to, *A. deliciosa*. *A. arguta purpurea* is hardy to about 0 degrees F and produces sweet purple fruits that are easy to spot beneath the green foliage. Several cultivars of *A. arguta* are available.

A. deliciosa's best cultivar is 'Hayward'. This species must be grown south of Zone 5 but far enough north to allow some winter chilling.

Plant kiwifruits in the early spring on a southeastern exposure protected from the wind. Set kiwi plants with their crowns slightly above

'Issai'	Hardy to Zone 6.
'119-40'	Self-fertile. Hardy to Zone 4.
'124-40'	Hardy to Zone 4. Pollinate with '127-40'.
'127-40'	Male pollenizer for '124-40' and '125-40'. Hardy to Zone 4.
'125-40'	Vigorous female plant. Hardy to Zone 4.
'Meader #1'	Female. Hardy to Zone 4.
'Ananasnaja'	A *kolomikta* x *arguta* cross that is hardy to Zone 4 and tastes like a pineapple.
'Longwood'	Male and female plants of this cultivar are vigorous and hardy to Zone 4.
'Geneva #1 and 2'	Hardy to Zone 4.
'74-8'	A female plant that does best with either '74-46' or '74-52' as pollenizers.

the soil. The plants can produce up to 15 to 20 feet of new growth per season, so give them lots of room. Space northern species about 10 feet apart within the row and 15 feet apart between rows. Space plants of *A. deliciosa* about 20 feet apart each way.

Kiwifruits have very shallow feeder root systems located within 2 inches of the soil surface, so limit cultivation to scraping only. Mulching with a nonpacking organic material can be advantageous but can cause crown rot in some areas. Don't let the mulch contact the vine trunk.

Fertilizer requirements vary according to location and environmental conditions. For most areas, a split application of 1 pound of ammonium nitrate (33–0–0) per mature plant in the spring, with two-thirds of the fertilizer being applied early and the final third after bloom, is adequate. Excessive fertilizer can be detrimental, particularly on northern plantings, because it causes new growth that may not be winter hardy.

Propagate new plants from softwood cuttings.

Because kiwi is a woody vine, it must be trained to a trellis or arbor. The most common method is to construct a five-wire, crossbar trellis 6 feet above the ground. Sink end posts about 3 to 4 feet into the ground, 20 feet apart, and anchor them firmly. Mount a 5-foot pressure-treated 2 x 4 onto each end post and string five 12-gauge wires between them.

Kiwifruits need to be trained to a trellis or other support to produce the best crops. The supports should be tall enough to allow you to walk beneath them.

Use turnbuckles to keep the wires taut. Center the plants beneath the central wire.

The first year, train the vine to a single trunk up to and above the wires. When it reaches 4 inches above the central wire, cut it back to 4 inches below the wire, forcing two strong shoots in a Y shape. Train these *cordons* to grow along the central wire in either direction. Head them to about 36 inches during the winter of the first season.

As growth resumes the following season, laterals develop from the cordons. Space the strongest laterals on either side of the cordon about 24 inches apart. Remove the weakest ones. Tie both the cordons and the laterals loosely to the wires. Do not wrap them around the wires. Twisting the shoots reduces production. Handle the wood carefully because it's very brittle.

Kiwifruit plants bleed profusely. Prune only in very early spring, cutting out twisted and crossing branches, suckers, and fruiting wood older than three years. Removing the oldest third of the wood each spring ensures young, fruitful wood. Shape the vine to conform to the size and reach of the trellis.

The kiwifruit takes up to eight years to come into bearing and another eight years to produce a full crop. It flowers between mid-May and mid-July only on the current season's shoots out of one-year-old wood. Older wood, and current shoots from older wood, generally do not flower.

In warm climates, kiwifruit plants, particularly those of *A. deliciosa*, can require up to 25 gallons of water per day, or 35 to 45 inches of rain or irrigation, during the growing season.

Kiwifruits have few pests. Leaf rollers and scale may be problems. Crown gall and root rot might develop in poorly drained soils, and root knot nematodes sometimes cause trouble. Like grapes, the kiwi is susceptible to *Botrytis cinerea* in damp weather. The worst pest is the house cat. The roots of *Actinidia* spp. produce a substance that has the same effect upon cats as catnip, and they often claw, rub, chew, and dig the plants to death. Although not all cats react to kiwi in such a destructive manner, it is safer to place chicken-wire cages around the vines for the first three years.

A mature female plant of *A. deliciosa* can produce up to 300 pounds of fruit. Plants of the northern species are somewhat smaller and produce less. But with the average U.S. per capita consumption at only ¼ pound a year, that's a whole lot of kiwifruit to eat. Fruits ripen from September to early December, depending upon the area, and can be harvested when slightly immature and stored for several months in a cool place with good air circulation. Place them in egg cartons and store them in the refrigerator away from apples and other ethylene-producing fruits.

Protect the trunk to reduce winter damage. After a few good frosts near the end of the first season, wrap the trunks with tree wrap to prevent sunscald. This is particularly important on northern species. Leave the wrap on the trunks until the plants are mature, or for at least the first three years.

LINGONBERRIES

Native Americans relished lingonberries (*Vaccinium vitis-idaea*), and Thoreau ate them stewed with sugar in the Maine woods. They're rich in vitamin C, and both the Scandinavians and the Cree of northern Canada used them as a cold remedy. They make a superb topping for venison and roast goose, and pancakes drenched in lingonberry syrup are a Swedish tradition. For years the wild stock supplied market demand, but no more.

A native of northern temperate, boreal, and arctic regions, the lingonberry is a broad-leaved evergreen 12 to 18 inches high that is cold hardy to Zone 2 and drought-tolerant. Covered with insulating snow, it survives the coldest Canadian winters, but it won't take the heat of southern gardens.

Plant lingonberries in a sunny spot with good air and soil drainage. A southeastern exposure, where the bushes receive sun most of the day but have protection from drying winter winds beneath drifted snow, is ideal. An acid, highly organic soil with a pH of 5 produces the best crops. Plants make their best growth when 5 to 7 pounds of peat moss or compost have been incorporated into the soil in each 100 square feet of row.

There are two varieties of lingonberries. The wild North American variety blooms only in the spring. The European variety blooms in spring and again in midsummer and is more commonly found in nurseries. This double bloom period is great, because the May bloom produces fruit that ripens in midsummer, and the summer bloom, which occurs when fruit from the first bloom is ripening, produces fruit for harvest in late September and October. Because blooming flowers are hardy only to 30 degrees F, the first bloom is often frost-killed.

Order European-variety plants early from a reputable nursery. Older plants, available in small pots, take better and are worth the extra cost.

'Koralle' is the most popular cultivar and makes up most of the European commercial production. 'Red Pearl' ripens fruit one to two weeks earlier than 'Koralle'. 'Sussi', 'Erntedank', 'Erntekrone', and 'Erntesegen' all produce large, mild-flavored fruit. 'Masovia', my all-time favorite, grows rampant and lush in my garden.

The lingonberry trails along the ground sending up vertical shoots (uprights) that produce fruit at their tips. It's an acid-loving, slow-growing plant that takes a long time to fill in a bed.

Plant in the spring after danger of severe spring cold has passed, setting the plants as deeply as they grew in the nursery, about 12 inches apart in rows 36 inches apart. By the second year, plants begin to spread, sending up risers increasingly distant from the crown. Your aim is to establish a small hedgerow 18 inches wide.

Lingonberries cannot compete with weeds. Hand pulling is the only way to remove weeds without injuring the lingonberry's shallow root system. Mulching helps to control weeds. Plants mulched with organic materials produce stronger growth and up to four times the yield of unmulched plants. A peat moss mulch, applied a couple of inches deep right after planting and increased in thickness each year, works well. Rhizomes will spread through its lower layers.

Like other members of the blueberry family, lingonberries require little fertilizer. If shoots grow vigorously and risers grow erect for several inches, fertility is right. If growth is soft with large, dark green leaves, you've overfertilized. If risers are short and their foliage is pale yellow or red, feed your plants a small handful of complete fertilizer, such as 5–10–10 or an organic equivalent. Apply it in a circle around a mature plant (older than 3 years) in the early spring. Use smaller amounts for younger plants. Lingonberries are sensitive to chlorides, so keep deicing salt, water from chlorinated pools, and fertilizers containing potassium chloride far away.

Propagate the plants by crown division, transplanting clumps every few years, or older plants will become crowded and unthrifty. Leave part of the rhizome attached to the clump to allow for the rapid spread of the plant. Stem or rhizome cuttings produce plants that won't spread rapidly. The only pruning required is the removal of dead and damaged shoots every spring. Lingonberries are relatively free of insects and diseases.

Plants will be in full production after a few years. A normal fall fruit yield, with about 50 percent fruit set, is 10 pounds per square yard of row. Cross-pollination is necessary, and bumblebees are the best pollinators.

Pick the firm, cranberrylike fruits singly into a pint container and store them in the refrigerator for up to three weeks. They can be frozen or preserved as sauce for later use.

RIBES

Currants, gooseberries, and jostaberries all belong to the genus *Ribes* and have similar cultural requirements.

Currants—red, white, and black—are native to colder climates. They were first mentioned as being grown and used medicinally in Germany in 1484, and by 1600 they were common in English gardens, where they were called "currants," probably because they resembled the small dried grapes exported from the Greek port of Corinth and known by that name.

The currant bears long clusters of red, white, or black fruits. Harvest the entire cluster, and strip the berries off during processing.

The white currant is a color mutation of the red. The black currant, however, belongs to a separate species. The black currant has never been popular in this country, partly because of its strong flavor, partly because of its greater susceptibility to blister rust, and partly because our forefathers thought the fruit bred worms in the stomach. It has four times the vitamin C of an orange and greater medicinal value than its red or white cousins. Europeans today drink black currant juice as we drink grape juice, but Americans are most familiar with it is as crème de cassis, a currant-flavored brandy liqueur. The musky flavor of the fruit is most pronounced in currants grown near the southern limit of their range and decreases the farther north they are grown.

Like currants, *gooseberries* (*R. grossularia*) are native to northern regions. They were first mentioned in English writings in 1557. They were used in sauces and as appetizers, and were thought especially helpful to pregnant women. European gooseberries grew poorly in this country, but Native Americans and early trappers sometimes ate the fruits of native species. Around the time of the Civil War, nurserymen developed improved cultivars of our American species to satisfy the small demand for plants. Today there are an estimated five thousand gooseberry cultivars, although only a few hundred are commonly grown.

The *jostaberry* is a hybrid of the black currant and gooseberry. Developed by the German scientist Rudolf Bauer in the 1950s, jostaberries have a unique flavor and a very high vitamin C content. The fruits

The gooseberry is armed and dangerous. Wear gloves when you pick the fruits, which are borne singly along the spiny stem. The dried flower parts protrude at the blossom end of both gooseberries and currants.

resemble black currants, and the thornless plant has hybrid vigor and resistance to many of the pests that plague its parents.

The compact plants of *Ribes* gained a certain amount of popularity in the United States in the early part of this century. Around the time of World War I, however, realizing that *Ribes* were an alternate host for the white pine blister rust, a fungus that was decimating five-needled pines, the federal government banned their planting and mustered the Boy Scouts, CCC, and WPA to destroy both wild and cultivated plants.

In 1966, the federal government rescinded its ban, but states with economically important stands of white pine continue to restrict their planting. Delaware, Maine, New Jersey, and North Carolina prohibit the importation of all *Ribes*. Massachusetts, New Hampshire, New York, Rhode Island, and Vermont allow plantings in certain areas by permission only. If you live in one of these states, contact your state department of agriculture for information. Regardless of where you live, you may want to check with your state department of agriculture just to be sure.

Because of their northern origins, *Ribes* plants grow well in Zones 3 to 5, provided you have at least a 120-day growing season. They'll take winter temperatures as low as -31 degrees F but will drop their leaves when summer temperatures rise much above 86 degrees F. This is not a plant for southern gardens.

Plant *Ribes* in partial shade or on the cooler northern, northeastern, or northwestern sides of a building, hedge, or hill. All *Ribes* are sensitive to chloride, so keep them away from swimming pools and walks or drives where deicing salt is used. Cool, moist, humusy, well-drained silt or clay loams at least 2 feet deep are best. Work in plenty of compost before planting. Bushes on light, droughty soil make poor growth, drop their leaves in midsummer, and ripen bland fruit prematurely.

Order one- or two-year-old plants in the spring prior to fall planting. You may have to show a permit issued by your state department of agriculture allowing the planting of *Ribes* in your area.

Although the red and white currants, gooseberries, and jostaberries are self-fruitful, they'll bear larger, earlier-ripening crops with cross-pollination. Plant at least two different cultivars of each kind. Black currants are usually self-sterile and must be cross-pollinated.

'Cherry', 'Minnesota 71', and 'Red Lake' are outstanding cultivars of red currants, and 'White Imperial' is one of the best white currants. 'Consort' is a self-fertile black currant thought to be immune to white pine blister rust. Several jostaberry cultivars are available, including 'Jostaki', 'Jostagranda', and 'Jostina'. 'Pixwell' and 'Poorman' are standard gooseberry cultivars; 'Welcome' is a relatively new one that has fewer thorns than the others.

All *Ribes* begin growth very early in the spring. If your garden doesn't dry out early enough, plant them in mid to late fall, after the growing season has ended but before the ground freezes. Fall planting allows the root system to become established before the spring burst of growth. Be sure to mulch heavily to reduce heaving. Set currant and gooseberry plants about 5 feet apart. Cut the tops back to about 8 inches from the soil line. This first pruning is optional, but I believe in it; it prevents too many leaves from demanding too much from the small root system. Jostaberry plants grow much larger, so plant them 6 to 8 feet apart in rows spaced 8 feet apart.

Because these plants do best under cool conditions, maintain a thick organic mulch around them. If you have good soil and use composted manure as a mulch, you won't need to fertilize. Renew the mulch around each plant every spring. If you are not using organic mulches and can't get manure, use a commercial fertilizer such as 10–10–10 early each spring. Don't fertilize the year of planting. Give a very small handful the second year, and a large handful each year after that. Don't get too fussy. These are hardy plants and don't need coddling.

Currants and gooseberries are easily pruned by removing a few old canes each spring to make room for the growth of new canes.

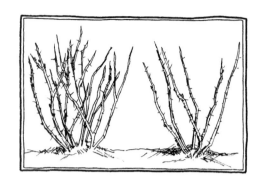

Propagate *Ribes* from hardwood cuttings. Plant the cuttings into the soil with just their upper buds showing. Keep them watered and weeded, and about half of them will quickly root. You can also propagate by tip layering and clump division.

Prune in late winter. Red and white currants and gooseberries produce flower buds at the base of one-year-old shoots and on spurs on older canes. Canes up to three years old are the most productive. Black currants bear more heavily on one-year-old wood. Jostaberries are somewhere in between.

Remove canes that droop to the ground or that are diseased, dead, or broken. Then remove canes older than three years. Next, cut out weak canes that made less than 6 inches of growth the previous season. Lastly, thin the remaining canes so that a half-dozen one-year-old, three two-year-old, and three three-year-old canes remain.

Few pests bother these plants. Leaf drop in summer is more likely the result of hot, dry weather than of a virus.

Harvest begins in June or July of the second year after planting. Plants in good condition are considered mature and in top production in their fifth year, and with proper care, they'll bear good crops for at least thirty years. The fruit ripens over a two-week period and hangs well.

Currants bear clusters of one to two dozen fruits each. Twist off the entire cluster, or strig. Strip the fruit from the strig into a container. You'll have to pick gooseberries and jostaberries individually. Don gloves before you delve into a gooseberry bush. If you're planning to eat the fruit fresh or to press it into tangy juice, pick the berries when they are fully colored, slightly softened, and dead ripe; if it's jelly you want, pick them slightly underripe and firm, when their pectin content is highest. No *Ribes* will ripen further off the bush, so don't pick them too soon or they'll be too tart to eat.

Most *Ribes* fruits don't store well, so use them quickly; jostaberries keep for about a week in the refrigerator.

STRAWBERRIES

Like many other small fruits, the strawberries (*Fragaria* spp.) were used for centuries but not cultivated until relatively recently. Ancient Greeks and Romans enjoyed the wild strawberry but confused the plant with *Arbutus*. French gardeners began to cultivate it in the fourteenth century. By the sixteenth century, the strawberry was a popular European garden plant. Considered a delicacy, the fruits were eaten with sugar and cream or turned into wine, and eating the dried leaves was thought to cure depression. Another species, the Alpine strawberry (*F. rosacea*), was grown in European gardens by the mid-eighteenth century and praised for its long fruiting season.

The wild American strawberry (*F. virginiana*), that highly flavored but tiny red jewel of the fields, was enjoyed by the earliest colonists and sent to France in 1624. Nine decades later, the larger Chilean strawberry (*F. chilensis*) found its way into France from the coasts of South America. The resulting hybrids were the ancestors of our modern cultivars.

The modern strawberry is like the onion; cultivars have been developed for different parts of the country, and planting the wrong cultivar in the wrong spot spells disaster. It has the greatest specificity of planting location of any fruit plant. There are cultivars that grow well in Zone 3 and those that do best in Zone 10. Southern cultivars are short-day plants, not winter hardy, and need little chilling. Northern cultivars are long-day plants, hardy, and need considerable chilling. In fact, temperature and day length are major factors in strawberry culture. In general, long days and high temperatures encourage leaf and runner development, while short days and low temperatures encourage flower formation in June bearers. Day length makes no difference to everbearers or the newer day-neutral types.

Because strawberry plants grow close to the ground and are prone to frost damage during early bloom, it is important to choose a site with very good air drainage. Strawberries will grow well on any soil type, as long as it is well drained and well supplied with humus. Wet soil encourages red stele disease and overstimulates vegetative growth. Dense foliage cover increases fruit rot.

Don't plant strawberries where raspberries, peas, potatoes, tomatoes, beets, eggplants, peppers, or other strawberries grew previously because of the possibility of disease carryover in the soil. Avoid sites formerly planted with peaches and cherries because of nematodes and formerly sodded sites because of the near-certain presence of white grubs. If you suspect your soil is infested with root-knot nematodes, plant rye, corn, or hairy vetch for a year or two to starve them out. If you have white grubs, a crop or two of buckwheat, beans, or clover will get rid of them.

Build up the soil's organic matter by adding compost or manure. Just before planting, broadcast about 25 pounds of 5–10–10 or equivalent and till it in.

Virus infection is common, causing otherwise healthy-looking plants to remain unproductive and stunted. Buy only certified, virus- and nematode-free one-year-old plants to start your bed.

There are three types of strawberry plants: June bearers, everbearers, and day-neutrals. *June bearers* produce a single crop each year, usually around June. The fruits are very flavorful and generally freeze well. *Everbearers* produce a few berries throughout the season, with peaks of production in early and late summer. The fruits are not as flavorful as those of the June bearers, but harvest is spread out over a longer period. Everbearers are shy runner producers. *Day-neutrals* are similar to everbearers in that they bear fruit throughout the summer, but they do so at a more steady rate. A crop is produced every six weeks or so instead of having early- and late-summer peaks. Fruit size remains constant and does not drop off as in other cultivars. The plants produce up to Thanksgiving in milder climates, and fruit quality is better than in the everbearing types.

There are hundreds of strawberry cultivars, and they change as fast as those of tomatoes. Check with your county agent for the latest recommendations for your area.

Plant only those adapted to your area. Southern June-bearing cultivars have short chilling requirements, set flower buds under short days, and tolerate high heat. Everbearers do poorly in the South. Northern June-bearing cultivars have a long rest requirement, are cold hardy, and produce under long days. Everbearers do well in the North. Because of diseases, most eastern cultivars don't tolerate western conditions, and vice versa. Day-neutrals like 'Tristar' and 'Tribute' generally do well in northern states, while 'Mrak', 'Yolo', and 'Selva' work for California and similar climates.

Strawberry cultivars change frequently. Check with your county agent for newer selections especially adapted to your area. E = everbearer; DN = day-neutral.

Region	Cultivars
NORTHEAST	Catskill, Fairfax, Sparkle, Surecrop, Midway, Earliglow, Redcoat, Honeoye, Guardian, Redchief, Vesper, Bounty, Ozark Beauty (E), Gem (E), Tribute (DN), Tristar (DN)
MID-ATLANTIC	Catskill, Fairfax, Sparkle, Albritton, Sunrise, Ozark Beauty (E)
SOUTHEAST	Albritton, Sunrise, Blakemore, Pocahontas
GULF COAST	Daybreak, Florida Ninety, Tangi, Tioga
MIDWEST	Catskill, Guardian, Midway, Ogallala (E)
ROCKY MOUNTAINS	Fort Laramie (E), Sparkle, Ogallala (E)
NORTHWEST	Fairfax, Blakemore, Sparkle, Catskill, Northwest
CALIFORNIA AND SOUTHWEST	Fresno

The strawberry plant has leaves and roots emerging from a crown. The mother plant produces runners that root to form runner (daughter) plants. These in turn produce runners to form more plants.

Plant strawberries in the fall and winter in the South but in the early spring in other areas. Earliness is the trick to starting a good bed. The sooner you get them into the ground, the faster they develop root systems and become established. Most gardeners use a matted-row system, with plants set 18 inches apart in rows spaced 4 feet apart. For June-bearers, pinch off all the blossoms the first year. For everbearing types, pinch off the blossoms for the June crop, then let the plants flower for a fall crop. As the plants run, let the row widen to 18 inches, leaving 1-foot walkways between rows.

You can also try the hill system or the spaced row system. The hill system produces the largest fruits and is especially useful for everbearers. The spaced row system is a combination of the matted-row and hill systems. Hold the runners in place with bobby pins, which soon rust away and present no problems, as would stones or clothespins.

Day-neutrals are planted on raised beds about 6 inches high by 24 inches wide, with centers about 4 feet apart. Plant two rows per bed, 1 foot apart. Remove all runners. Pinch off all the blossoms for the first two years to encourage uniform bearing habits.

Set strawberry plants in a shallow furrow and fan the roots out. Roots laid in parallel to the soil surface with plants bent up at a 90-degree angle produce very weak growth and may not survive the first season. Set the plants so that the base of the crown is at soil level and no roots are exposed. If the soil is fertile, water the plants in with clear water. If it's a little sandy, use ½ pint of soluble fertilizer. Once growth begins, side dress the plants very lightly.

Because they have such small, shallow root systems and can't forage well for nutrients, strawberries quickly become nutrient deficient. Too much fertilizer, however, may cause excessive foliage growth that interferes with fruit set and increases fruit rot. If your plants are not growing vigorously, broadcast about 80 pounds of 5–10–10 per 1,000 square feet

Plant strawberries in a double- or triple-row hill system to produce the largest fruit. In a spaced row system, the mother plants are spaced about 2 feet apart in rows spaced about 42 inches apart. Six runners are allowed to form and are spaced to produce plants about 6 inches apart. All other runners are removed. Hold the runners in place with bobby pins until they root.

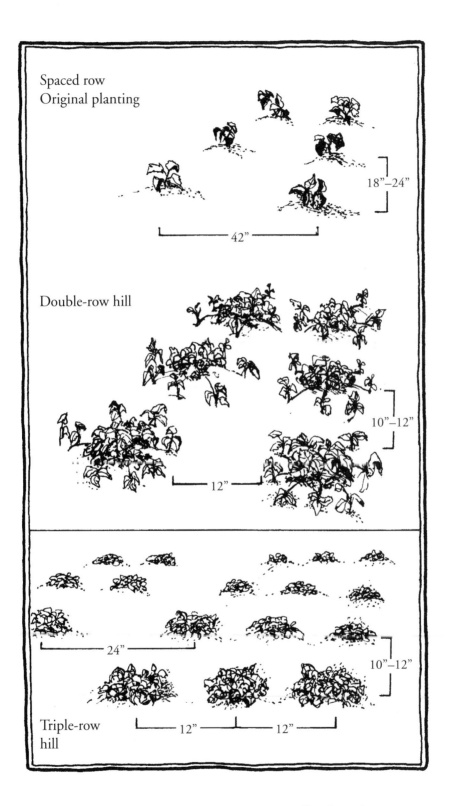

Spaced row
Original planting

18"–24"

42"

Double-row hill

10"–12"

12"

24"

10"–12"

12"   12"

Triple-row
hill

after harvest. Do it when leaves are dry, and brush the granules off the foliage by dragging a burlap bag across the plants. I don't recommend spring fertilization because that can overstimulate the foliage. Use of strawy manure as a winter mulch may be all the fertilizer you need on a sandy soil but could be too much on a fertile one.

Fertilize day-neutrals by applying about 10 pounds of 10–10–10 or equivalent per 1,000 square feet in early August of the year of planting. The following spring, apply about 20 pounds of 10–10–10 per 1,000 square feet. Continue this feeding regimen each year for the few years that the plants will remain productive.

Strawberry plants cannot compete with weeds. Because of their small and shallow root systems, any cultivation you do must be careful and light. Use an organic mulch to control weeds, but compensate for nitrogen depleted from the soil as the mulch breaks down. Black plastic should be avoided; strawberries cannot set runners through the plastic, and in very hot climates the plastic may cause the fruit to scald.

If you need more weed-control help and have the room, try geese. One goose per 1,000 square feet should do. Mature geese eat some types of weeds, such as crabgrass and foxtail, but won't harm the strawberries.

Remove the blossoms for the entire first season (June-bearing plants), for the first crop (everbearing plants), or for the first few weeks after planting (day-neutral plants). Early flowering stunts the vegetative growth and delays the plant's establishment.

A fence will keep the geese in and dogs out. Put water at one end of the row and some corn at the other. The geese will waddle back and forth between them, eating juicy weeds along the way. Believe me, geese really work; just watch where you step.

Strawberries need an inch of water a week, preferably through drip irrigation to avoid wetting the foliage and fruit when weather is cool. If the temperature is above 95 degrees F, turn on the sprinklers to cool the foliage and fruit for best production.

Strawberries have many

pests, but because the plants don't usually occupy a site for long periods of time, pests often don't have the chance to build up. If you choose your site carefully and keep it clean and weed-free, you may not have to spray at all.

Powdery mildew will cause strawberry leaves to turn purple and curl upward. Use lime-sulfur for control, but stop spraying about two weeks before harvest. Catfacing or nubbins—small, deformed berries—are caused by poor pollination or, more rarely, disease. If your bed is old, renovate it or replant a new bed in a different location.

Propagate June bearers and day-neutrals from runners. Plunge a flowerpot filled with compost into the soil next to a strawberry plant, stick the runner tip into it, let the daughter plant develop, remove the pot, clip the runner, and transplant the new plant. Because everbearers don't produce many runners, they are usually propagated through crown division. Alpine strawberries are usually propagated by seed.

Strawberries taste best when they're fully red, though fruit picked three-quarters red will ripen off the vine. Fruit picked only half colored tastes bad, even though it will eventually develop a full red color. Pick the fruit by placing the thumb and forefinger on the stem and twisting, lifting, and pulling at the same time to detach the fruit with 1/2 inch of stem and the green calyx, or cap, intact. Picking without the cap intact will cause the fruit to rot very quickly. Cap the fruits just before eating. Hold only one or two fruits in your hand at once, and place them into a shallow basket to prevent crushing.

Ripening continues over a two- to three-week period. You'll have to harvest every day, or at least every other day. A ripe fruit remains edible for about two days, depending upon cultivar and weather.

After three or four years, you'll notice your strawberry bed running out, or declining in vigor and yield. If you suspect a viral infection, turn under the plants and forget about strawberries in that spot. The more usual cause of running out is crowding, weeds, and the production of inferior seedlings. This means it's time to renovate.

Right after harvest, mow your entire bed to a height of 2 inches with a rotary lawn mower. Be careful not to injure the crowns. Rake out the debris vigorously and cart it away, pull out weak plants and weeds, thin the remaining plants to stand about 8 inches apart, and reestablish walkways with a rototiller. Top dress the bed with your regular annual fertilizer application and water it in well. Vigorous new growth will begin in a few

Raised beds make day-neutral strawberries easier to grow because the soil warms faster in spring. Make the beds about 6 inches high and 2 feet wide, with the centers of the beds 4 feet apart, leaving a 2-foot-wide walkway between beds.

12"

6"

24"

24"

8"

12"

weeks. A bed can be renewed twice in this manner. After that, your strawberries will have been in the same spot for too long and pests will have begun to build up. Then it's better to move the bed to another location.

Hardened strawberry plants will tolerate -10 degrees F, but they are apt to heave because of their shallow root systems. Apply a winter mulch. In the fall, after a few hard freezes but before the temperature drops to 20 degrees F, spread about 3 inches of clean straw, pine needles, or cornstalks over the plants. The plants should appear to be about half covered. Too much mulch will cause ice to form near the plants, and insulation will be lost. The mulch keeps the soil frozen to reduce heaving and helps trap snow for insulation. In the spring after new growth begins, pull off half the mulch and leave it in the walkways to reduce weed growth. The remaining mulch won't hurt the strawberry plants; they'll grow through it, and you may damage them if you try to remove it.

Be sure to use clean straw. If you're not sure how weed-free it is, stack the bales near the bed in September and cut them open. Water them or wait for a soaking rain, then cover them with clear plastic. Heat will

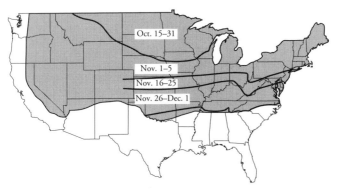

Mulching should begin by the first date listed for your area and be completed by the last date listed. Strawberries in the southern United States and along the Pacific Coast usually need no winter mulch protection.

build up and, combined with the dampness, cause any seeds to germinate. Subsequent cold will kill the seedlings.

Because of their low growth habits and their early bloom, strawberry blossoms are often killed by late frosts. If you expect a spring frost during bloom, pull the winter mulch back over the plants, or set up your garden sprinkler to water the plants. Turn it on when the temperature drops to 34 degrees F, and don't turn it off until the ice that coats the flowers melts. The blossoms will be protected down to 22 degrees F.

HIGHBUSH CRANBERRIES

The fruit of the highbush cranberry (*Viburnum trilobum*), also called the cranberry tree, Guelder rose, or whitten tree, has long been used as a substitute for cranberries (*Vaccinium* spp.) They're eaten with honey and flour in Scandinavia, where they are also made into a liqueur. They are used today for jelly and sauce and are a reasonable substitute for the real cranberry, to which they are not related.

Highbush cranberries will succeed anywhere the weather is cool and moist, from New Brunswick to British Columbia and across the northern United States from New York to South Dakota and the Pacific Northwest. They'll take the cold, but they won't take drought. Although they will tolerate partial shade, they produce the best crops in full sun. Plant them in good soil adjusted to a pH of 6.0 to 7.5.

'Andrews', 'Wentworth', 'Hahs', and 'Manitou Pembina' are worthy cultivars. The fruit of 'Phillips', developed at the University of New

Hampshire, does not produce the musky odor of other cultivars and makes a very fine, clear jelly.

In the early spring, plant one-year-old plants at the depth at which they grew in the nursery, 7 feet apart in rows 15 feet apart. Water them in well, and water them frequently to promote rapid growth the first year.

You can propagate the plants by softwood cuttings taken in midsummer, but let them develop good root systems before you transplant them to the garden. The base of the current season's growth produces good plants by simple layering in midsummer.

Pruning is minimal. Remove only dead, damaged, or crowded wood. There are few pests to worry about. Occasionally a tarnished plant bug might deform the blossoms and young fruit.

You'll have a limited harvest in the third season, but it will be full-blown by the fifth. Pick the fruit when they're fully mature but before they've been hit by a frost.

SASKATOONS

There are several species of *Amelanchier* used for food and ornamental purposes, including *A. arborea*, the eastern serviceberry (Juneberry, shad-bush, or sweet pear), but *A. alnifolia*, or saskatoon, is the dominant one. Native Americans added the saskatoon berries liberally to pemmican, and early settlers considered them a major source of fresh fruit. Today, this blueberrylike fruit is used in preserves, pies, jelly, and syrup, and it has reached some commercial importance in Canada.

This fruit is well adapted to Canada and the northern and north-central prairie states south to New Mexico and California. It does well in Zones 3 through 8. It tolerates most soils except for those very poorly drained or poorly aerated and is not fussy about pH, growing well in a range of 6 to 7.5. Saskatoons are among the first fruit trees to bloom; be sure you have good air circulation and drainage to prevent frost damage.

There are numerous cultivars that bear delicious fruit. Try 'Pembina' and 'Sturgeon'. Plant well-branched plants 6 to 12 inches tall and head them back to about 3 inches. Space plants 8 feet apart in rows 8 feet apart. Use an organic mulch.

You probably won't have to fertilize, but if your soil and plant growth are poor, try applying about $1/2$ pound of 10–10–10 per plant each year per year of plant age up to a maximum of 5 pounds. Don't overfertilize, particularly if fire blight is present in your area.

You can propagate the plants by suckers, root cuttings, or softwood cuttings. Dig dormant suckers, shorten them to 3 inches, and plant them in a nursery row for a year before transplanting. Take root cuttings about $^1/_2$ inch in diameter and 5 inches long in early spring and plant them stem end up less than $^1/_4$ inch deep. Water well.

Pruning is simple. Retain about a half-dozen vigorous canes on each new bush. As the plant matures, remove low branches and top it at 6 feet. Fruit is borne on the previous year's growth or older, so leave old wood intact. Occasionally remove a few of the oldest canes as they become unproductive.

Plants in this genus are related to the apple and get many of the same diseases. Several rusts, which have as alternate hosts the red cedar, the southern white cedar, and the common juniper, sometimes cause problems. Remove these alternate hosts where possible, or plant as far from them as you can. Fire blight occasionally devastates a planting; remove the blighted portions, disinfect your pruning shears after each cut, and don't fertilize. Feeding encourages the tender new growth most susceptible to fire blight.

The plants begin to bear after two to four years and reach maximum production after ten years, when you'll harvest from 10 to 15 pounds of fruit per bush in midsummer. For jelly, harvest the berries slightly underripe, when pectin is high; for wine, pick them fully ripe, when sugar content is at its peak.

JUJUBE

The jujube (*Ziziphus jujuba*) is a native of China, where its fruit has been used for over four thousand years. This fruit resembles a date with a pit and can contain about 22 percent sugar. Pliny said they were brought from Syria to Rome at the end of Augustus's reign. From there they spread over southern Europe and were introduced into North Carolina in 1837.

They will tolerate a wide range of soil conditions and temperatures—extremes of -25 to 120 degrees F when planted in a sunny location on a southern exposure. 'Lang', 'Li', and 'Silverhill' are popular cultivars.

Plant the trees in the early spring, about 30 feet apart. Mulch but don't cultivate them, because that will produce excessive suckering. The trees require cross-pollination and bloom late, usually escaping late frosts. To propagate, try root cuttings and grafts, because seedlings grow slowly.

A mature tree produces about 100 pounds of fruit that ripens over a month or more. Pick jujubes every few days as the fruit turns red-brown. They'll keep in storage for about two months at 50 degrees F.

NANKING CHERRIES
The Nanking cherry (*Prunus tomentosa*), also known as mountain cherry, Manchu cherry, Mongolian cherry, or Chinese bush cherry, is a native of China and Manchuria introduced into the United States in 1882.

Most seedlings produce good fruit, so there are not many cultivars to choose from. The Nanking cherry has been crossed with the western sand cherry (*P. besseyi*) to produce the cultivars 'Leto' and 'Damanka'.

This plant tolerates semiarid conditions, winters at -40 degrees F, and broiling heat. You can grow it from Zones 3a to 6b with little problem. In fact, it does well in the high plains, where not much else will grow. Nanking cherries bloom early and are susceptible to late frosts. They need cross-pollination for the best fruit set.

Set the plants in full sun in well-drained soil. Keep them open and well aerated to reduce fungal diseases. Periodically rejuvenate the plants by cutting them to the ground. To propagate, plant the seeds in the fall or stratify them for three months in the refrigerator. You can also take both hardwood and softwood cuttings.

After several years, you will harvest up to 15 pounds of cherries per bush. Leave the stems attached to the plant when you harvest; to pull them off may damage the reproductive wood for the next crop.

BUFFALOBERRIES
Buffaloberry (*Shepherdia argentea*) is one of the few plants that thrives in the high plains of eastern Montana and bordering states. Also called the Nebraska currant, it is a slow-growing, thorny shrub that reaches heights of 6 to 18 feet. Its small, red fruits were used by Native Americans and early settlers to make a fine relish that was eaten with fresh buffalo meat, hence the name. They are native to the Great Plains north to Manitoba and Saskatchewan and south to New Mexico, Kansas, and Nebraska.

Buffaloberries require well drained soil and thrive along riverbanks. They need no pruning and are propagated by sowing seeds outdoors in the autumn or by taking hardwood cuttings in October that will root by the following October. The plants are dioecious; plant one male to five females for good crops.

Because most buffaloberries are propagated from seed, there is great variability among the plants and fruits. The scarlet (and sometimes yellow) berries will hang in clusters well into the winter but should be protected from birds if you want to use them. A light frost improves their flavor, which is somewhere between that of a red currant and a grape. They retain their flavor nicely when dried. Extract the single seed and turn the fruit into jelly, juice, syrup, or relish for your buffalo steaks.

GRAPES

Grapes are as old as civilization. Archaeologists have found grape seeds in Egyptian mummies and in Bronze Age Swiss Lake dwellings. Both the Greeks and the Romans honored a god of vines and wine, and the Greek poet Hesiod gave directions for growing grapes. Virgil described fifteen cultivars, and Pliny, ninety-one. By the early Christian era, the European grape, or *Vitis vinifera*, had become the chief cultivated plant among the Greeks and Romans.

European grapes were carried to North America by Spanish missionaries, who planted them throughout New Mexico, Arizona, and California. Lord Delaware urged its planting in Virginia in 1616, and by 1619, the Virginia Colonial Assembly had compelled every householder to plant ten cuttings and learn grape culture. But because the European grape wasn't adapted to eastern North America it succumbed to pests and diseases common in the humid East and South. The wine industry flourished only in the dry, hot areas of California. When Louisiana Jesuits finally established a successful winery, they did it with native grapes.

There are several species of grapes native to North America. Of these, the muscadine (also called bullace or scuppernong) and the fox grapes are the most important. Because they are lower in sugar, more acidic, and have a stronger flavor than the European grapes, they make a better juice and dessert grape but a poorer-quality wine. And because they're native, they have resistance to pests that ravaged the European grape.

Despite this inborn adaptation to pests and diseases, the American grapes were not cultivated until 1722; the first cultivars were described around 1800, and by 1830, the viticulture industry had become firmly established in the United States—with American grapes. Prior to 1850 grapes were cultivated exclusively for wine, but by the Civil War jams, juice, and other products had begun to appear on the market.

The European grape is hardy to Zone 6 but thrives only in the drier

Decide first which grape species grows best in your area, then which cultivars are right for you. Here's a list of American grapes adapted to different regions.

NORTHEAST
> Beta, Blue Jay, Red Amber

MID-ATLANTIC
> Brighton, Catawba, Concord, Delaware, Fredonia, Moore Early, Niagara, Ontario, Portland, Seneca, Van Buren, Worden

MIDWEST
> Brighton, Catawba, Concord, Delaware, Fredonia, Golden Muscat, Lenoir, Niagara, Norton, Portland, Sheridan, Worden

SOUTHEAST
> Blue Lake, Catawba, Champanel, Concord, Delaware, Ellen Scott, Extra, Fredonia, Lenoir, Niagara

ROCKY MOUNTAINS
> Beta

LLANO ESTACADO
> Campbell Early (Island Belle), Concord, Delaware, Ellen Scott, Golden Muscat, Niagara, Worden

NORTHWEST
> Campbell Early, Concord, Golden Muscat, Niabell, Niagara, Worden

SOUTHWEST
> Concord, Niabell

areas of the western United States and won't tolerate temperatures much below 0 degrees F. It's grown commercially in California, Arizona, the Pacific Northwest, and some areas of the Northeast as far north as coastal Massachusetts. It needs a two- to three-month rest period. The earliest-maturing cultivars need to accumulate about one thousand six hundred degree days to ripen properly.

Muscadine grapes thrive where most other grapes do not—in the South Atlantic states from eastern North Carolina to Florida, the Gulf states, Arkansas, southeast Oklahoma, and eastern Texas. They tolerate temperatures down to about 10 degrees F.

American grapes of species other than the muscadine are widely adapted. Most cultivars are derived from the fox grape, but some origi-

European grapes are highly specialized for wine. Some are also good for table use, but you'll find them difficult to grow well in most areas.

WINE GRAPES		TABLE GRAPES
RED	WHITE	
Carignane	Muscat	Emperor
Grenache	Sauvignon Blanc	Cardinal
Mission	Sevillon	Perlette
Zinfandel		Ribier
		Thompson Seedless
		Red Flame

Muscadine grapes do best in the southern United States. Plant mostly pistillate-flowered plants, but you do need some perfect-flowered plants for pollination. 'Thomas', 'Magoon', 'Dearing', and 'Burgaw' are best for the home garden.

PISTILLATE-FLOWERED	PERFECT-FLOWERED
Creek	Dulcet
Eden	Tarheel
Flowers	Noble
James	Pride
Mish	Wallace
Hunt	Willard
Topsail	Magnolia
Higgins	Yuga
Thomas	Chowan
	Carlos
	Magoon
	Dearing
	Burgaw

nate from other American species. Those from *V. riparia* are better adapted to colder areas of the United States. They also make reasonably good wine. Cultivars of *V. champini, V. lincecumii, V. rupestris,* and *V. bourquiniana* are better adapted to warmer areas.

The fox grape thrives as far north as Zone 5, but you can extend its range a little by choosing the right cultivars. It's a good grape for the Pacific Northwest and areas east of the Rocky Mountains and does especially well in the North and Northeast. This grape requires a 160-day growing season and an average summer temperature of 65 degrees F. It needs many sunny days in August, September, and October to ripen the fruit. Areas that receive more than 6 inches of rain during May, June, and July and more than 5 inches during August, September, and October are not great for fox grapes because of the increased incidence of disease.

French hybrid grapes are crosses of the European grape with one of several species of American grapes. They have characteristics intermediate to those of their parents and are more widely adapted than the European grapes. They make better wine than American grapes, but not as good as the European grapes. They are more resistant to pests than the European but less resistant than the American. The crosses *V. vinifera* x *V. lince-cumii* (turkey grape) and *V. vinifera* x *V. rupestris* (sand grape) grow in ranges intermediate between those of their parents.

Researchers in California have given a big boost to the raisin industry by creating a grape that shrivels into high-quality raisins right on the vine. The cultivar, named 'DOVine', is an early-season white seedless grape. It is the first hybrid developed from a cross of two seedless cultivars ('P79-101' x 'Fresno Seedless'). By snipping the canes when the fruit matures but leaving the fruit on the trellis to shrivel and increase in sugar, you can make raisins without the postharvest drying common for centuries. You can do this with other cultivars as well, but they won't make such fine raisins as 'DOVine'. If you like raisins and live in a warmer region of the country, plant 'DOVine' and see what happens.

All grapes are late bloomers, so spring frost is not usually a problem. Because grapes ripen late, however, early fall frosts can be. High temperatures and high humidity, especially in late summer, will ruin your crop.

Locate your vineyard in full sun and on a slope with good air drainage. Don't replant to old vineyard sites that might be infested with pests. If you can't plant somewhere else, put the area into grass for at least two years before replanting with grapevines.

French hybrid grapes make good wine and are easier to grow than the European species. Many cultivars were originally designated with the name of the breeder followed by a number; their alternate names appear in parentheses.

Red	White
Seibel 13053	Seibel 5279 (Aurora)
Kuhlmann 188-2 (Foch)	Seyve-Villard 5376 (Seyval)
Baco 1 (Baco Noir)	Seibel 4986 (Rayon d'Or)
Seibel 9549 (De Chaunac)	
Seibel 1000 (Rosette)	
Seibel 5898 (Rougeon)	

Although the fox grape tolerates poor soil drainage, all grapes do best in well-drained soil. In fact, good soil drainage should be your primary concern, as grape roots can extend to depths of 15 feet and spread up to 32 feet from the trunk. Loams high in organic matter make the best grape soils, and some growers claim that clay loams give the sweetest, best-flavored grapes. Lighter soils promote early ripening and very sweet fruit but weak growth and low yields. The secret to growing good grapes is organic matter. Turn under as much as you can when preparing the soil for planting. Turn under composted manure or leaves, then plant a cover crop of winter rye in the fall prior to spring planting. Adjust soil pH to between 4.5 and 5.5. Don't overfertilize; excessive fertility causes rampant shoot growth that might winter-kill and small, poorly colored, flat-tasting grapes that ripen late and are highly susceptible to rots.

One-year-old plants are best; two-year-old plants are okay if conditions are good, but they may be culls. Fox and muscadine grapes should be on their own roots, but European grapes should be grafted to phylloxera- and nematode-resistant stock. 'Dogridge' is one popular rootstock. Most grapes are self-fruitful. Muscadine grapes are available in both imperfect- (pistillate-) and perfect-flowered cultivars. Most of your muscadine plants should be pistillate flowered, which produce the finest grapes. Plant only enough perfect-flowered vines for good pollination, one for every six to eight pistillate vines.

Plant in the early spring. Run rows north to south to get the best light distribution. If you must plant your rows east to west, space them slightly farther apart to allow as much light penetration through the vines as possible. Space the vines about 8 feet apart. Set self-rooted plants of American species about 2 inches deeper than they grew in the nursery. Set plants of European grapes as deep as they grew in the nursery, with the graft union above the soil line. Water the plants well but don't fertilize them, since grapes are very sensitive to salts. Cut the vines back to two buds; try to leave a short side stub to hold the twine for training.

Use an organic mulch to control weeds and to keep the soil moist and cool. Established grapevines will do well in sod that's kept mown. If the vines are growing too luxuriously near the end of the season, stop mowing and let the grass growth reduce water and nutrients in the soil to slow vine growth and speed hardening. If you mulch your vines, sow an annual cover like spring oats or buckwheat into the mulch at summer's end. These will also compete with the vine for water and nutrients but will not interfere with vine growth the following spring.

My grandfather used to say that a vine must struggle to make good wine. That's not far from the truth. Grapes are strong growers and can easily be overstimulated by too much water or too-high fertility. Fertilize them only when necessary, and use only enough to give satisfactory growth. Manure is an excellent grape fertilizer, especially on young vines, but be sure to apply it only in the late fall or early spring. If you have no manure, apply $1/2$ pound of 10–10–10 to a one-year-old vine, 1 pound to a two-year-old vine, and $1^1/2$ pounds to a three-year-old or older vine. Do this about two to three weeks before spring growth begins. With mature plants, broadcast the fertilizer in a broad band 6 feet wide on either side of the row. Depending upon the cultivar, new shoots of fox grapes should grow 6 to 8 feet per season, and those of muscadines, 2 to 3 feet. Shoots of European vines should be somewhere between these in length.

Don't overwater. Vines that have just enough water will have soft, green shoot tips. If water is inadequate, the shoot tips harden and darken to a gray-green. If the vines are extremely dry, the leaves curl, dry, and drop. A slight shortage during ripening will slow shoot growth and hasten ripening, but a severe shortage delays ripening and might interfere with proper hardening.

Grapes are one of the easiest plants to propagate. Hardwood cuttings work well, and tip layering is a good way to replace missing vines within a row. Because of nematodes and phylloxera, *vinifera* vines must be grafted onto resistant stocks, such as 'Dogridge', 'St. George', '1613', or 'AxR #1'.

Grapes need support to produce good fruit. Over the centuries, a number of different methods have been used to support grapevines. The four-arm Kniffin system is simple and can be used for any variety. Construct a trellis at planting using posts of decay-resistant wood such as black locust, cedar, or redwood. Immediately after planting, tie a length of twine to the vine and run it up to the first wire to give the shoot something to grow on. Rub off any suckers that rise from the roots. By the end of the first season, the shoots should be two or more feet long, depending on the cultivar.

Prune early the following spring by removing all canes but the strongest. Cut this cane back to the lower wire, to which it is tied. If the cane grew less than 3 feet the first year, cut it back to two buds. After two seasons in the field, train two new canes to the first wire and head them to about four buds each. Tie a third new cane to the second wire and head it back to the wire.

After three seasons, three of the arms and the fruiting canes have been formed. The arms are 6 to 10 inches long, with two extending in opposite directions from the trunk along each wire. Each summer, new shoots arise from buds on the arms and will bear fruit the next season. Another shoot on each arm is cut back to a short stub bearing two buds. This is called the renewal spur. The vine should be mature by the fourth year, and you'll simply have to maintain the established framework.

You must fully understand the fruiting habit of grapes to prune a mature vine correctly. By the end of the season, compound buds have formed at the nodes of new shoots. These give rise to shoots the following spring. These shoots bear from two to four flower clusters that form

Grapevines are most frequently grown on trellises. The end posts must be anchored firmly to keep the trellis from collapsing. A diagonally set post supported by a deadman at the end of the row is a good anchor but gets in the way of mowing and other chores.

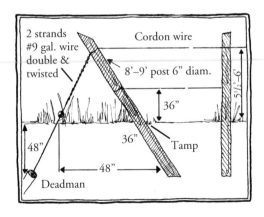

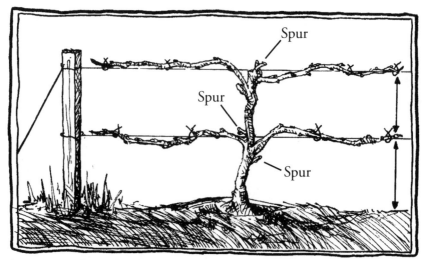

Common and simple, the four-arm Kniffin training system allows only four canes to remain after pruning. These are trained along wires and produce a full crop. Spurs remain at the vine trunk to form the buds from which replacement canes will grow. This system uses two wires in the trellis, the lower about 30 inches above the ground and the upper about 24 to 30 inches above the lower.

fruits that ripen at the end of the summer. Meanwhile, new compound buds are forming on the new shoots to bear a crop the following year. If the primary fruiting shoots are killed by a spring frost, secondary shoots form and bear a partial crop.

What if you do not prune your vines? Four canes, each having twenty buds, will produce eighty shoots the first year. If you allow each of these to produce twenty buds, your vine will have sixteen hundred shoots the following year. Each year your grapes will get smaller and be of poorer quality. This is why the grape is the most heavily pruned of all the fruit crops; pruning regulates the cluster, fruit size, and spread of the plant.

Prune grapes with a vengeance in the early spring. Cut all canes 4 feet from the trunk. Select four canes, one originating from each arm, slightly thicker than a pencil. These will bear the crop. If there is more than one suitable cane on each arm, choose the one closest to the trunk. If there are none, choose one arising from the trunk near the arm.

Shorten these canes to bear ten to fifteen buds each, for a total of forty to sixty buds per vine. Leave fewer buds on weaker vines and slightly more on vigorous vines. Tie the canes to the wire with twine,

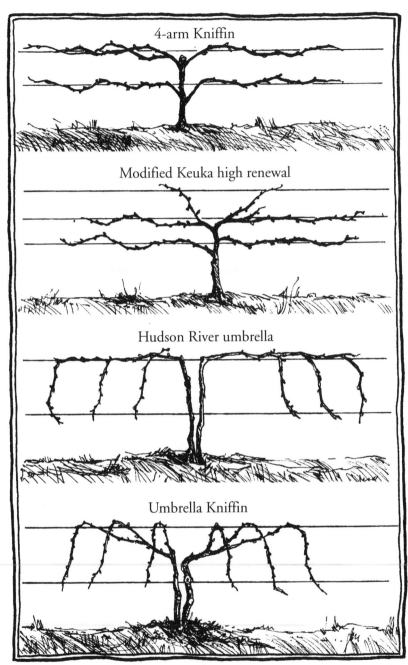

Other training systems—the modified Keuka, Hudson River umbrella, and umbrella Kniffin—are shown along with the four-arm Kniffin. Note the three wires in the modified Keuka system.

which is durable enough to last one season but will rot off by the second. Don't use nylon stockings or wire ties. Tie the trunk to both wires for good support, and renew these ties each year.

Next, choose four more canes near the base of each arm or on the trunk near each arm, and head them to two buds each. These renewal spurs provide new shoots for the following season. The stronger cane to arise is allowed to bear the crop the following year. Remove all other canes and old tendrils. Remove old arms every few years by choosing a cane growing directly from the trunk for the replacement arm.

Arbors are popular in home gardens but compromise fruit quality for beauty. If you want one, follow the pruning for the four-arm Kniffin system, but extend the vine to more arms, depending upon the size of the arbor.

Grapevines can be trained to cover an arbor through an extension of the four-arm Kniffin, employing the development of as many arms as necessary to cover the arbor. Set two or more vines on each side of the arbor and train them to meet in the middle of the top.

If you have a neglected vine you want to save, cut it off at the base. Some of the shoots may have tip-layered themselves, so be sure you get all the plants out. Fertilize the stump well and it will throw vigorous shoots. Train the best of these to form a trunk, and you're back in business. I once rejuvenated 260 grapevines with a chain saw and lost only one.

There are lots of grape pests. Diseases are rampant in the humid East. I once had a person ask me where she could buy a raisin vine like her neighbor's; actually, her neighbor's 'Concord' vines were infected with black rot, a fungus that causes grapes to blacken, shrivel, and resemble hard raisins. A potassium deficiency can cause leaves to turn black or purple near the season's end. Have your soil tested and add potash if necessary. Japanese beetles love grape leaves, and birds will eat your grapes as soon as they are sweet. The only good way to keep birds out is to drape the vines with netting three weeks before the fruit ripens.

Grapevines also are very susceptible to air pollution. Ozone causes oxidant stippling between the veins on the upper surface of mature leaves. 'Delaware' seems resistant; 'Catawba', 'Niagara', and 'DeChaunac' are highly susceptible; 'Concord' is somewhere in between.

Grapes are ripe when the stems brown, the seeds turn brown-black, the skin slips easily on American types, and the fruit gives off a full, heavy aroma. They won't ripen further off the vine. Don't rely on color, because the fruits often turn color long before they're ripe. You can allow a small crop the third year and a full crop the fourth year and thereafter.

Harvest European and most American grapes by cutting the cluster from the shoot. Pick muscadine grapes by shaking them onto a sheet or by picking individual berries from the cluster. Light fall frosts usually don't bother the crop because it's protected by the heavy leaf canopy.

If your cultivars are not fully adapted to your area, you'll have to provide winter protection. Train them to two trunks so that if one winter-kills, the other might survive. Bank soil around the crown. Choose early-ripening cultivars to allow the vine time to harden off in the fall. Provide a windbreak, especially in dry areas. If some of your new shoots suffer severe spring frost damage, strip all new growth from the vine. This will force vigorous secondary shoot growth and the vine will not suffer much. If you let some of the primary growth remain, shoots will be too vigorous and secondary growth suppressed, resulting in a few long shoots and a ragged-looking vine that might take a few years to recover.

Index

Almonds, 184–85
Apples
  antique cultivars, 145, 146
  best regions for, 140
  biennial bearing, 152
  clonal stock, 141–44
  color strains, 145, 148
  cultivars by region, 144
  diseases, 147–48, 150–51
  double-worked, 145
  dwarf, 144
  fertilizing, 150
  fruit drops, 24, 151–52
  fruiting habits, 19
  growing tips for, 149
  harvest dates, 141
  harvesting, 152
  limb bending, 18
  low-chill, 148
  midwinter thaws and, 27
  mulching, 150
  Mutsu, pollen of, 21
  partially self-fruitful, 149
  planting distances, 150
  pollen sterile, 149
  pollinating, 150
  propagating, 32, 34
  pruning, 151
  purchasing, 140–41
  scab-resistant cultivars, 145
  seedling stock, 141
  single-worked, 145
  soil requirements, 63, 140
  spur-type strains, 145–48
  storage period, 136
  thinning, 25
  water requirements, 89
Apricots, 162–63
  midwinter thaws and, 27
  thinning, 25

Bacillus thuringiensis, 127, 128
Biennial bearing, 19
Blackberries

cultivars by region, 204
fertilizing, 204
hardiness zones, 203
harvesting, 206
pests, 205
propagating, 31, 34, 205
pruning, 205
soil requirements, 203–4
water requirements, 205
winter protection, 205
Blueberries
  cultivars by region, 196–97
  fertilizing, 198–99
  fruiting habits, 19
  hardiness of, 197
  hardiness zones, 194
  harvesting, 202
  landscaping cultivars, 201–2
  mulching, 88
  pests, 202
  planting, 194–95
  pollinating, 198
  propagating, 32, 199
  pruning, 108, 199–200
  purchasing, 195–98
  from seed, 31
  soil requirements, 10, 63
  water requirements, 200–2
  yields, 48, 202
Boysenberries, 203
Buffaloberries, 238–39
  salt-tolerant, 68
  from seed, 28

Cherries
  cultivars, 166, 168
  diseases and pests, 169–71
  dwarf, 166
  fruit drops, 24, 167
  hardiness zones, 164
  harvesting, 167–69
  planting, 165
  pollinating, 169
  propagating, 32, 34

pruning, 167
purchasing, 165–66
rootstocks, 166
from seed, 28
species, 164
water requirements, 165
Cherry-plums, 164
Chestnuts, 185–87
Cover crops, 69
  acid soil, 71
Cranberries, highbush, 235–36
  soil requirements, 10
Cultivation, 85–86
Cultural requirements, 7
  light, 7–8
  nutrients, 9–11
  soil pH, 9, 10–11
  temperature, 8
  water, 10, 11
Currants, 222–23
  propagating, 32
  from seed, 31
Cuttings
  hardwood, 31–32
  propagating, 32–34
  root, 34

Dormancy, 25–26
  cold hardiness and chilling during, 26–27
  midwinter thaws and, 27
Drainage, 56–57

Elderberries, 213–14
Ethylene gas, 138

Fertilizers, 73
  classes and analyses of, 74
  commercial vs. organic, 73–76
  foliar, 81
  requirements, 76–80
  side dressing, 81, 82
  tips concerning, 82–83
  when and how to apply, 80–81

Figs, 214–16
  storing, 136
  temperature requirements, 8
  winter protection, 100
Filberts, 187–88
Flower bud formation, 15–18
  forcing, 18–19
  critical temperatures for, 104
Fruit drop, 24
Fruit set, 23–24
Fruiting habits, 19–20
Fruits
  bearing ages, 13
  classification of, 1–5
  common pests, 117–18
  container-grown, 57–59
  critical minimum temperatures for,
    101–2, 104
  definition of, 1
  general symptoms, 119–22
  grafting stock combinations, 40
  indicators of maturity, 134
  nutrient deficiency symptoms in,
    77, 78–79
  pollination methods, 22
  soil conditions, 57
  soil pH range, 65
  storage period, 135, 136
  suggested number of plants, 49
  wet-soil tolerance scale, 58
  yields, 48–49

Glyphosate, 84–85
Gooseberries, 223
  fruiting habits, 19
  harvesting, 133
  propagating, 34
  temperature requirements, 8
Grafting, 36–38
  budding, 38–41
  cleft, 38, 39
  combinations, 40
  interstocks, 41–42
  whip, 37, 38
Grapes
  arbors, 248
  cultivars by region, 240
  diseases and pests, 249
  DOVine, 242
  European, 241
  fertilizing, 244
  fox, 242
  French hybrid, 243
  hardiness zones, 239–42
  harvesting, 249
  mulching, 244
  muscadine, 240, 241
  planting, 243–44
  propagating, 34, 38, 244–45
  purchasing, 243
  site selection, 242
  soil requirements, 243
  species, 239–42
  supporting, 245
  training and pruning, 245–48
  water requirements, 244
  winter protection, 100, 249

Growth and development
  reproductive adult phase, 12–14
  seedlings, 12
  vegetative adult phase, 12–14

Hardiness and chilling, 26–27
Hardiness zones, 5–6
Harvesting, 133
  indicators of maturity, 134
Herbicides, 84–85
Huckleberries, propagating, 34

Jostaberries, 223–24
Jujube, 237–38

Kiwifruits
  cultivars, 217, 218
  fertilizing, 218
  harvesting, 220
  pests, 220
  planting, 217–18
  propagating, 218
  pruning, 219
  training, 218–19
  water requirements, 219
  winter protection, 220

Landscaping
  with blueberries, 201–2
  suggested fruit for, 50
Layering, 34–35
Light requirements, 7–8
Limb bending, 18
Lingonberries, 220–23
  mulching, 88
  soil requirements, 10, 63
  water requirements, 89
Loganberries, 203

Manure, moisture and nutrient
  content of, 76
Medlars, 160–62
  harvesting, 133
Microclimates, 52–53
Mulberries, 181–82
Mulches, 86–88

Nanking cherries, 238
Nectarines, 175
  cultivars by region, 176
  midwinter thaws and, 27
Nursery stock, 43–45
Nutrients, 9–11, 72
  carrier materials average content of,
    83
  deficiency symptoms, 77, 78–79
Nuts
  bearing ages, 13
  pollination methods, 22
  from seed, 28
  storage period, 137

Pawpaw, northern, 182–83
Peaches
  cultivars by region, 172
  dwarf, 173
  fertilizing, 174

fruit drops, 24
fruiting habits, 19
hardiness zones, 171–72
harvesting, 175
midwinter thaws and, 27
planting, 173
pollinating, 173
propagating, 32
pruning, 174–75
purchasing, 172
rootstocks, 172
from seed, 28, 31
soil requirements, 173
thinning, 25
training, 174
water requirements, 89, 175
winter protection, 174
Pears
  Asian, 157–58
  bearing, 156
  cultivars by region, 154
  dwarf, 154–55
  fertilizing, 156
  fire blight and, 156
  fruit drops, 24
  fruiting habits, 19
  hardiness zones, 153
  harvesting, 133, 157
  limb bending, 18
  pollinating, 155
  propagating, 32
  pruning, 156–57
  quince as rootstock for, 155
  rootstocks, 153–54
  soil requirements, 63, 155–56
  species, 152–53
  storing, 157
  thinning, 25
  water requirements, 157
Pecans
  cultivars by region, 189
  fertilizing, 190
  harvesting, 191
  nut drops, 190
  pests, 190–91
  planting, 190
  pollinating, 189–90
Persimmons, 183–84
Pest control, 116
  barriers and traps, 124–25
  common pests, 117–18
  general, 116–24
  mammal and bird, 131–32
  parasites, 126–27
  pathogens, 126–27
  pesticides, 127–30
  physical removal, 125
  predators, 126–27
  symptoms, 119–22
Pesticides, 127–28
  biological, 128
  botanical, 128
  cautions concerning, 130
  inorganic, 129–30
  organic, 129
Phloem interruption, 18–19
Photoperiodism, 7–8

Planting, 92–93
  care after, 99
  hole size, 94–97
  staking and support, 97–98
  when to do, 93–94
Plums
  cross-incompatible, 179
  cultivars, 178
  diseases and pests, 181
  dwarf, 178–79
  fertilizing, 180
  flower bloom, 180
  fruit drops, 24, 181
  harvesting, 181
  minor, 177
  planting, 180
  pollinating, 179–80
  propagating, 32, 33, 34
  pruning, 180–81
  purchasing, 178
  rootstocks, 178
  from seed, 31
  self-fruitful, 179
  self-unfruitful, 179
  species, 176–77
  thinning, 25
Pollen, types of, 21
Pollination, 20
  cross, 20–21
  improving, 23
  methods of, 21–22
  self, 20
  types of, 20–21
Propagating frame, 33
Propagation
  asexual, 31–36
  grafting, 36–43
  by seed, 28–31
Pruning, 106
  during reproductive adult phase,
    16–17
  during vegetative adult phase, 16
  equipment, 109–10
  how much to remove when, 108–9
  methods, 110
  to train, 111–15
  when to do, 106–8

Quinces, 158–60
  propagating, 32, 34

Raspberries
  cultivars, 208
  cultivars by region, 209
  diseases and pests, 212
  fertilizing, 209–10
  flower bud formation, 15
  growth habits, 210
  harvesting, 213
  mulching, 88
  planting, 207
  propagating, 31, 34
  pruning, 210–12
  purchasing, 208
  setting, 208
  soil requirements, 207

  training, 212
  weed control, 208–9
Ribes, 222–24
  cultivars, 225
  fertilizing, 225
  hardiness zones, 224
  harvesting, 226
  mulching, 225
  pests, 226
  planting, 224–25
  propagating, 226
  pruning, 226
  storing, 227
Ringing, 18, 19

Saskatoons, 236–37
Scoring, 18–19
Seed starting, 28–31
  stratification, 30–31
Seedlings, 12
Site selection, 46
  drainage, 56–57
  microclimates, 52–53
  planning and layout, 46–51
  winds and windbreaks, 54–56
Soil, 60
  alkali, 68
  carbon-to-nitrogen (C:N) ratios, 70
  clay, 61–63
  color, 56
  increasing humus content in, 68–70
  loam, 60–61
  moisture-holding capacity, 62
  moisture, testing for, 90
  pH, 9, 10–11, 63–67
  preparing, 70–71
  sandy, 61
  silty, 63
  testing, 61
  types, 60–63
  water infiltration rate, 57
Spring protection, 103–5
Storage, 133–36
  ethylene gas and, 138
  period, 135, 136, 137
  relative humidity, 137
  temperature, 136
  ventilation, 137–38
Stratification, 30–31
Strawberries
  after harvest care, 233–34
  cultivars by region, 229
  diseases and pests, 233
  fertilizing, 230–32
  flower bud formation, 15
  hardiness zones, 227
  harvesting, 233
  mulching, 88, 232
  photoperiodism and, 7–8
  planting, 230–31
  planting systems, 227
  propagating, 34, 233
  soil requirements, 228
  water requirements, 89, 232
  weed control, 232
  winter care, 234–35

Sunscald damage, 103

Tayberries, 203
Temperature
  hardiness zones, 5–6
  requirements, 8
Thinning, fruit, 24–25
Training, 111
  central leader system, 111–14
  espalier, 115
  modified central leader system, 112,
    114
  open-center system, 112, 114–15
Transpiration, 11

Walnuts, 191–93
  cultivars by region, 191
Water requirements, 10, 11
Watering, 89–90
  irrigation methods of, 90–91
Weed control, 84–85
  cultivation, 85–86
  mulches, 86–88
Winds and windbreaks, 54–56,
  102–3
Winter protection
  assessing cold damage, 105
  autumn watering, 100
  burying plants, 100–2
  critical minimum temperatures,
    101–2, 104
  early-spring, 103–5
  windscreens, 102–3

Youngberries, 203